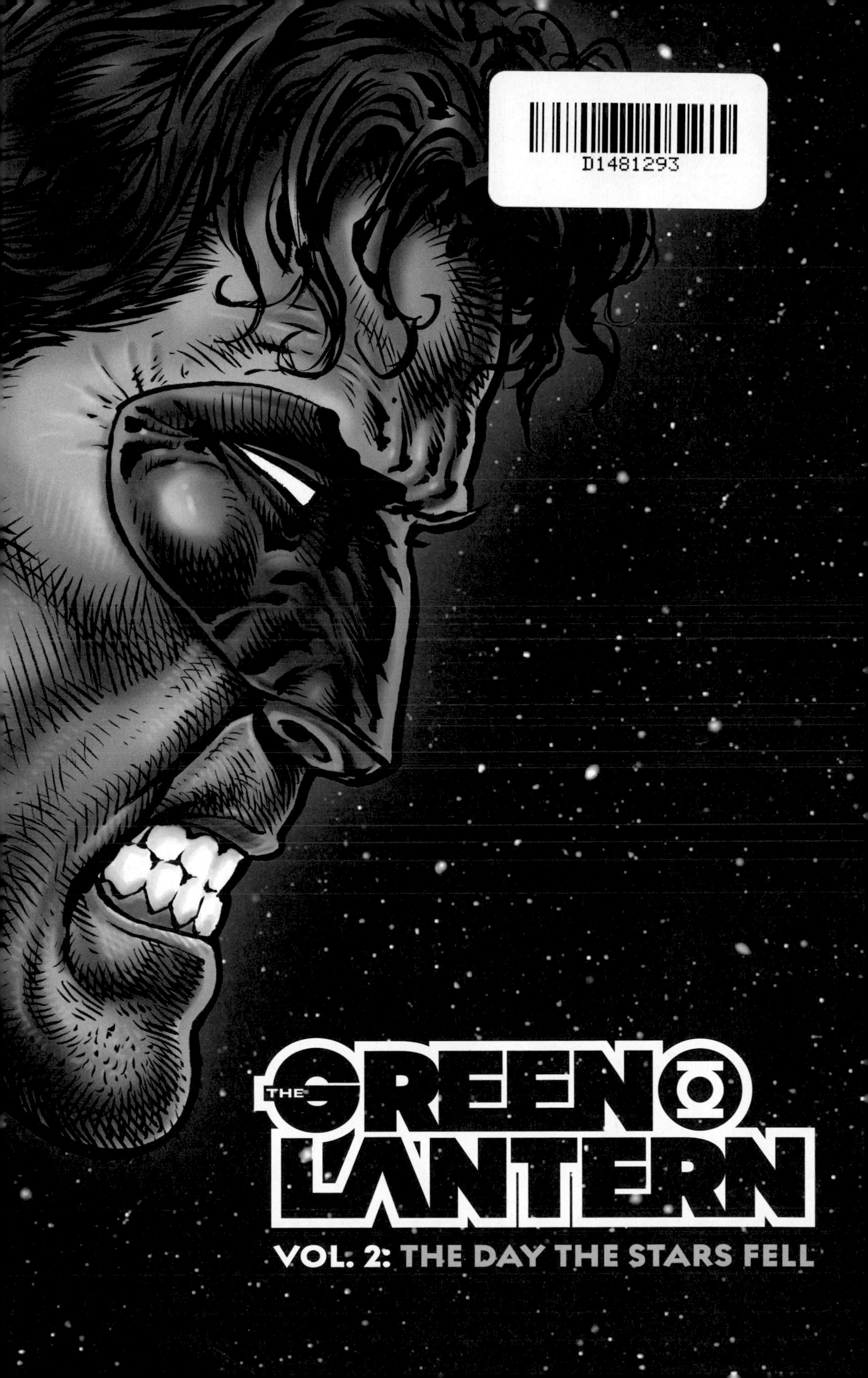

THE GREEN LANTERN

VOL. 2: THE DAY THE STARS FELL

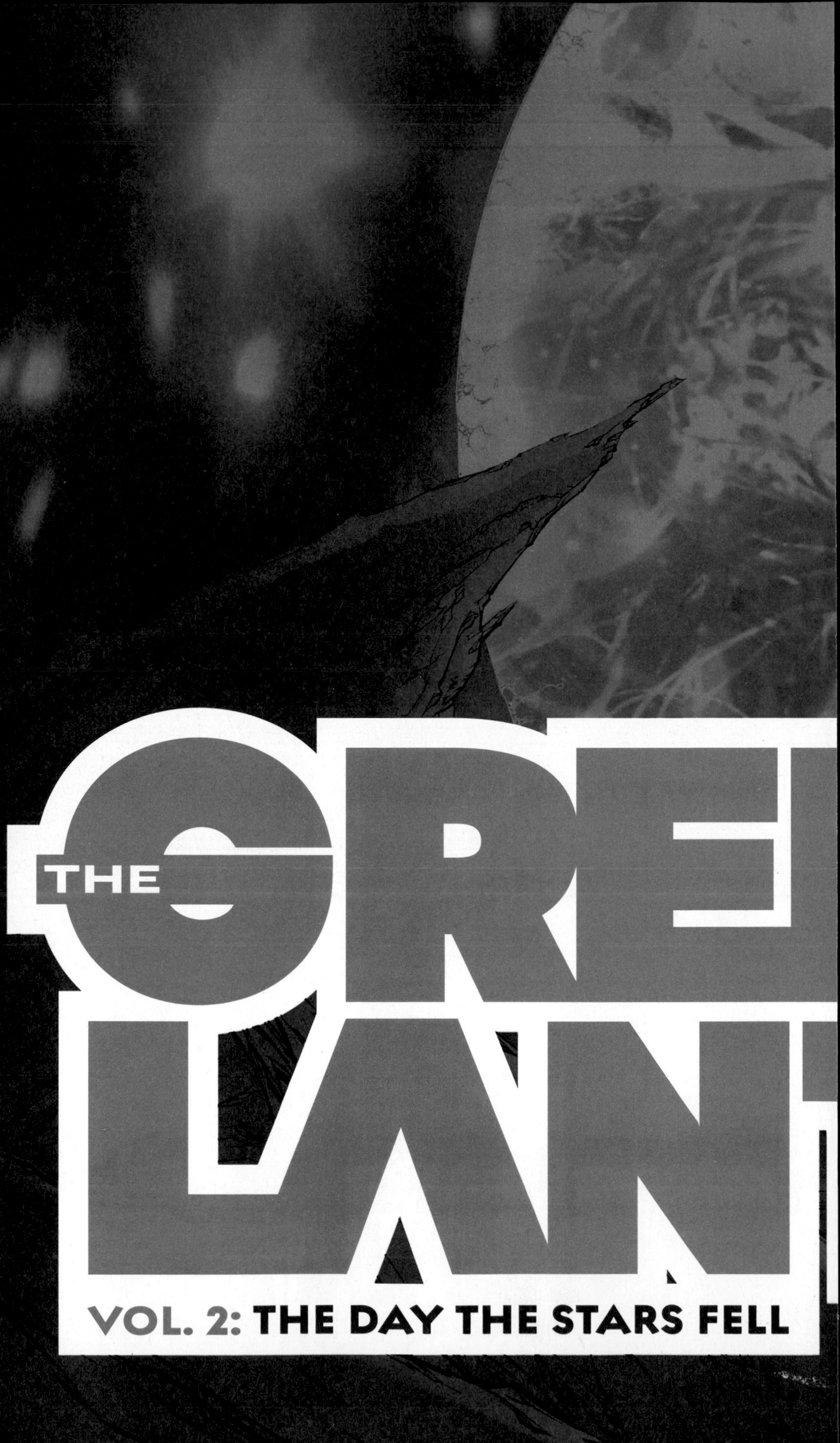
THE
VOL. 2: THE DAY THE STARS FELL

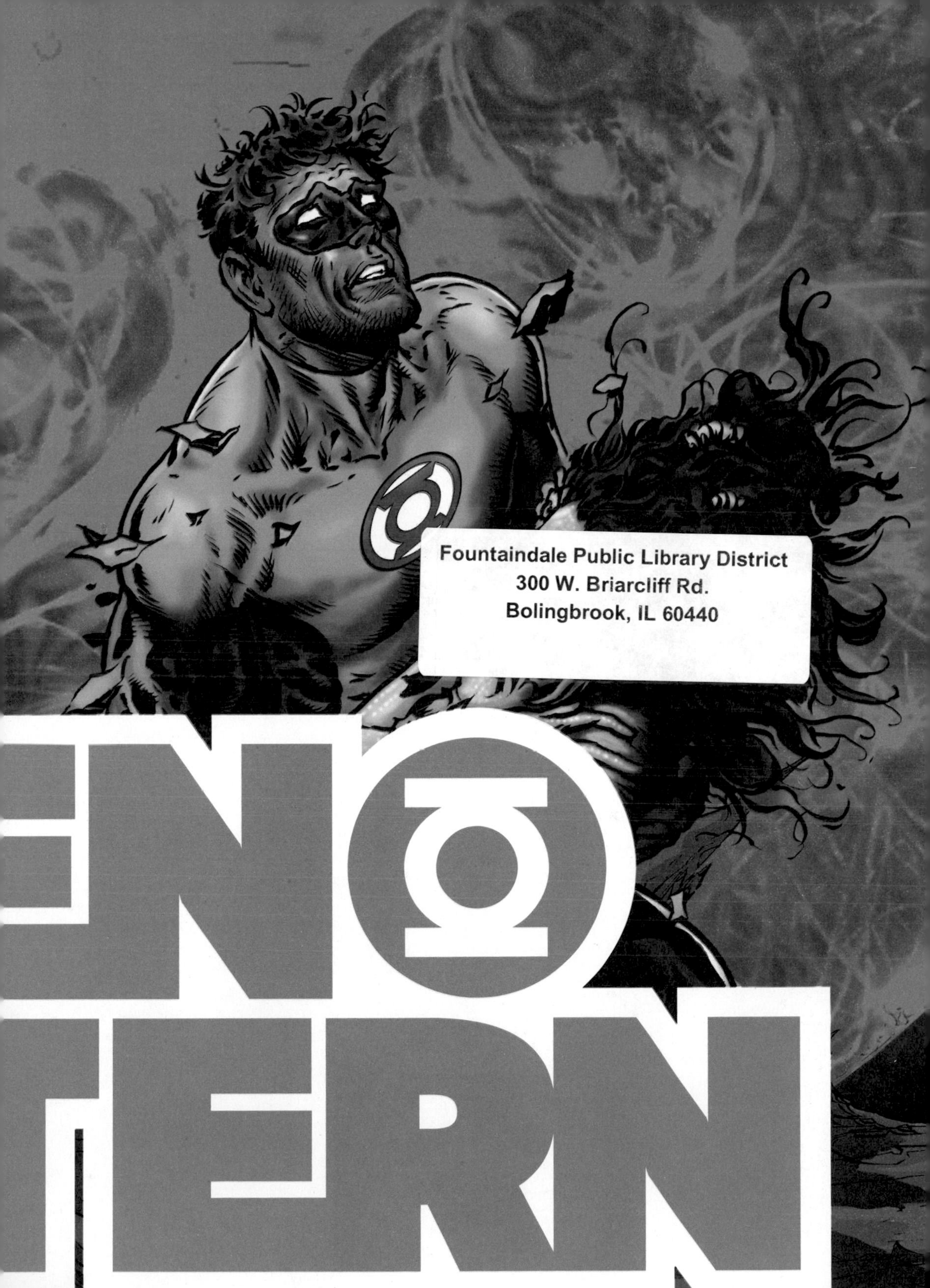

writer **GRANT MORRISON**
artists **LIAM SHARP** **GIUSEPPE CAMUNCOLI** **TREVOR SCOTT**
colorists **STEVE OLIFF** **LIAM SHARP**
letterer **TOM ORZECHOWSKI**
collection cover artist **LIAM SHARP**

BRIAN CUNNINGHAM Editor – Original Series
JESSICA CHEN Associate Editor – Original Series
JEB WOODARD Group Editor – Collected Editions
REZA LOKMAN Editor – Collected Edition
STEVE COOK Design Director – Books
GABRIEL MALDONADO Publication Design
SUZANNAH ROWNTREE Publication Production

BOB HARRAS Senior VP – Editor-in-Chief, DC Comics

DAN DiDIO Publisher
JIM LEE Publisher & Chief Creative Officer
BOBBIE CHASE VP – New Publishing Initiatives
DON FALLETTI VP – Manufacturing Operations & Workflow Management
LAWRENCE GANEM VP – Talent Services
ALISON GILL Senior VP – Manufacturing & Operations
HANK KANALZ Senior VP – Publishing Strategy & Support Services
DAN MIRON VP – Publishing Operations
NICK J. NAPOLITANO VP – Manufacturing Administration & Design
NANCY SPEARS VP – Sales
JONAH WEILAND VP – Marketing & Creative Services
MICHELE R. WELLS VP & Executive Editor, Young Reader

THE GREEN LANTERN VOL. 2: THE DAY THE STARS FELL

DC Comics, 2900 West Alameda Ave., Burbank, CA 91505
Printed by LSC Communications, Owensville, MO, USA. 5/29/20. First Printing.
ISBN: 978-1-77950-268-1

Library of Congress Cataloging-in-Publication Data is available.

PEFC Certified

This product is from
sustainably managed
forests and controlled
sources

PEFC

PEFC/29-31-337   www.pefc.org

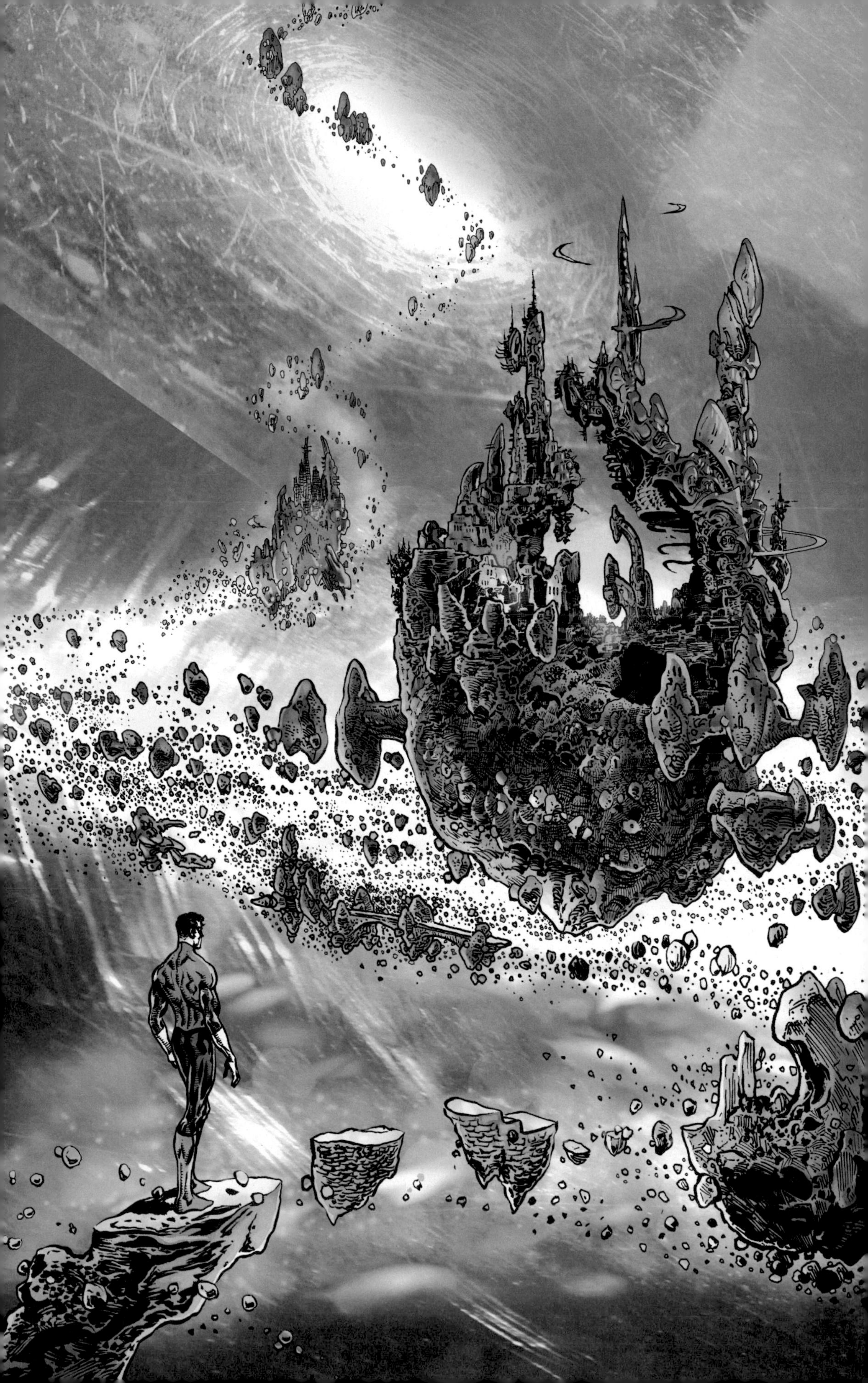

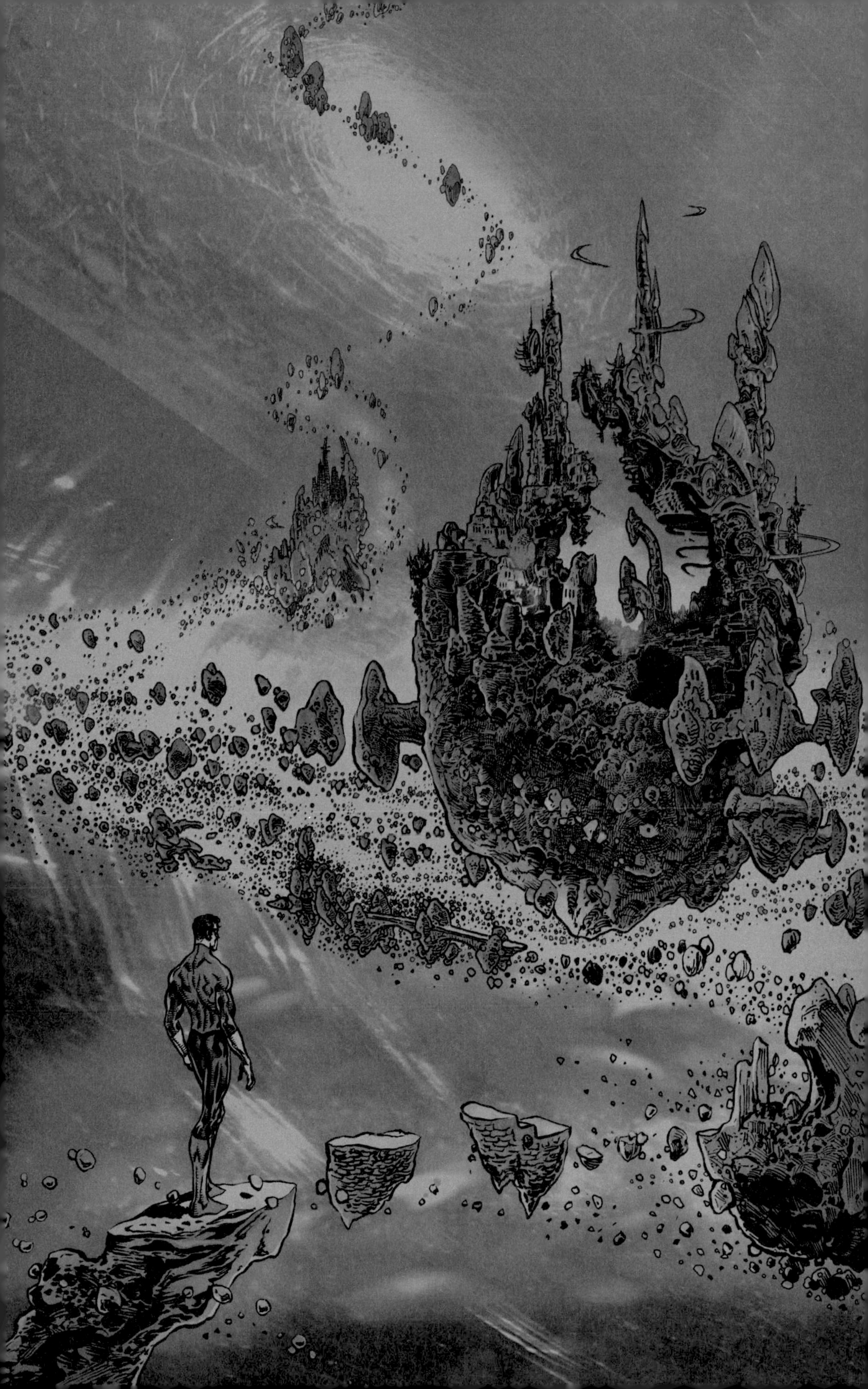

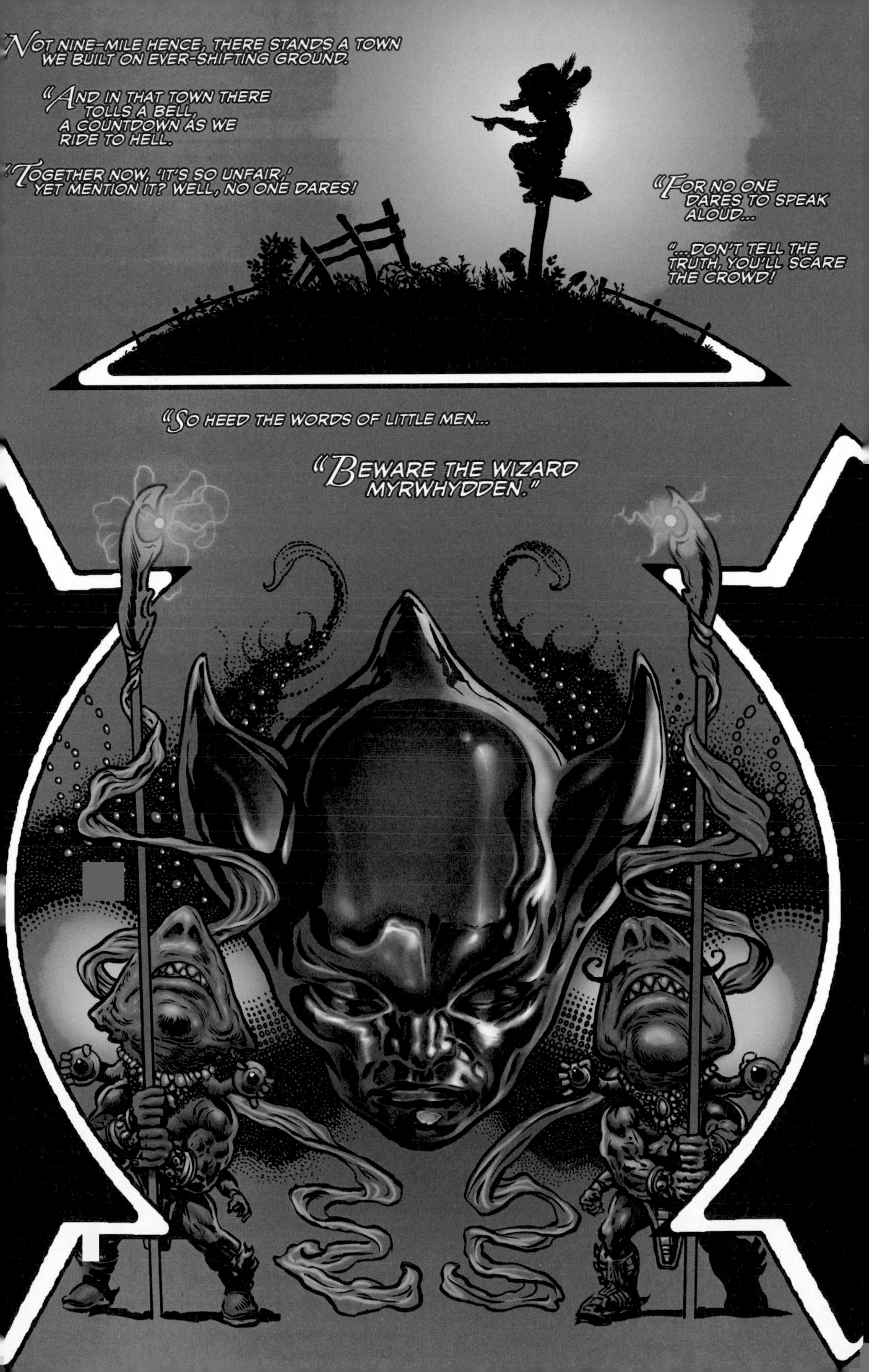
"NOT NINE-MILE HENCE, THERE STANDS A TOWN WE BUILT ON EVER-SHIFTING GROUND.
"AND IN THAT TOWN THERE TOLLS A BELL, A COUNTDOWN AS WE RIDE TO HELL.
"TOGETHER NOW, 'IT'S SO UNFAIR,' YET MENTION IT? WELL, NO ONE DARES!
"FOR NO ONE DARES TO SPEAK ALOUD...
"...DON'T TELL THE TRUTH, YOU'LL SCARE THE CROWD!
"SO HEED THE WORDS OF LITTLE MEN...
"BEWARE THE WIZARD MYRWHYDDEN."

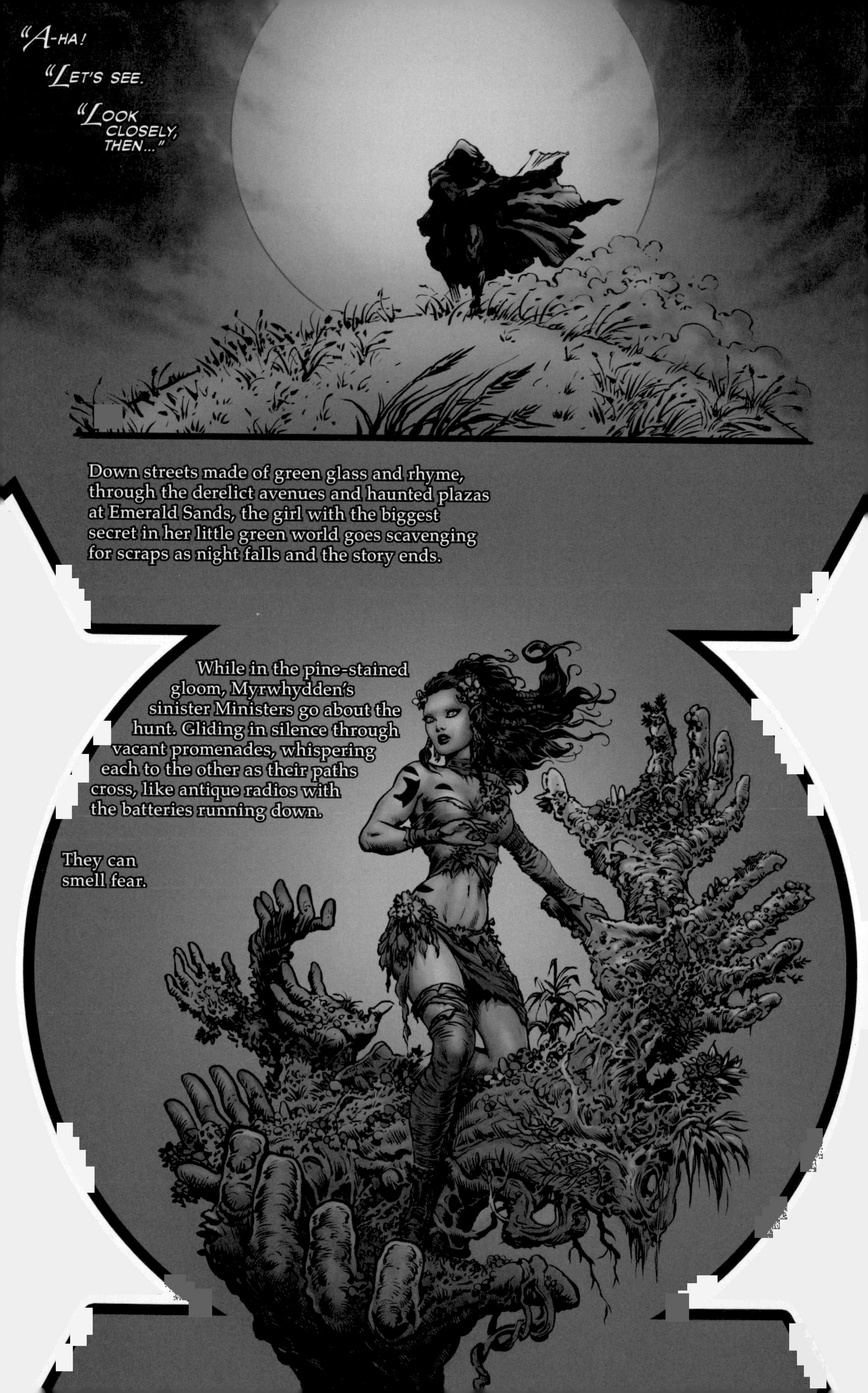
"A-HA!
"LET'S SEE.
"LOOK CLOSELY, THEN..."
Down streets made of green glass and rhyme, through the derelict avenues and haunted plazas at Emerald Sands, the girl with the biggest secret in her little green world goes scavenging for scraps as night falls and the story ends.
While in the pine-stained gloom, Myrwhydden's sinister Ministers go about the hunt. Gliding in silence through vacant promenades, whispering each to the other as their paths cross, like antique radios with the batteries running down.
They can smell fear.

The girl with no fear, the girl with the secret not even she knows, the witch-girl Pengowirr, holds her breath as Myrwhydden's Ministers pass by, crackling softly through sullen moss-dark shadows that lie as dense as greenwood.

Once there were bright, clean peppermint skies overhead. Once there were a thousand shades of radiant, dreaming paint-chart green to choose from. Chartreuse and lime, aquamarine and viridian.

Once, Myrwhydden slept, content.

But now the Wizard turns uneasily in his fretful slumber.

...and all his little nightmares, taken shape, serve as his Ministers.

While the Sorcerers of Emerald Sands, once filled with purpose, instead replay familiar gestures over and over, insensate ghosts repeating...

Pengowirr takes shelter from the glass-storm that scours away the accustomed contours of the Emerald Sands resort, dissolving in unremembered fragments, the world that once seemed so secure.

Before a creeping, indifferent magic came to steal it all away--piece by piece, grain by grain, atom by atom.

Sense by sense.

Half-blind, all but mute, deaf by degrees, Pengowirr does her best to stay alive, not certain why.

What makes her different from the others?

She must surely be insane, she thinks, alone in a dying city on the emerald edge of nowhere.

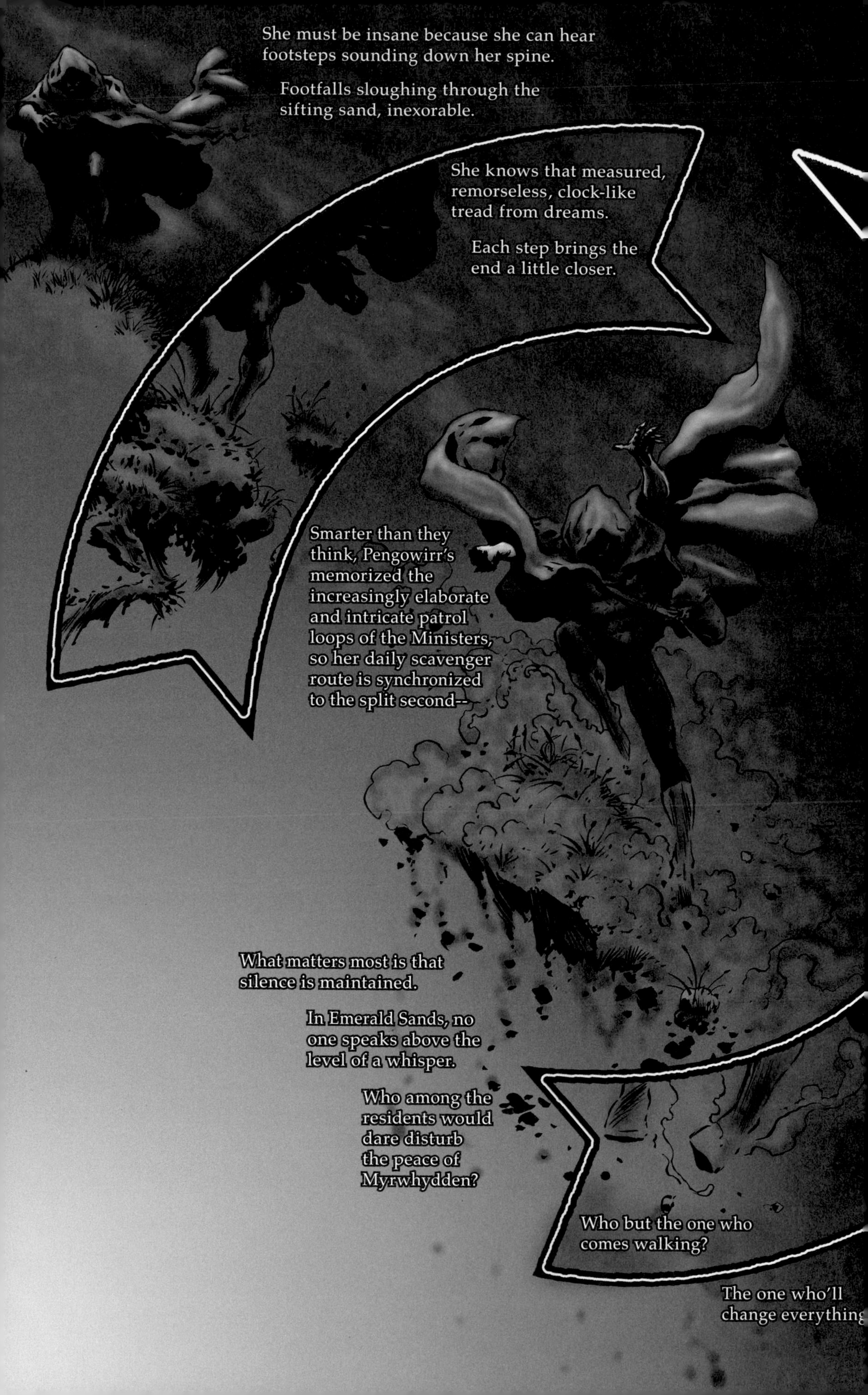
She must be insane because she can hear footsteps sounding down her spine.
Footfalls sloughing through the sifting sand, inexorable.
She knows that measured, remorseless, clock-like tread from dreams.
Each step brings the end a little closer.
Smarter than they think, Pengowirr's memorized the increasingly elaborate and intricate patrol loops of the Ministers, so her daily scavenger route is synchronized to the split second--
What matters most is that silence is maintained.
In Emerald Sands, no one speaks above the level of a whisper.
Who among the residents would dare disturb the peace of Myrwhydden?
Who but the one who comes walking?
The one who'll change everything

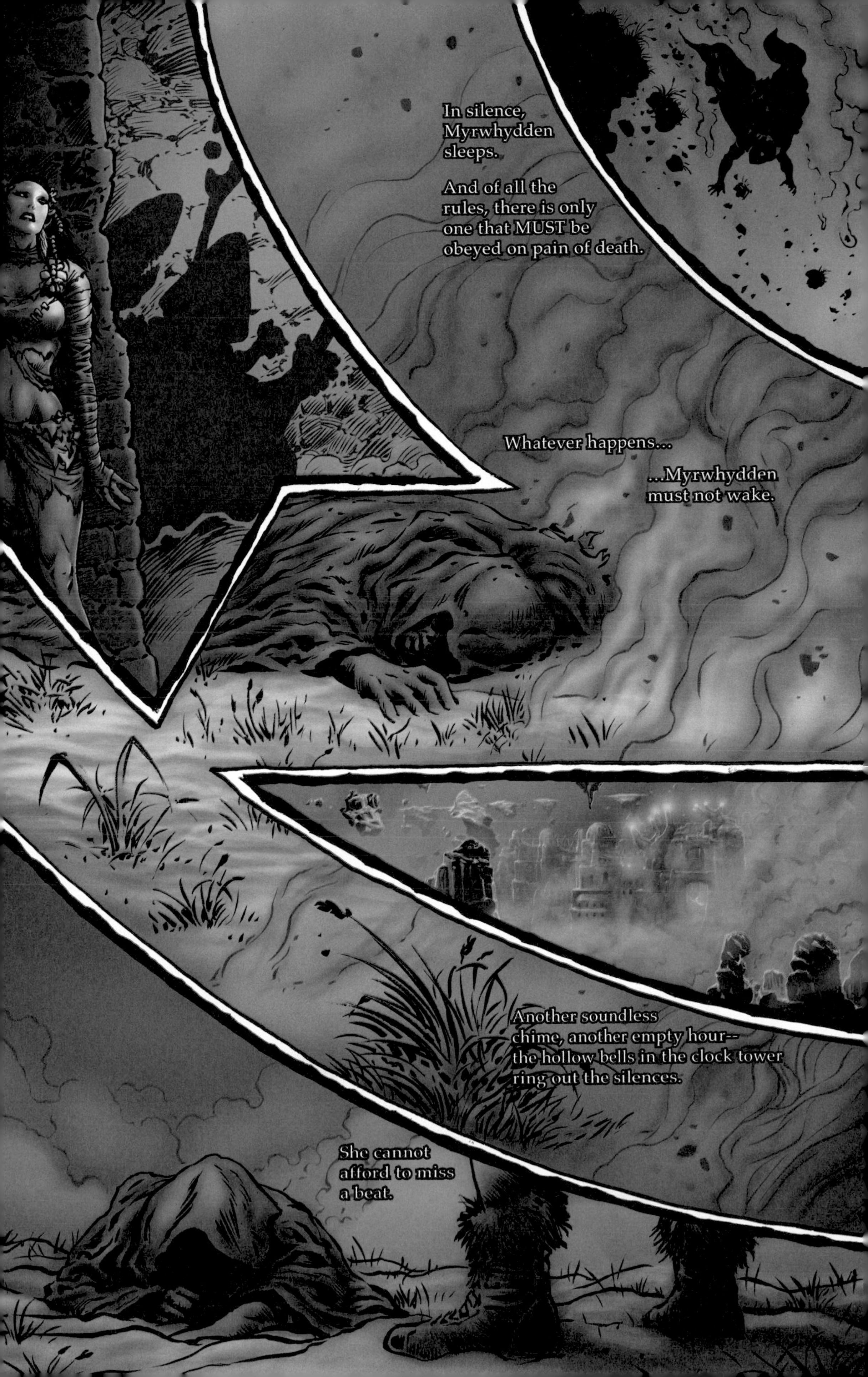
In silence, Myrwhydden sleeps.
And of all the rules, there is only one that MUST be obeyed on pain of death.
Whatever happens...
...Myrwhydden must not wake.
Another soundless chime, another empty hour-- the hollow bells in the clock tower ring out the silences.
She cannot afford to miss a beat.

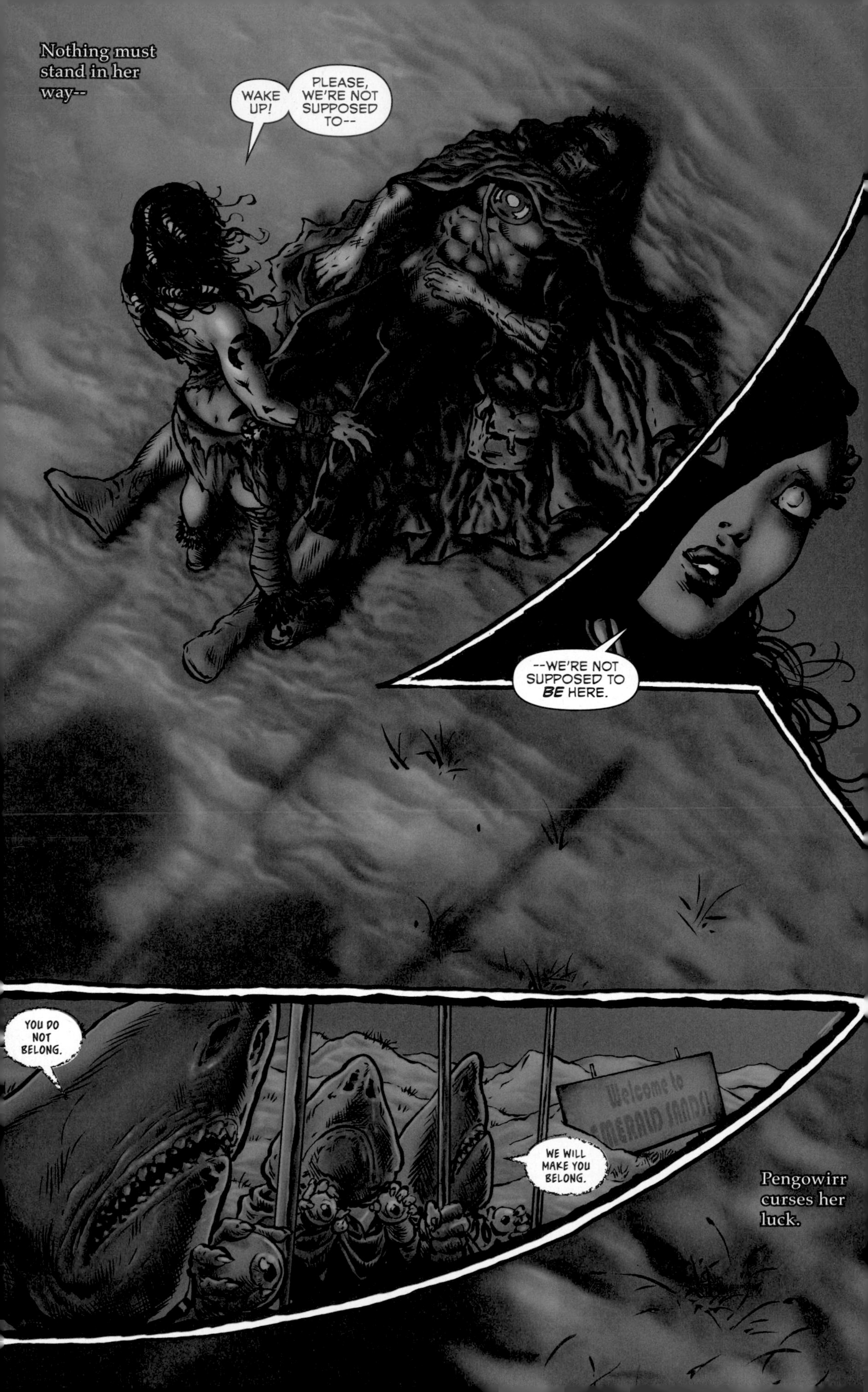
Nothing must stand in her way--
WAKE UP!
PLEASE, WE'RE NOT SUPPOSED TO--
--WE'RE NOT SUPPOSED TO *BE* HERE.
YOU DO NOT BELONG.
Welcome to EMERALD SANDS!
WE WILL MAKE YOU BELONG.
Pengowirr curses her luck.

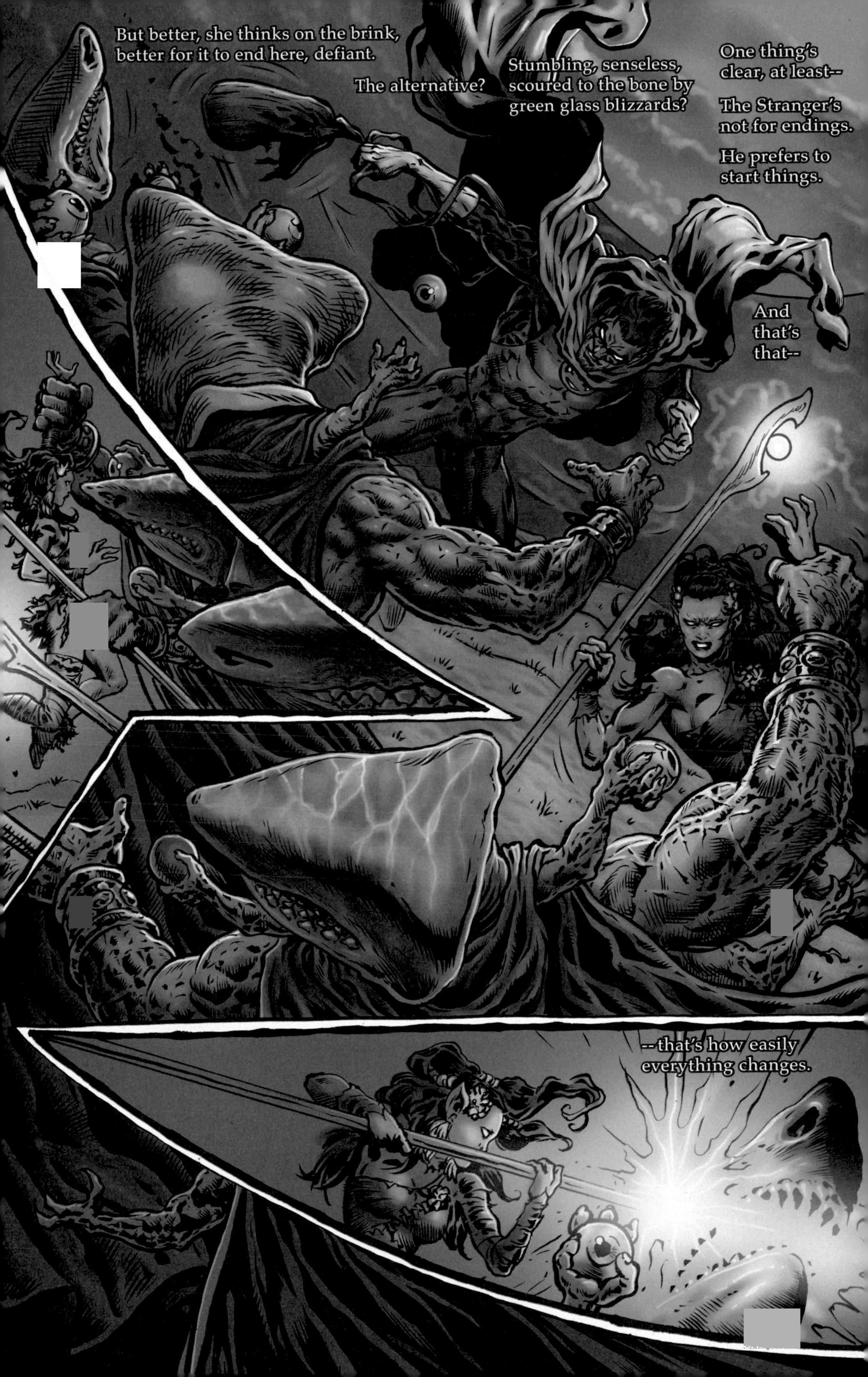
But better, she thinks on the brink, better for it to end here, defiant.
The alternative?
Stumbling, senseless, scoured to the bone by green glass blizzards?
One thing's clear, at least--
The Stranger's not for endings.
He prefers to start things.
And that's that--
--that's how easily everything changes.

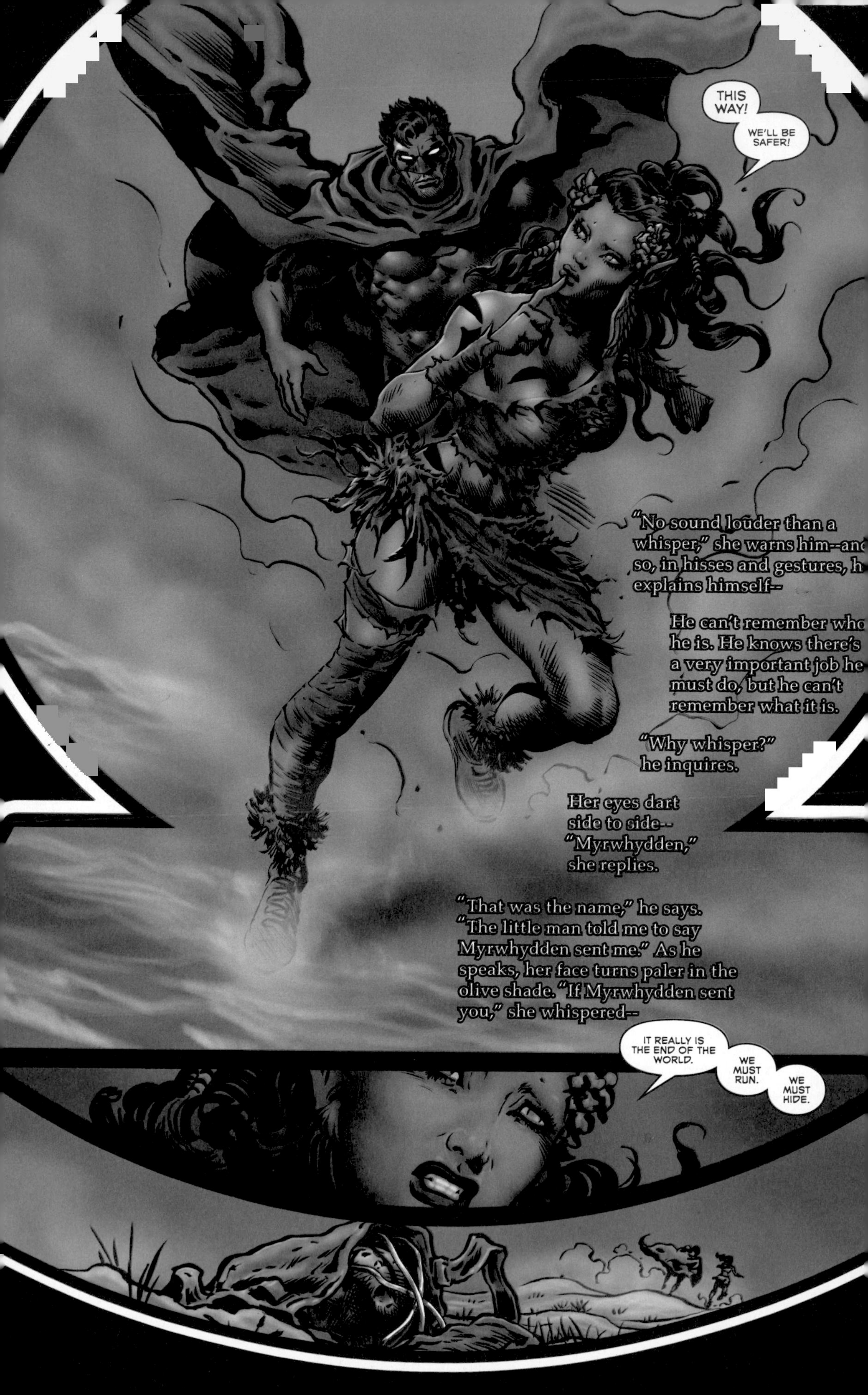
THIS WAY!
WE'LL BE SAFER!
"No sound louder than a whisper," she warns him--an so, in hisses and gestures, h explains himself--
He can't remember wh he is. He knows there's a very important job he must do, but he can't remember what it is.
"Why whisper?" he inquires.
Her eyes dart side to side-- "Myrwhydden," she replies.
"That was the name," he says. "The little man told me to say Myrwhydden sent me." As he speaks, her face turns paler in the olive shade. "If Myrwhydden sent you," she whispered--
IT REALLY IS THE END OF THE WORLD.
WE MUST RUN.
WE MUST HIDE.

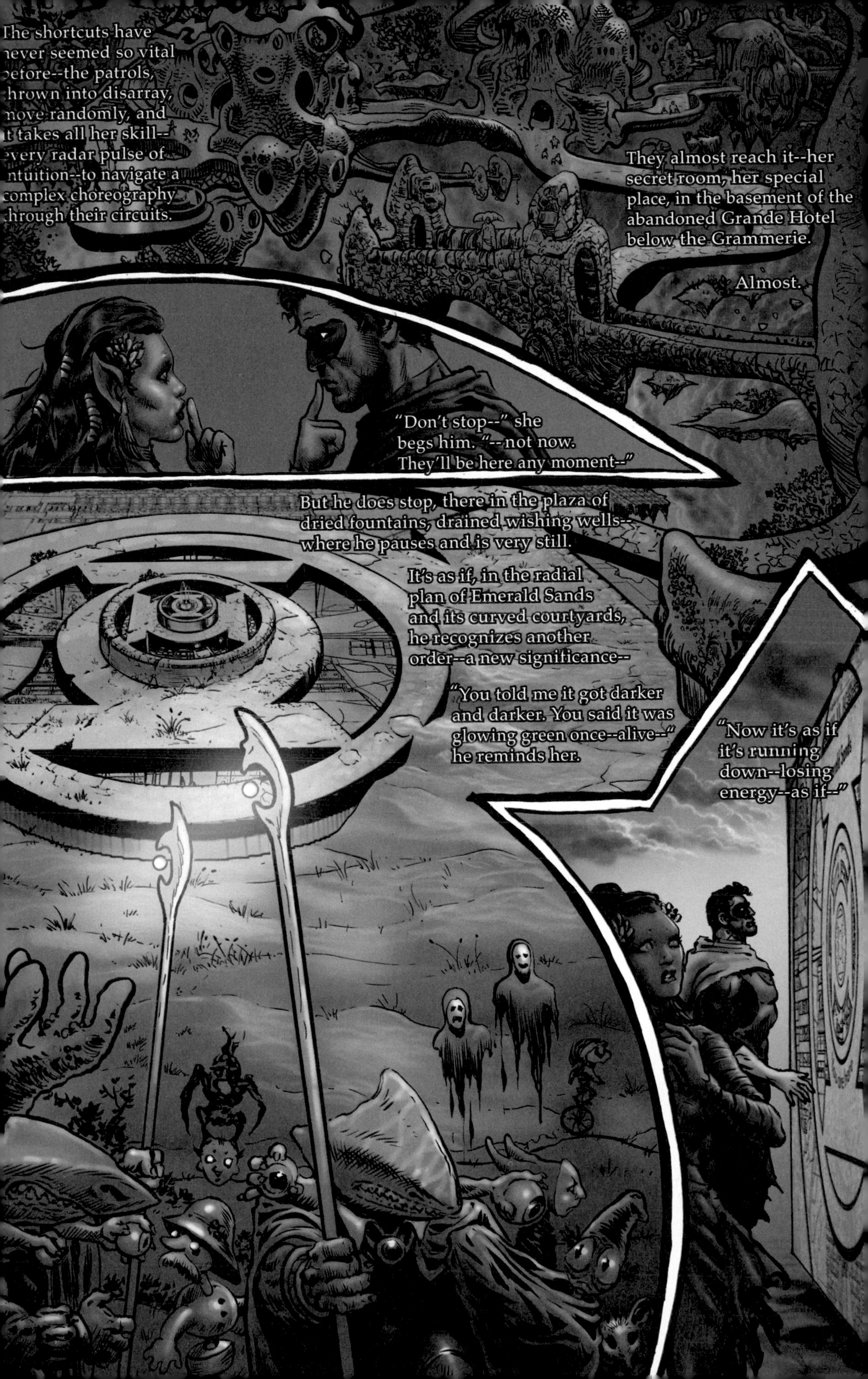

The shortcuts have never seemed so vital before--the patrols, thrown into disarray, move randomly, and it takes all her skill--every radar pulse of intuition--to navigate a complex choreography through their circuits.
They almost reach it--her secret room, her special place, in the basement of the abandoned Grande Hotel below the Grammerie.
Almost.
"Don't stop--" she begs him. "--not now. They'll be here any moment--"
But he does stop, there in the plaza of dried fountains, drained wishing wells--where he pauses and is very still.
It's as if, in the radial plan of Emerald Sands and its curved courtyards, he recognizes another order--a new significance--
"You told me it got darker and darker. You said it was glowing green once--alive--" he reminds her.
"Now it's as if it's running down--losing energy--as if--"

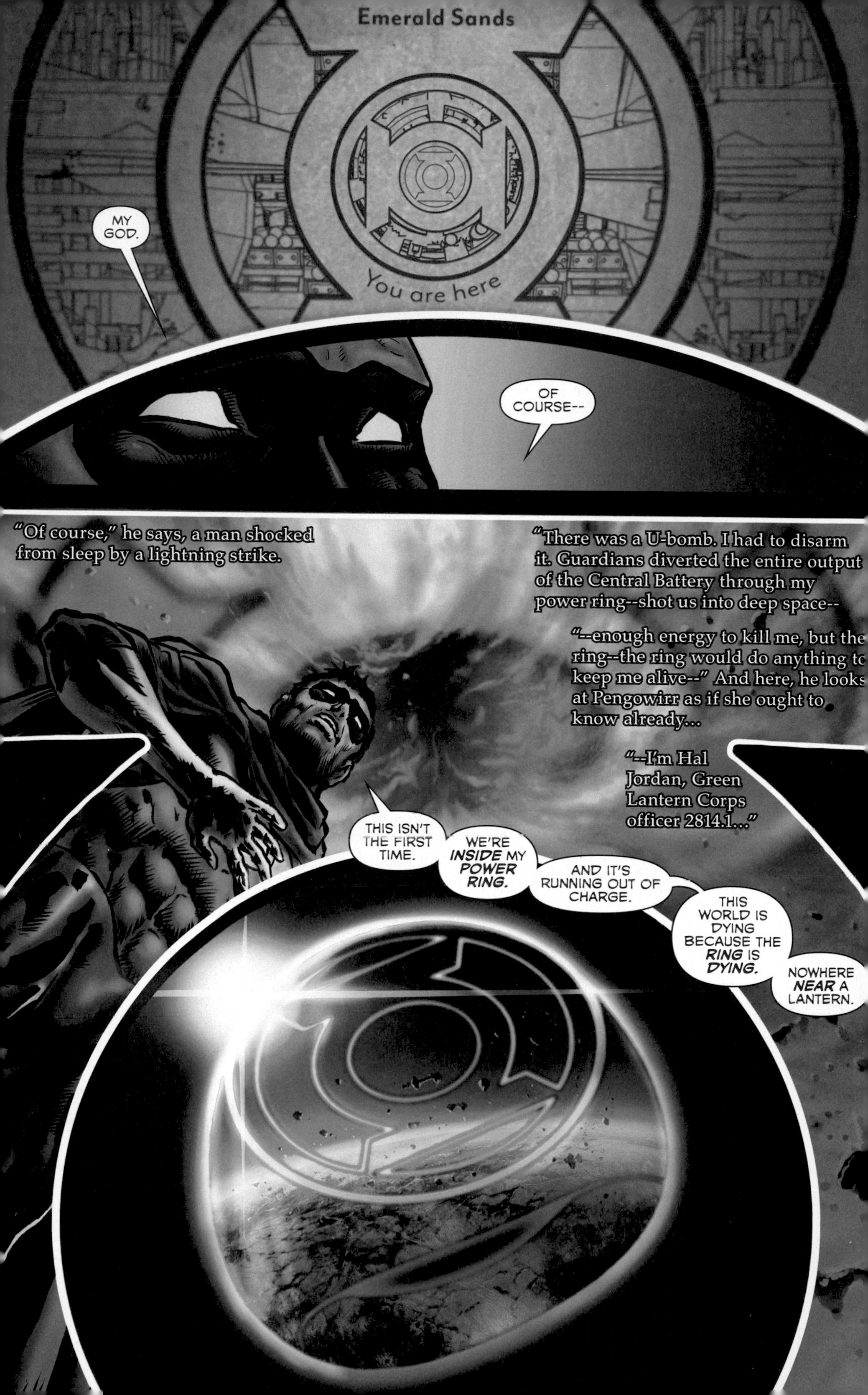

Emerald Sands
You are here
MY GOD.
OF COURSE--
"Of course," he says, a man shocked from sleep by a lightning strike.
"There was a U-bomb. I had to disarm it. Guardians diverted the entire output of the Central Battery through my power ring--shot us into deep space--
"--enough energy to kill me, but the ring--the ring would do anything to keep me alive--" And here, he looks at Pengowirr as if she ought to know already...
"--I'm Hal Jordan, Green Lantern Corps officer 2814.1..."
THIS ISN'T THE FIRST TIME.
WE'RE *INSIDE* MY *POWER RING.*
AND IT'S RUNNING OUT OF CHARGE.
THIS WORLD IS DYING BECAUSE THE *RING* IS *DYING.*
NOWHERE *NEAR* A LANTERN.

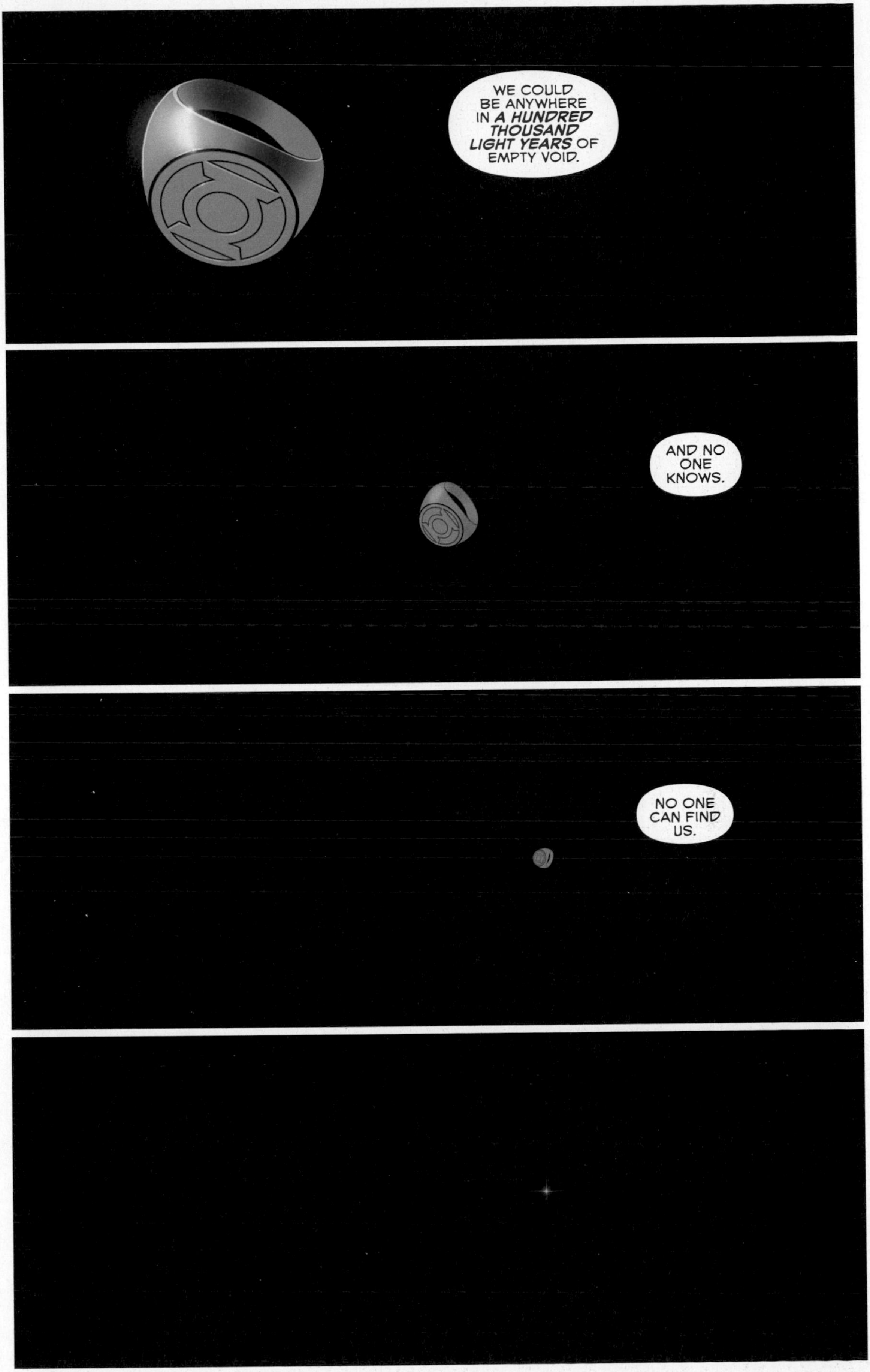
WE COULD BE ANYWHERE IN A HUNDRED THOUSAND LIGHT YEARS OF EMPTY VOID.
AND NO ONE KNOWS.
NO ONE CAN FIND US.

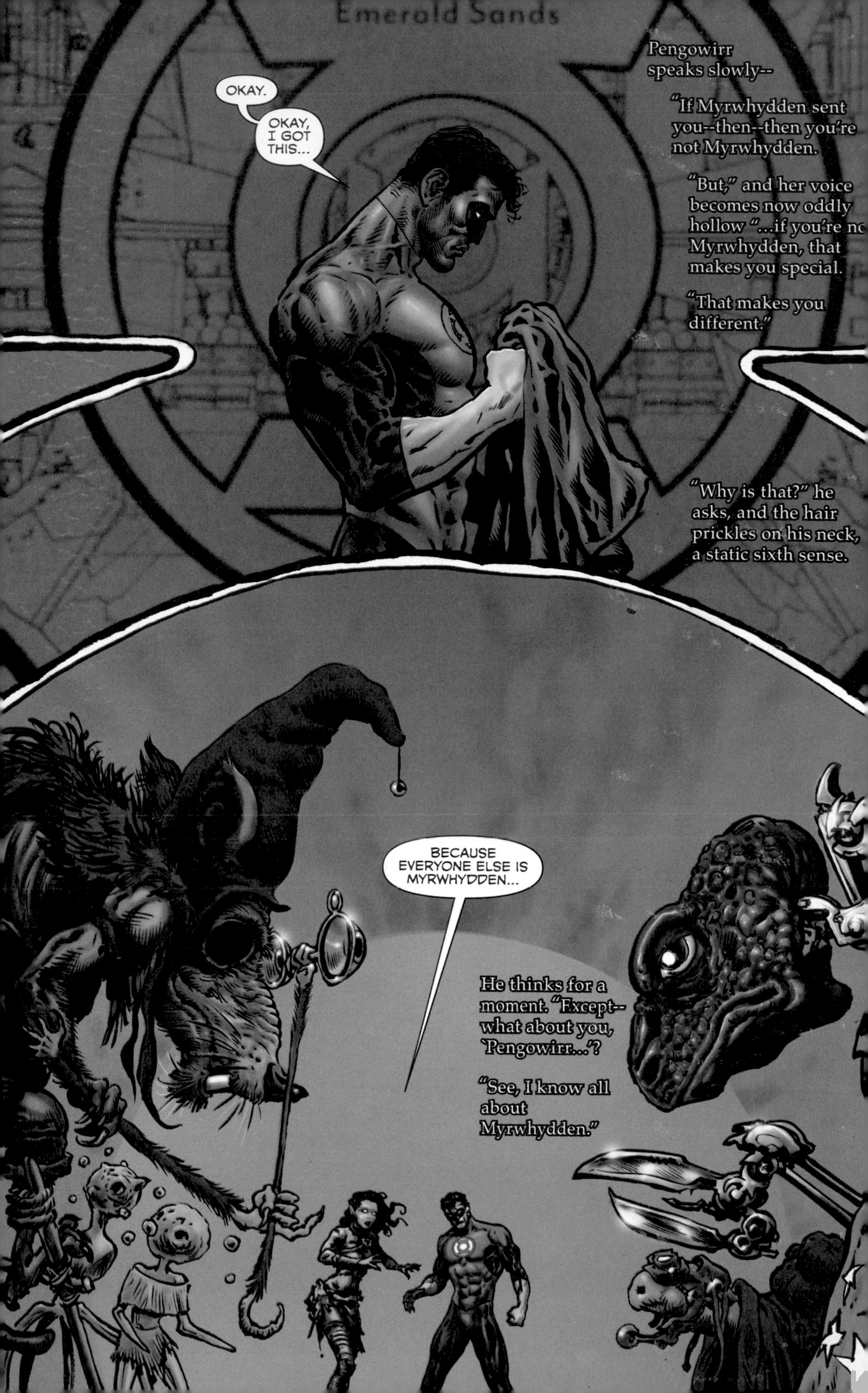
Emerald Sands
Pengowirr speaks slowly--
OKAY.
OKAY, I GOT THIS...
"If Myrwhydden sent you--then--then you're not Myrwhydden.
"But," and her voice becomes now oddly hollow "...if you're no Myrwhydden, that makes you special.
"That makes you different."
"Why is that?" he asks, and the hair prickles on his neck, a static sixth sense.
BECAUSE EVERYONE ELSE IS MYRWHYDDEN...
He thinks for a moment. "Except--what about you, 'Pengowirr...'?
"See, I know all about Myrwhydden."

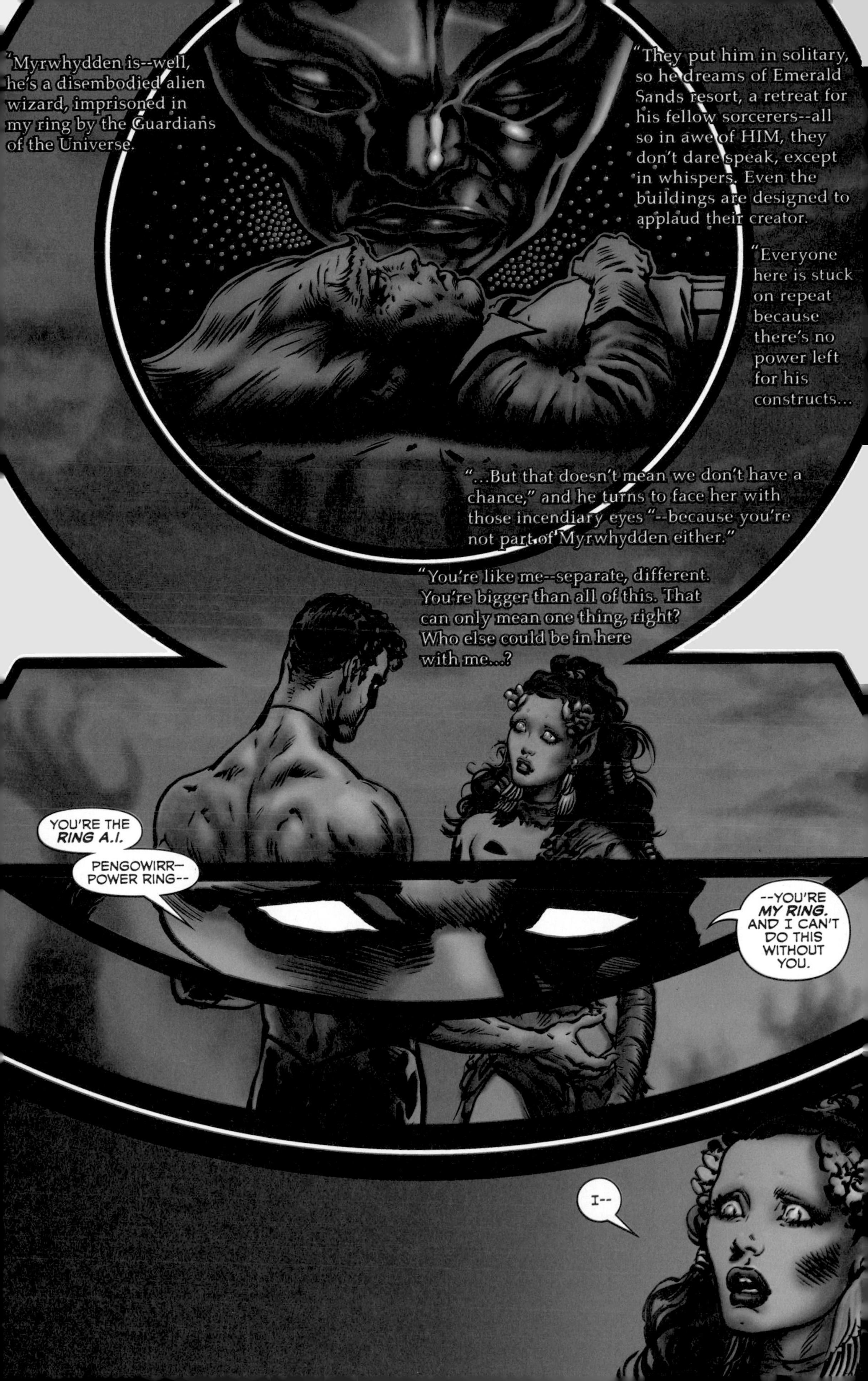
"Myrwhydden is--well, he's a disembodied alien wizard, imprisoned in my ring by the Guardians of the Universe.
"They put him in solitary, so he dreams of Emerald Sands resort, a retreat for his fellow sorcerers--all so in awe of HIM, they don't dare speak, except in whispers. Even the buildings are designed to applaud their creator.
"Everyone here is stuck on repeat because there's no power left for his constructs...
"...But that doesn't mean we don't have a chance," and he turns to face her with those incendiary eyes "--because you're not part of Myrwhydden either."
"You're like me--separate, different. You're bigger than all of this. That can only mean one thing, right? Who else could be in here with me...?
YOU'RE THE RING A.I.
PENGOWIRR—POWER RING--
--YOU'RE MY RING. AND I CAN'T DO THIS WITHOUT YOU.
I--

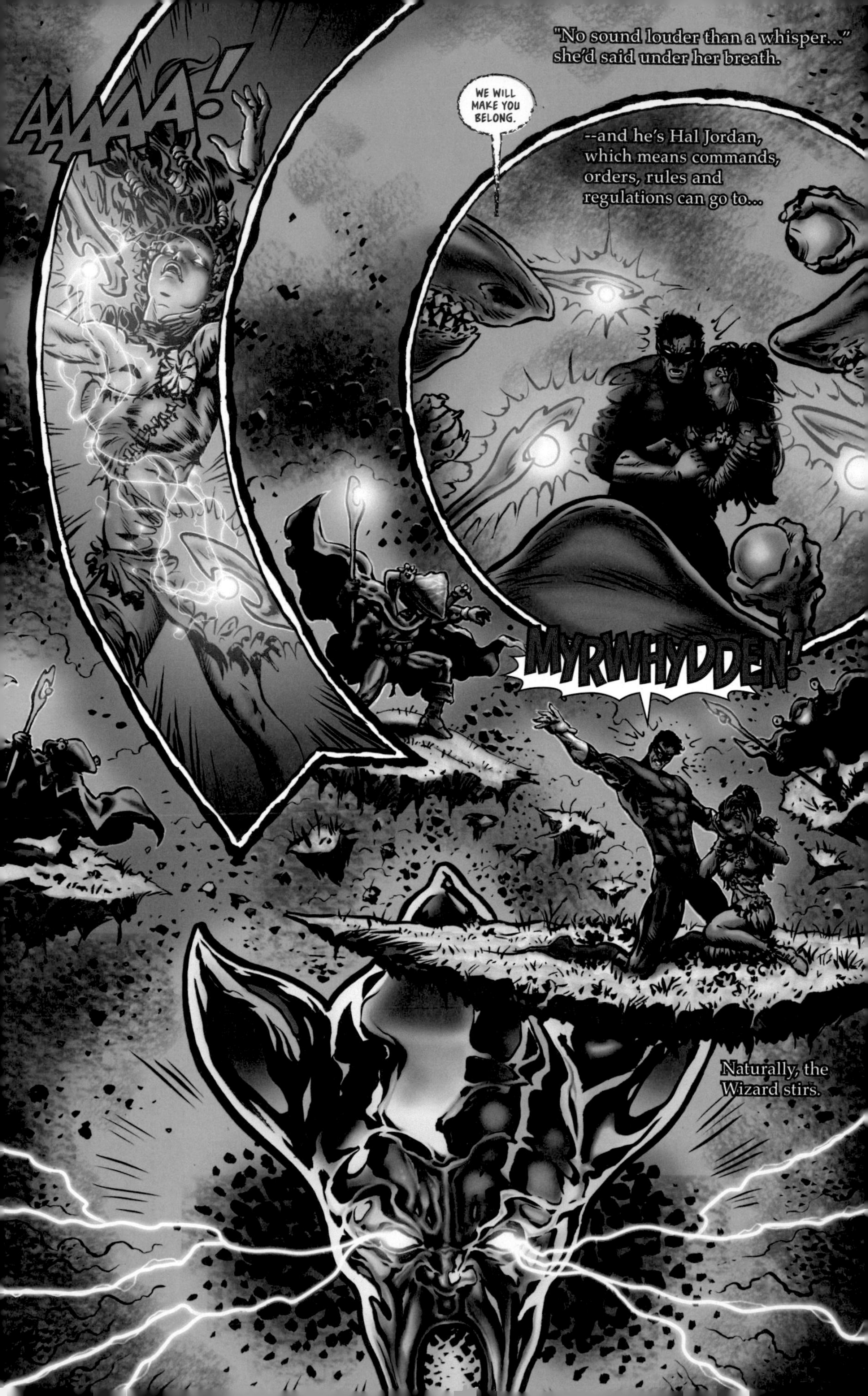
"No sound louder than a whisper..." she'd said under her breath.
AAAAA!
WE WILL MAKE YOU BELONG.
--and he's Hal Jordan, which means commands, orders, rules and regulations can go to...
MYRWHYDDEN!
Naturally, the Wizard stirs.

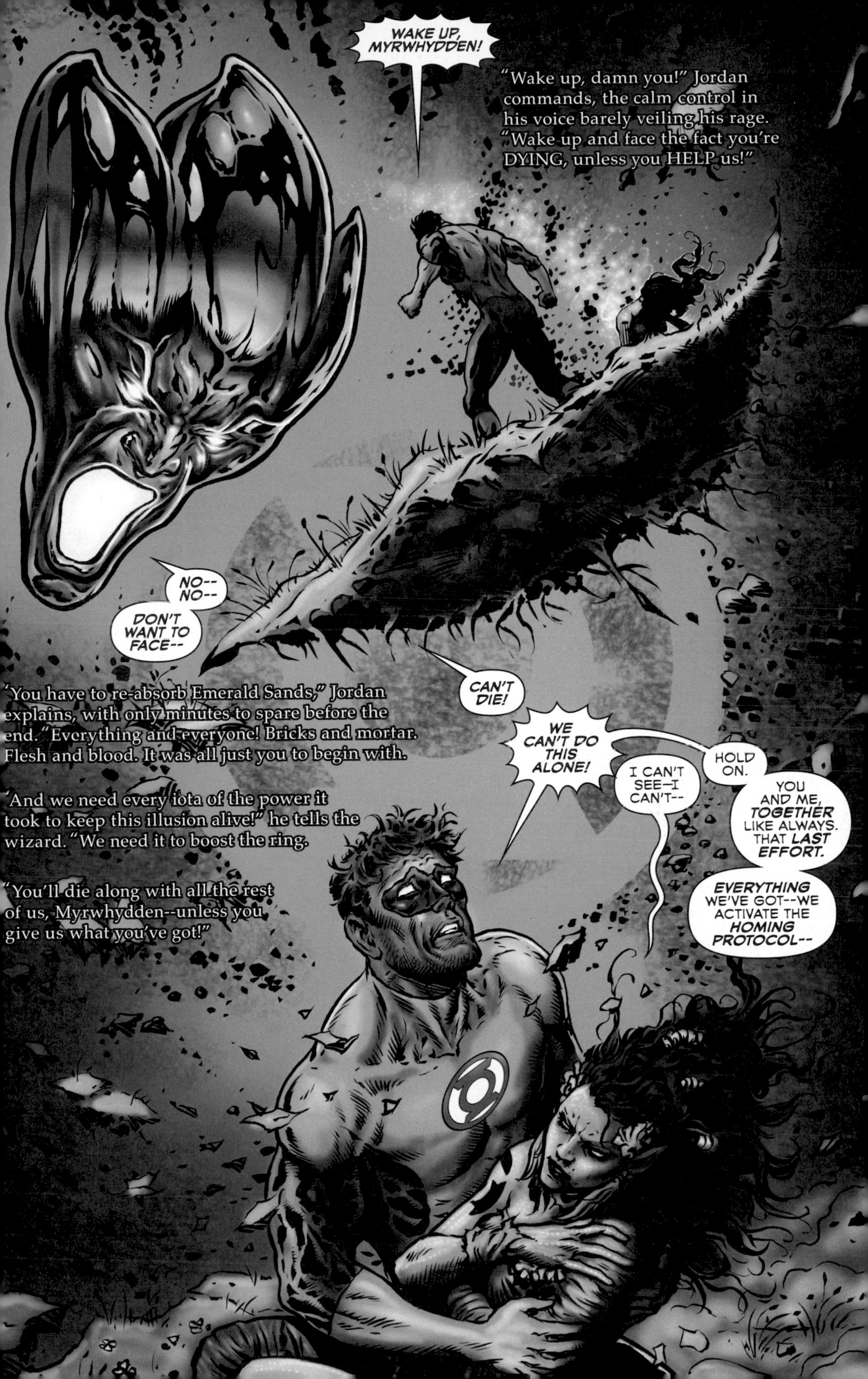
WAKE UP, MYRWHYDDEN!
"Wake up, damn you!" Jordan commands, the calm control in his voice barely veiling his rage. "Wake up and face the fact you're DYING, unless you HELP us!"
NO-- NO--
DON'T WANT TO FACE--
"You have to re-absorb Emerald Sands," Jordan explains, with only minutes to spare before the end. "Everything and everyone! Bricks and mortar. Flesh and blood. It was all just you to begin with.
"And we need every iota of the power it took to keep this illusion alive!" he tells the wizard. "We need it to boost the ring.
"You'll die along with all the rest of us, Myrwhydden--unless you give us what you've got!"
CAN'T DIE!
WE CAN'T DO THIS ALONE!
I CAN'T SEE—I CAN'T--
HOLD ON.
YOU AND ME, TOGETHER LIKE ALWAYS. THAT LAST EFFORT.
EVERYTHING WE'VE GOT--WE ACTIVATE THE HOMING PROTOCOL--

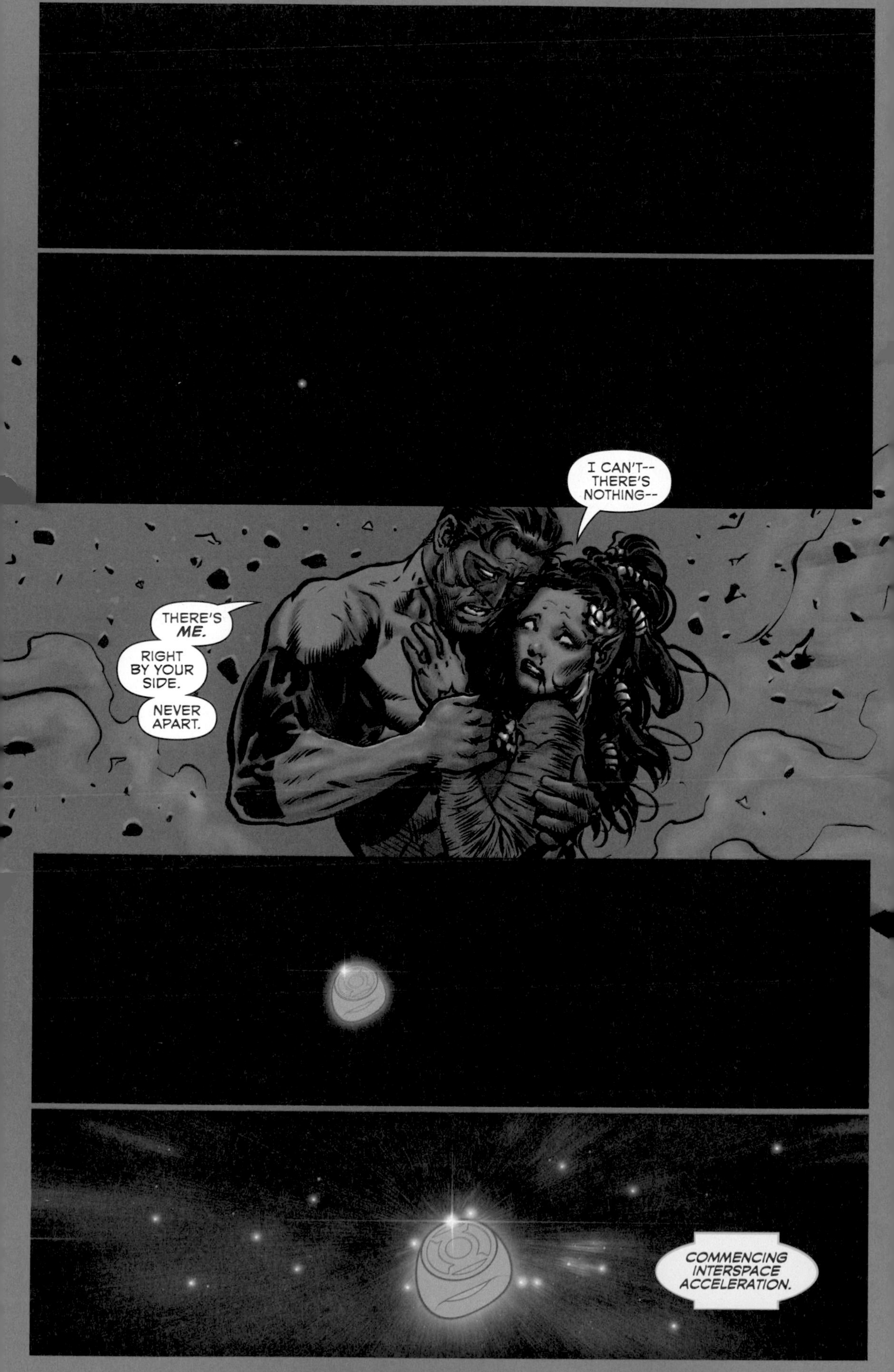
I CAN'T-- THERE'S NOTHING--
THERE'S *ME.*
RIGHT BY YOUR SIDE.
NEVER APART.
COMMENCING INTERSPACE ACCELERATION.

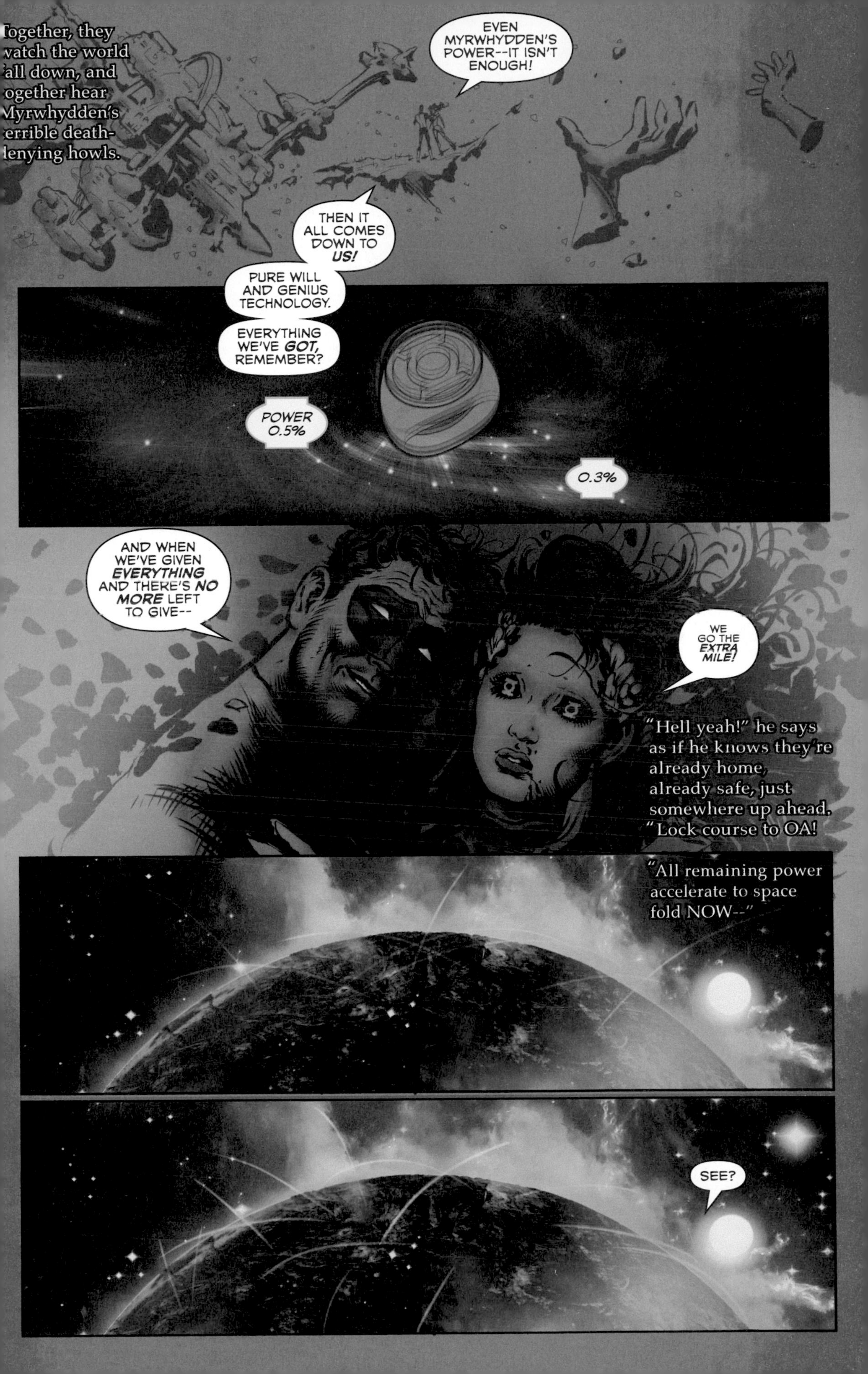

Together, they watch the world fall down, and together hear Myrwhydden's terrible death-denying howls.
EVEN MYRWHYDDEN'S POWER--IT ISN'T ENOUGH!
THEN IT ALL COMES DOWN TO US!
PURE WILL AND GENIUS TECHNOLOGY.
EVERYTHING WE'VE GOT, REMEMBER?
POWER 0.5%
0.3%
AND WHEN WE'VE GIVEN EVERYTHING AND THERE'S NO MORE LEFT TO GIVE--
WE GO THE EXTRA MILE!
"Hell yeah!" he says as if he knows they're already home, already safe, just somewhere up ahead. "Lock course to OA!
"All remaining power accelerate to space fold NOW--"
SEE?

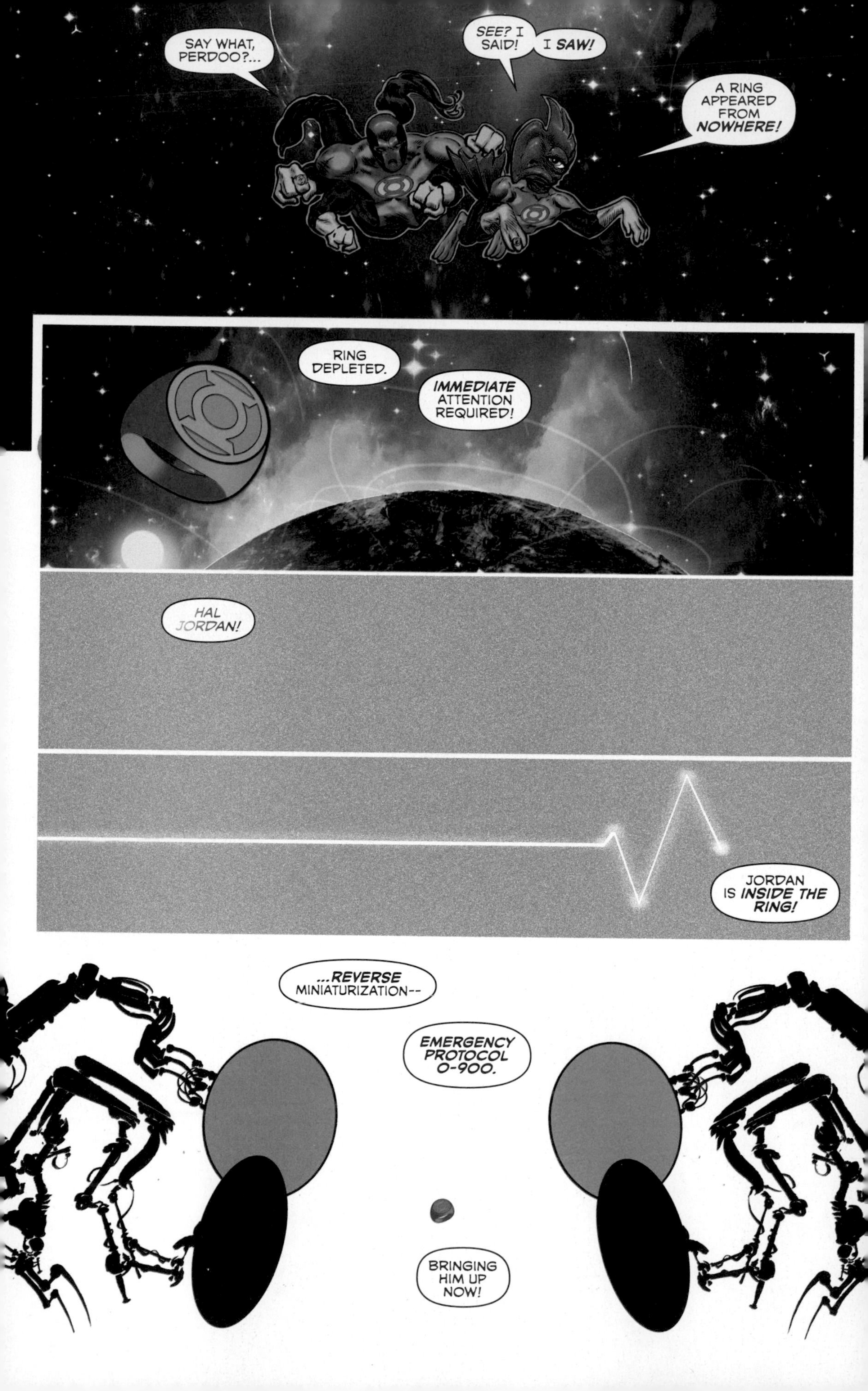
SAY WHAT, PERDOO?...
SEE? I SAID!
I SAW!
A RING APPEARED FROM NOWHERE!
RING DEPLETED.
IMMEDIATE ATTENTION REQUIRED!
HAL JORDAN!
JORDAN IS INSIDE THE RING!
...REVERSE MINIATURIZATION--
EMERGENCY PROTOCOL O-900.
BRINGING HIM UP NOW!

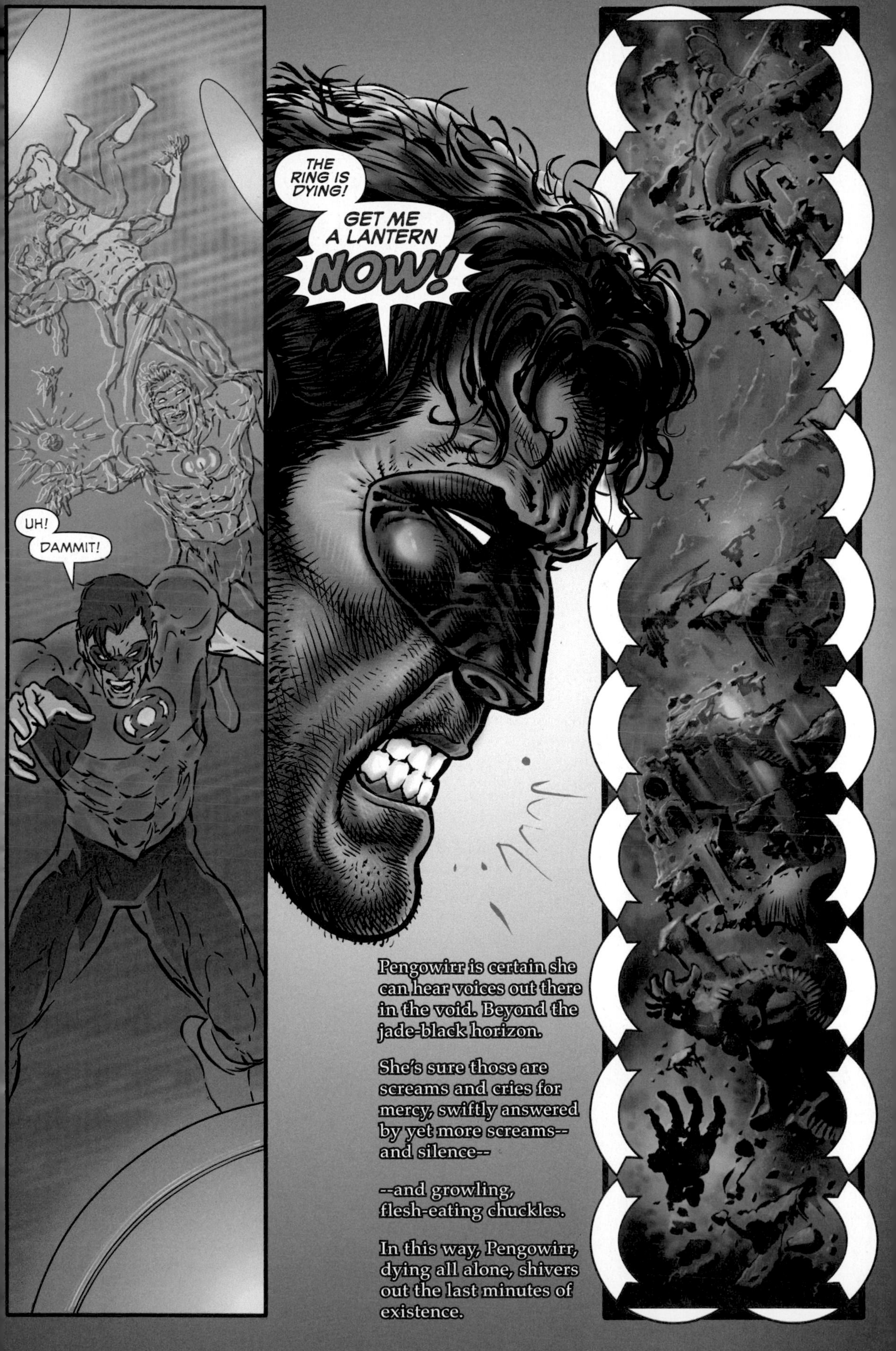
UH!
DAMMIT!
THE RING IS DYING!
GET ME A LANTERN NOW!
Pengowirr is certain she can hear voices out there in the void. Beyond the jade-black horizon.
She's sure those are screams and cries for mercy, swiftly answered by yet more screams-- and silence--
--and growling, flesh-eating chuckles.
In this way, Pengowirr, dying all alone, shivers out the last minutes of existence.

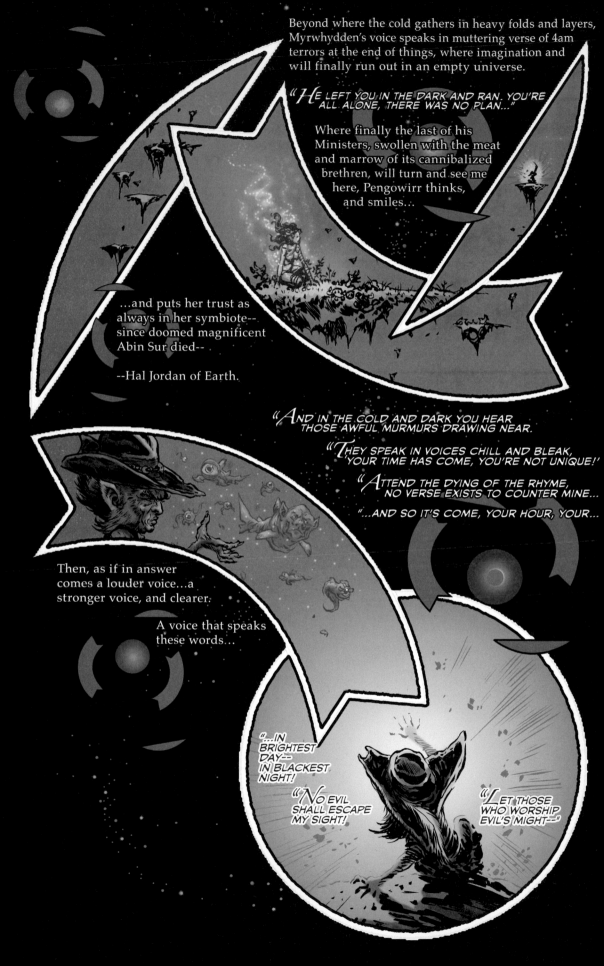

Beyond where the cold gathers in heavy folds and layers, Myrwhydden's voice speaks in muttering verse of 4am terrors at the end of things, where imagination and will finally run out in an empty universe.

"*He left you in the dark and ran. You're all alone, there was no plan...*"

Where finally the last of his Ministers, swollen with the meat and marrow of its cannibalized brethren, will turn and see me here, Pengowirr thinks, and smiles...

...and puts her trust as always in her symbiote-- since doomed magnificent Abin Sur died--

--Hal Jordan of Earth.

"*And in the cold and dark you hear those awful murmurs drawing near.*

"*They speak in voices chill and bleak, 'your time has come, you're not unique!'*

"*Attend the dying of the rhyme, no verse exists to counter mine...*

"*...and so it's come, your hour, your...*"

Then, as if in answer comes a louder voice...a stronger voice, and clearer.

A voice that speaks these words...

"*...In brightest day-- in blackest night!*

"*No evil shall escape my sight!*

"*Let those who worship evil's might--*"

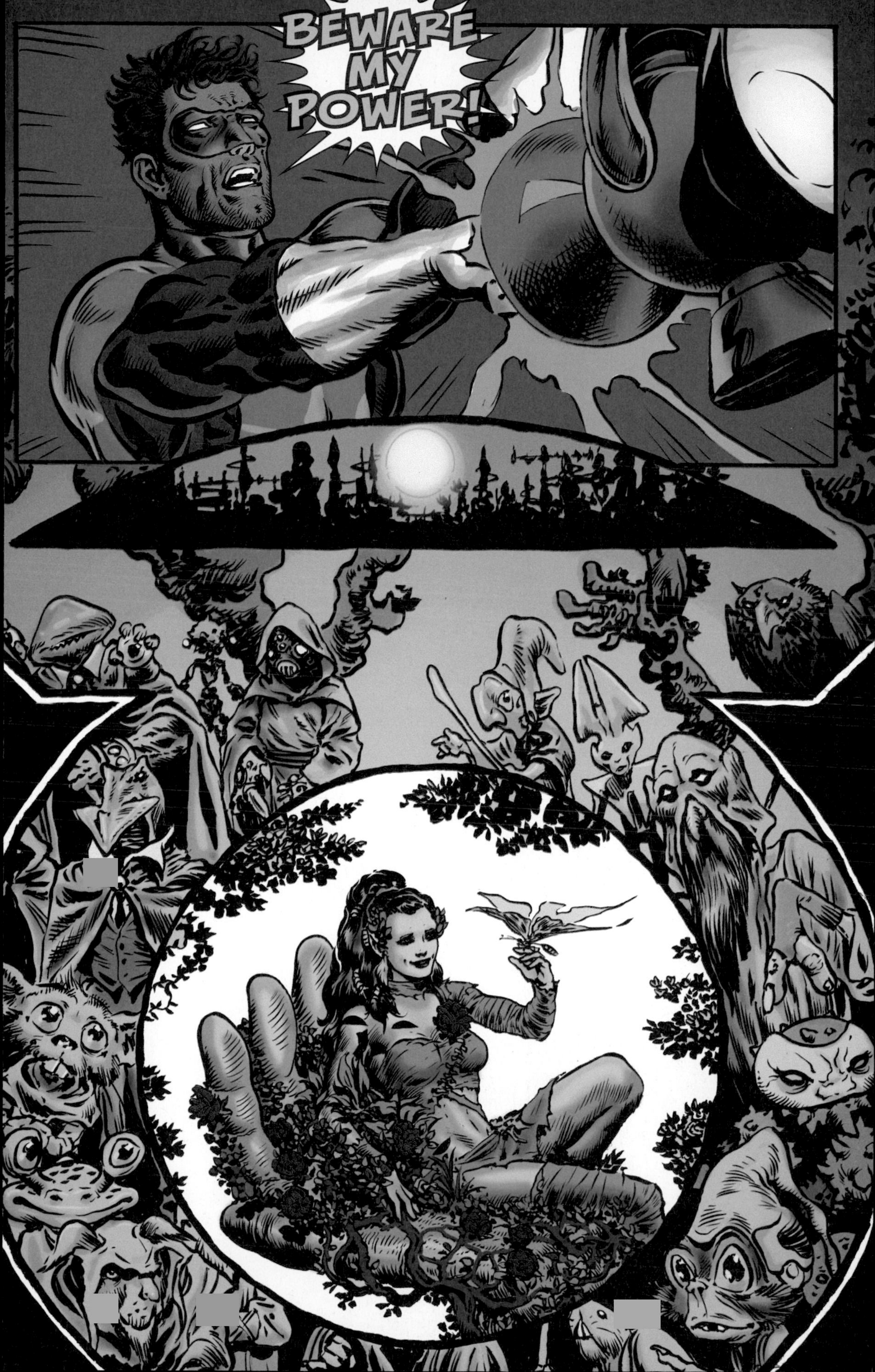
BEWARE MY POWER!

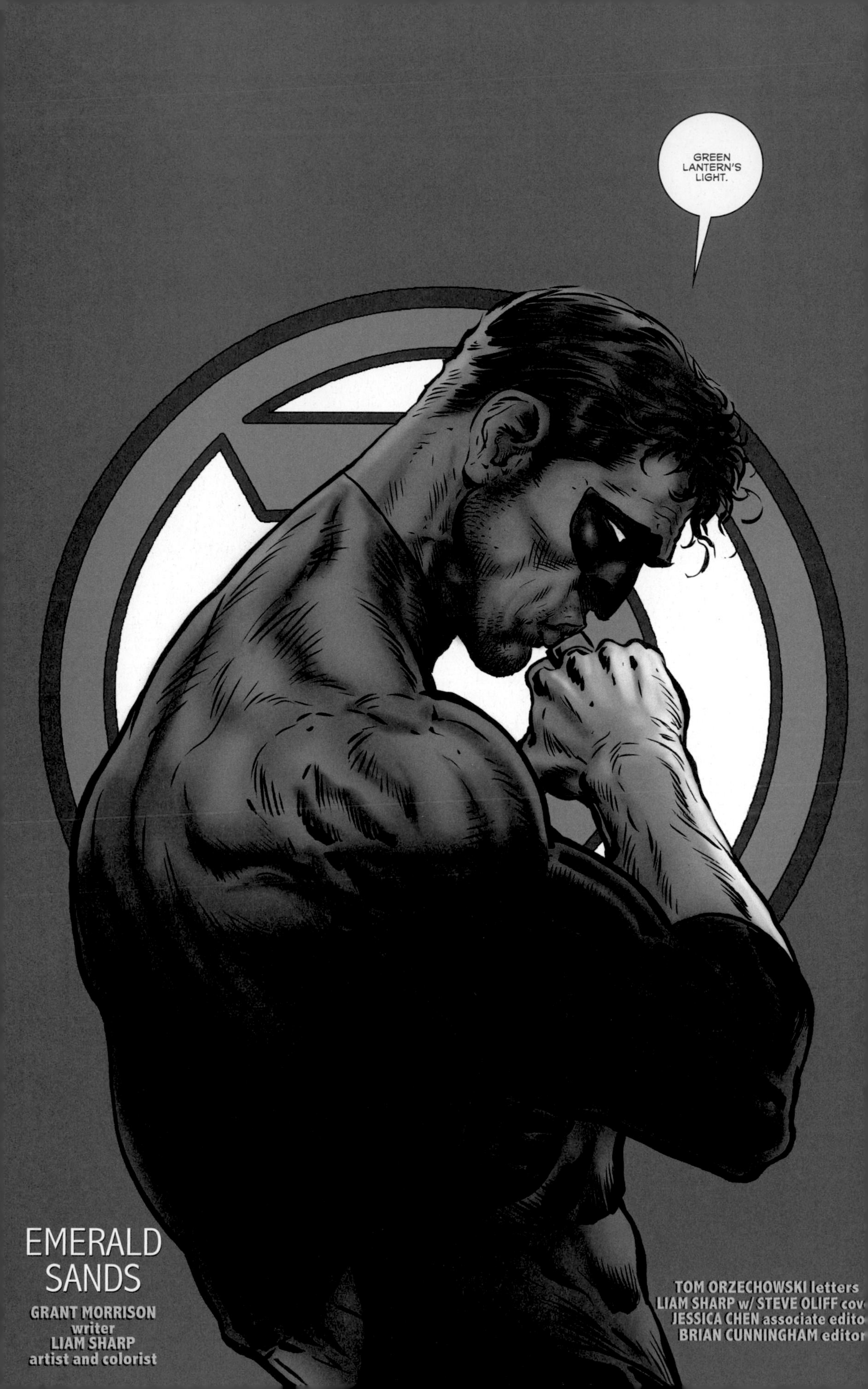
GREEN LANTERN'S LIGHT.
EMERALD SANDS
GRANT MORRISON writer
LIAM SHARP artist and colorist
TOM ORZECHOWSKI letters
LIAM SHARP w/ STEVE OLIFF cov
JESSICA CHEN associate edito
BRIAN CUNNINGHAM editor

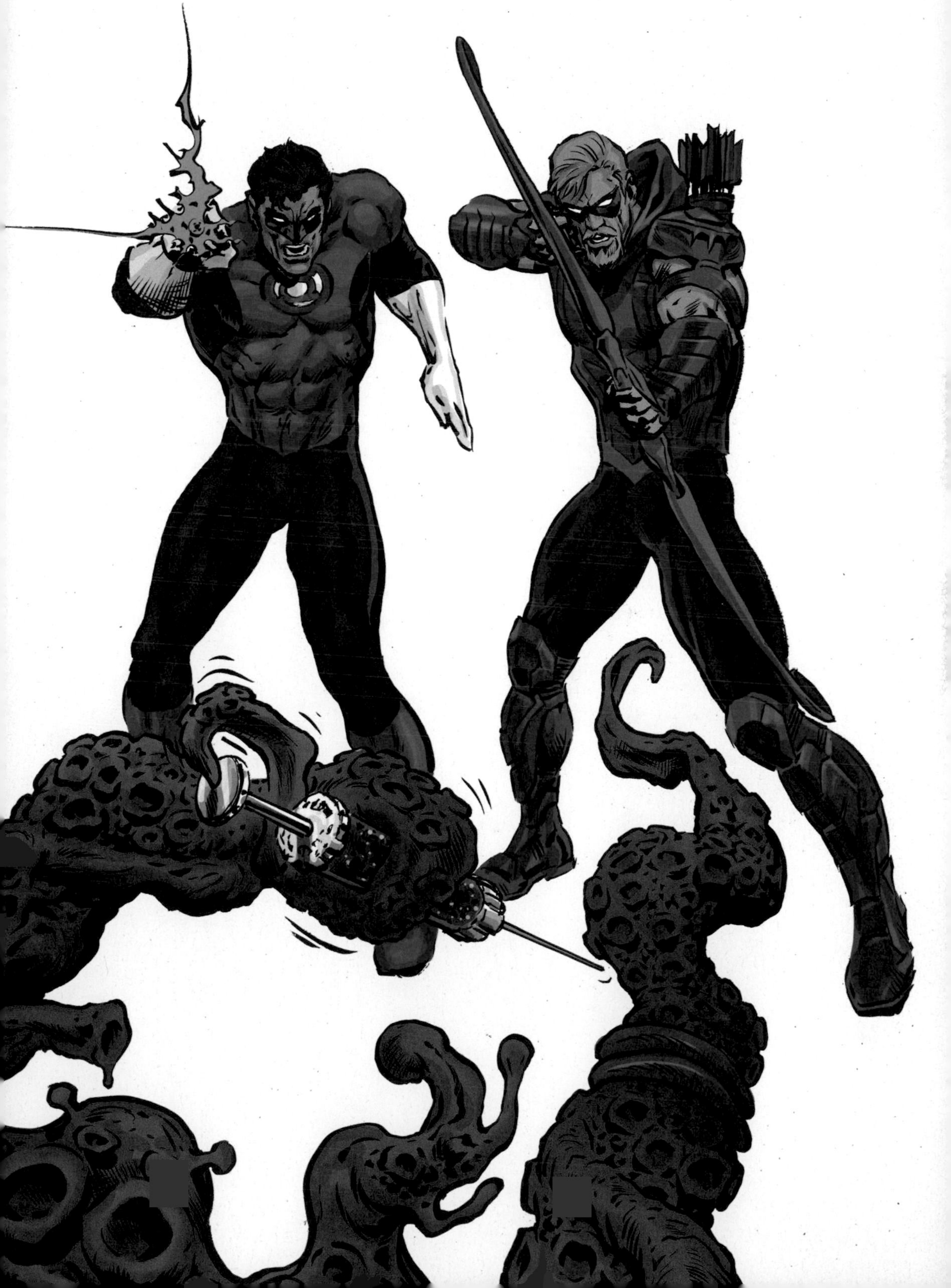

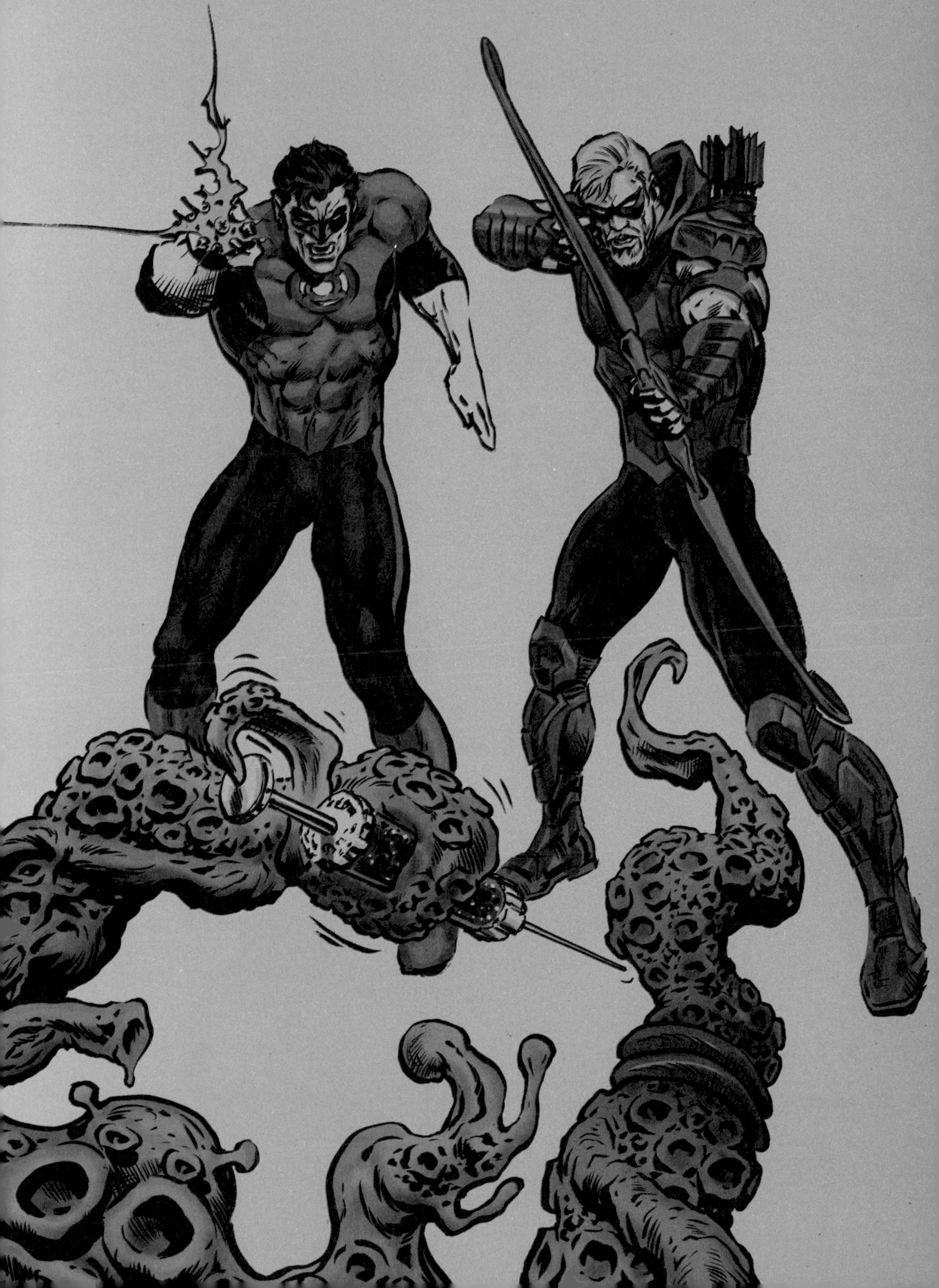

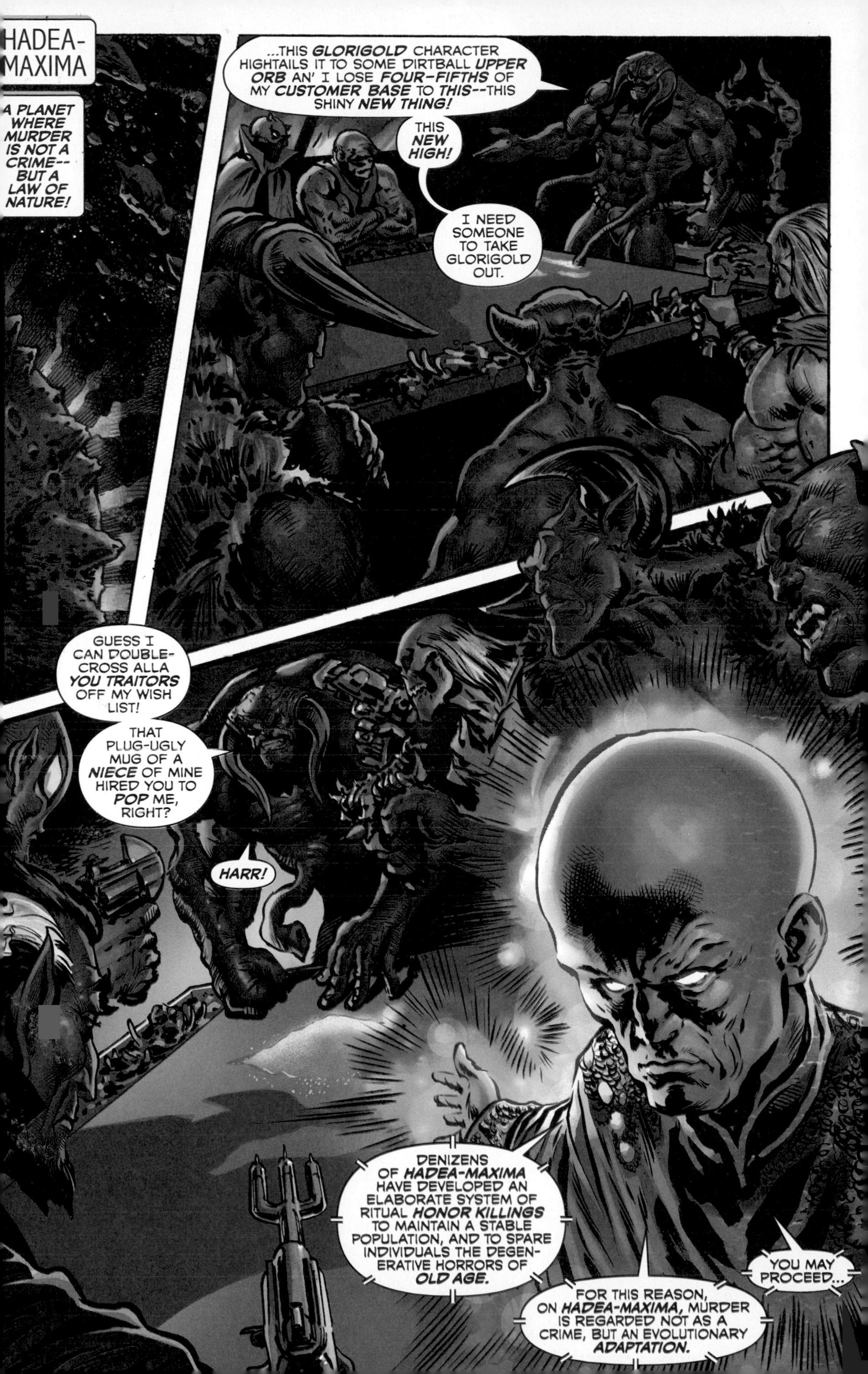
HADEA-MAXIMA
A PLANET WHERE MURDER IS NOT A CRIME--BUT A LAW OF NATURE!
...THIS GLORIGOLD CHARACTER HIGHTAILS IT TO SOME DIRTBALL UPPER ORB AN' I LOSE FOUR-FIFTHS OF MY CUSTOMER BASE TO THIS--THIS SHINY NEW THING!
THIS NEW HIGH!
I NEED SOMEONE TO TAKE GLORIGOLD OUT.
GUESS I CAN DOUBLE-CROSS ALLA YOU TRAITORS OFF MY WISH LIST!
THAT PLUG-UGLY MUG OF A NIECE OF MINE HIRED YOU TO POP ME, RIGHT?
HARR!
DENIZENS OF HADEA-MAXIMA HAVE DEVELOPED AN ELABORATE SYSTEM OF RITUAL HONOR KILLINGS TO MAINTAIN A STABLE POPULATION, AND TO SPARE INDIVIDUALS THE DEGENERATIVE HORRORS OF OLD AGE.
FOR THIS REASON, ON HADEA-MAXIMA, MURDER IS REGARDED NOT AS A CRIME, BUT AN EVOLUTIONARY ADAPTATION.
YOU MAY PROCEED...

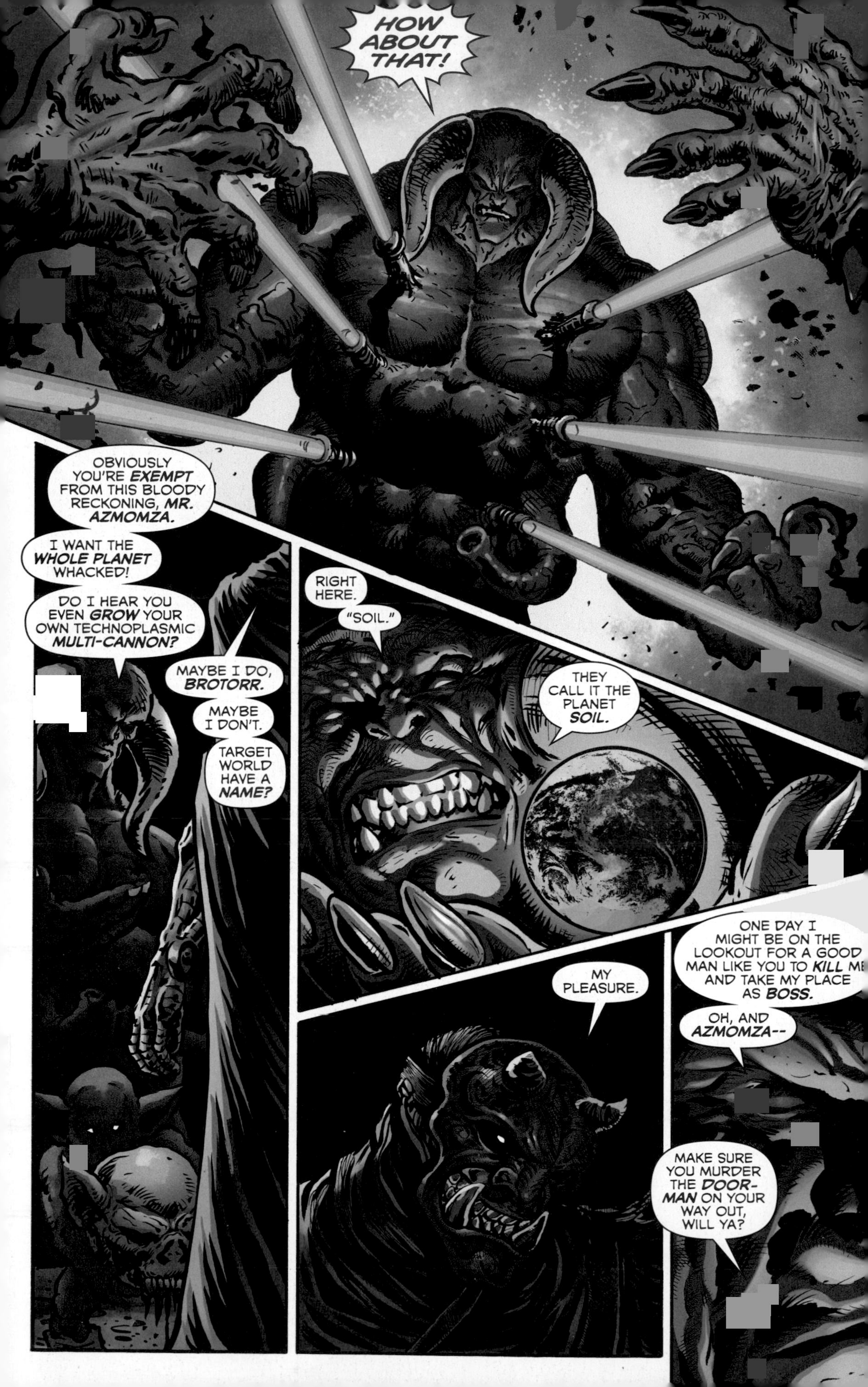
HOW ABOUT THAT!
OBVIOUSLY YOU'RE EXEMPT FROM THIS BLOODY RECKONING, MR. AZMOMZA.
I WANT THE WHOLE PLANET WHACKED!
DO I HEAR YOU EVEN GROW YOUR OWN TECHNOPLASMIC MULTI-CANNON?
MAYBE I DO, BROTORR.
MAYBE I DON'T.
TARGET WORLD HAVE A NAME?
THEY CALL IT THE PLANET SOIL.
RIGHT HERE.
"SOIL."
ONE DAY I MIGHT BE ON THE LOOKOUT FOR A GOOD MAN LIKE YOU TO KILL M
AND TAKE MY PLACE AS BOSS.
MY PLEASURE.
OH, AND AZMOMZA--
MAKE SURE YOU MURDER THE DOOR-MAN ON YOUR WAY OUT, WILL YA?

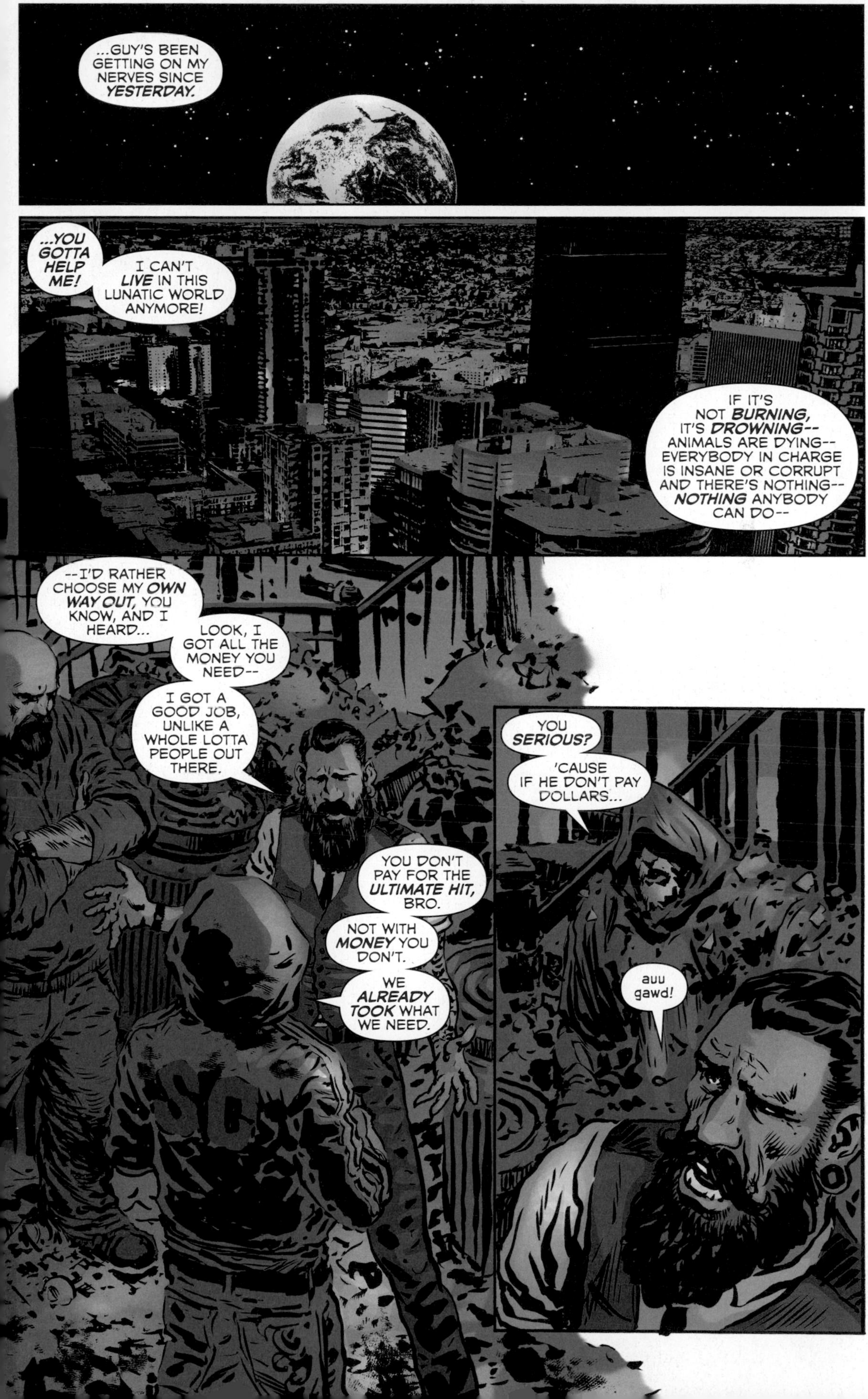
...GUY'S BEEN GETTING ON MY NERVES SINCE YESTERDAY.
...YOU GOTTA HELP ME!
I CAN'T LIVE IN THIS LUNATIC WORLD ANYMORE!
IF IT'S NOT BURNING, IT'S DROWNING-- ANIMALS ARE DYING-- EVERYBODY IN CHARGE IS INSANE OR CORRUPT AND THERE'S NOTHING-- NOTHING ANYBODY CAN DO--
--I'D RATHER CHOOSE MY OWN WAY OUT, YOU KNOW, AND I HEARD...
LOOK, I GOT ALL THE MONEY YOU NEED--
I GOT A GOOD JOB, UNLIKE A WHOLE LOTTA PEOPLE OUT THERE.
YOU DON'T PAY FOR THE ULTIMATE HIT, BRO.
NOT WITH MONEY YOU DON'T.
WE ALREADY TOOK WHAT WE NEED.
YOU SERIOUS?
'CAUSE IF HE DON'T PAY DOLLARS...
auu gawd!

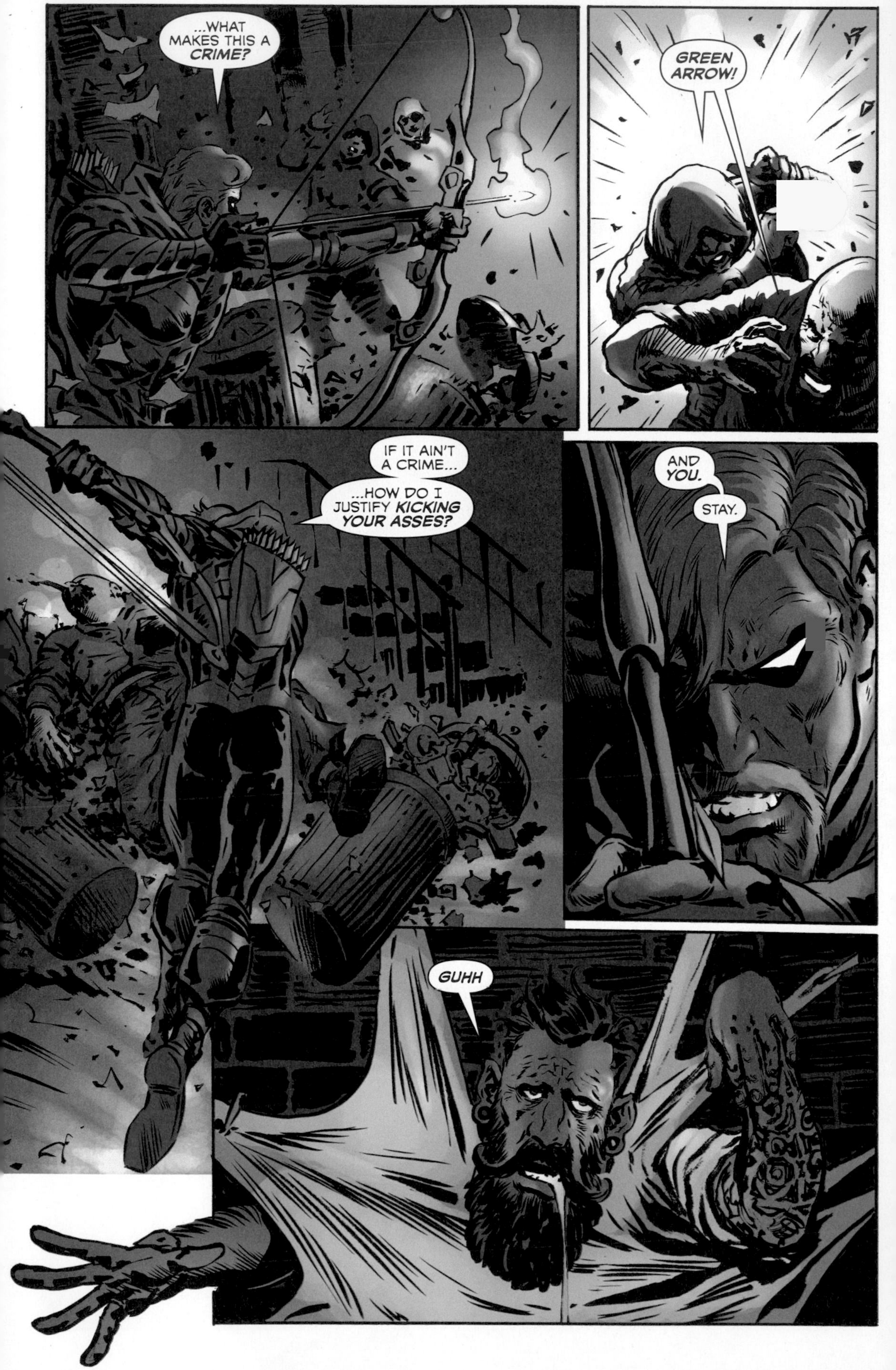
...WHAT MAKES THIS A CRIME?
GREEN ARROW!
IF IT AIN'T A CRIME...
...HOW DO I JUSTIFY KICKING YOUR ASSES?
AND YOU.
STAY.
GUHH

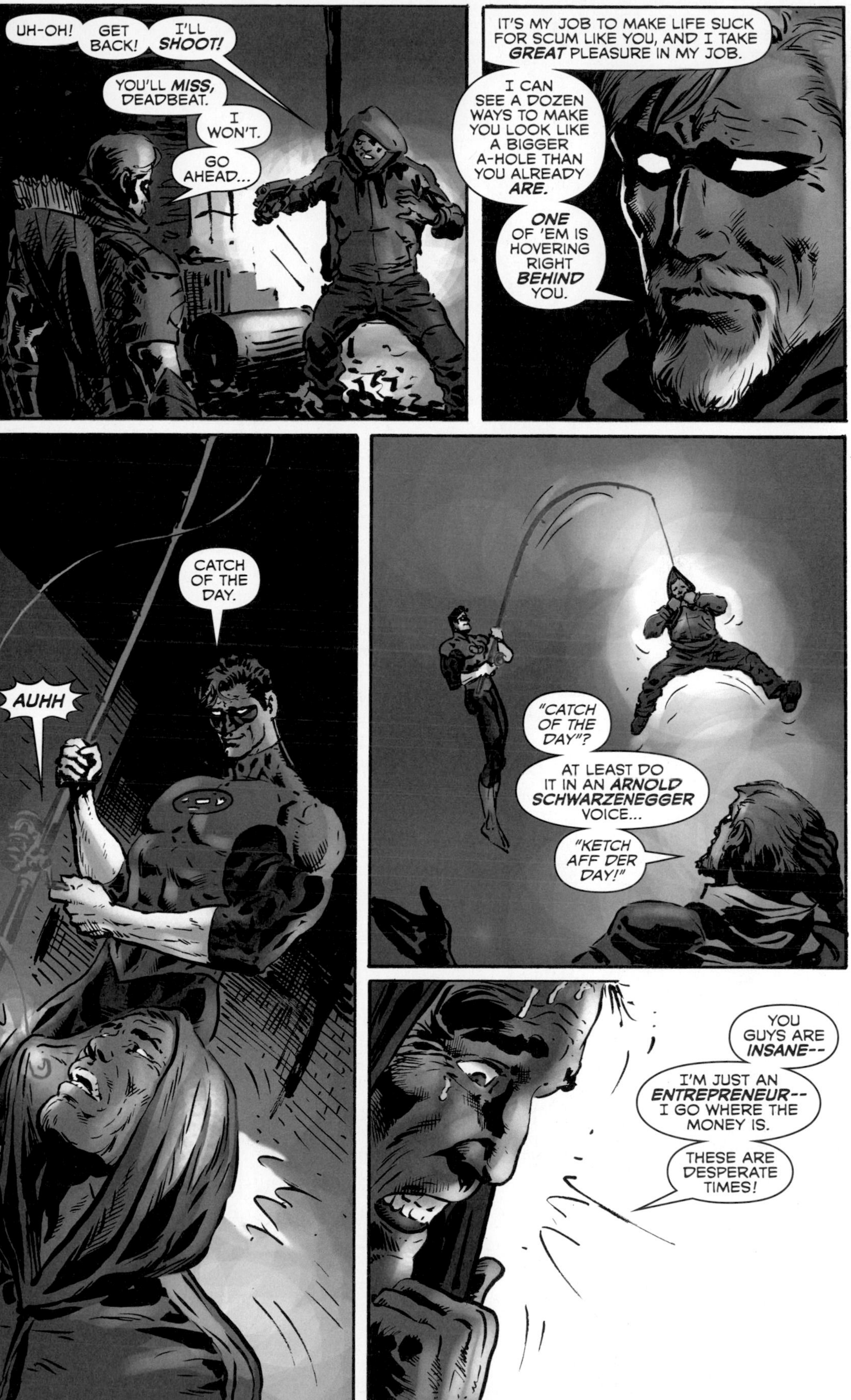
UH-OH!
GET BACK!
I'LL SHOOT!
YOU'LL MISS, DEADBEAT.
I WON'T.
GO AHEAD...
IT'S MY JOB TO MAKE LIFE SUCK FOR SCUM LIKE YOU, AND I TAKE GREAT PLEASURE IN MY JOB.
I CAN SEE A DOZEN WAYS TO MAKE YOU LOOK LIKE A BIGGER A-HOLE THAN YOU ALREADY ARE.
ONE OF 'EM IS HOVERING RIGHT BEHIND YOU.
CATCH OF THE DAY.
AUHH
"CATCH OF THE DAY"?
AT LEAST DO IT IN AN ARNOLD SCHWARZENEGGER VOICE...
"KETCH AFF DER DAY!"
YOU GUYS ARE INSANE--
I'M JUST AN ENTREPRENEUR-- I GO WHERE THE MONEY IS.
THESE ARE DESPERATE TIMES!

I DUNNO WHAT THEY *DID* TO THE BUYER.

GUY LOOKS ROUGH.

...ACCORDING TO MY *RING*, HIS ULTIMATE HIGH'S JUST A POWERFUL *ANESTHETIC*...

AND IT'S *WEARING OFF*...

ALL RIGHT! ALL RIGHT!

--*PIER 20*-- THAT'S WHERE THE STUFF COMES IN--

BUT YOU'RE *WAY* OUTTA YOUR DEPTH THIS TIME, *ARROW!*

AW, NO!

IT'S OKAY, BUDDY.

GOOD GUYS, SEE?

WE'RE YOUR GUARDIAN *ANGELS.*

ARROW, THEY'RE COMING!

I DON'T THINK HE'S SEEING *ANGELS.*

WHAT'S HE SO *SCARED* OF?

WE NEED TO GET THIS GUY TO A *HOSPITAL*--

HE'S *DEAD!*

WHAT'S THAT LIGHT AHEAD?

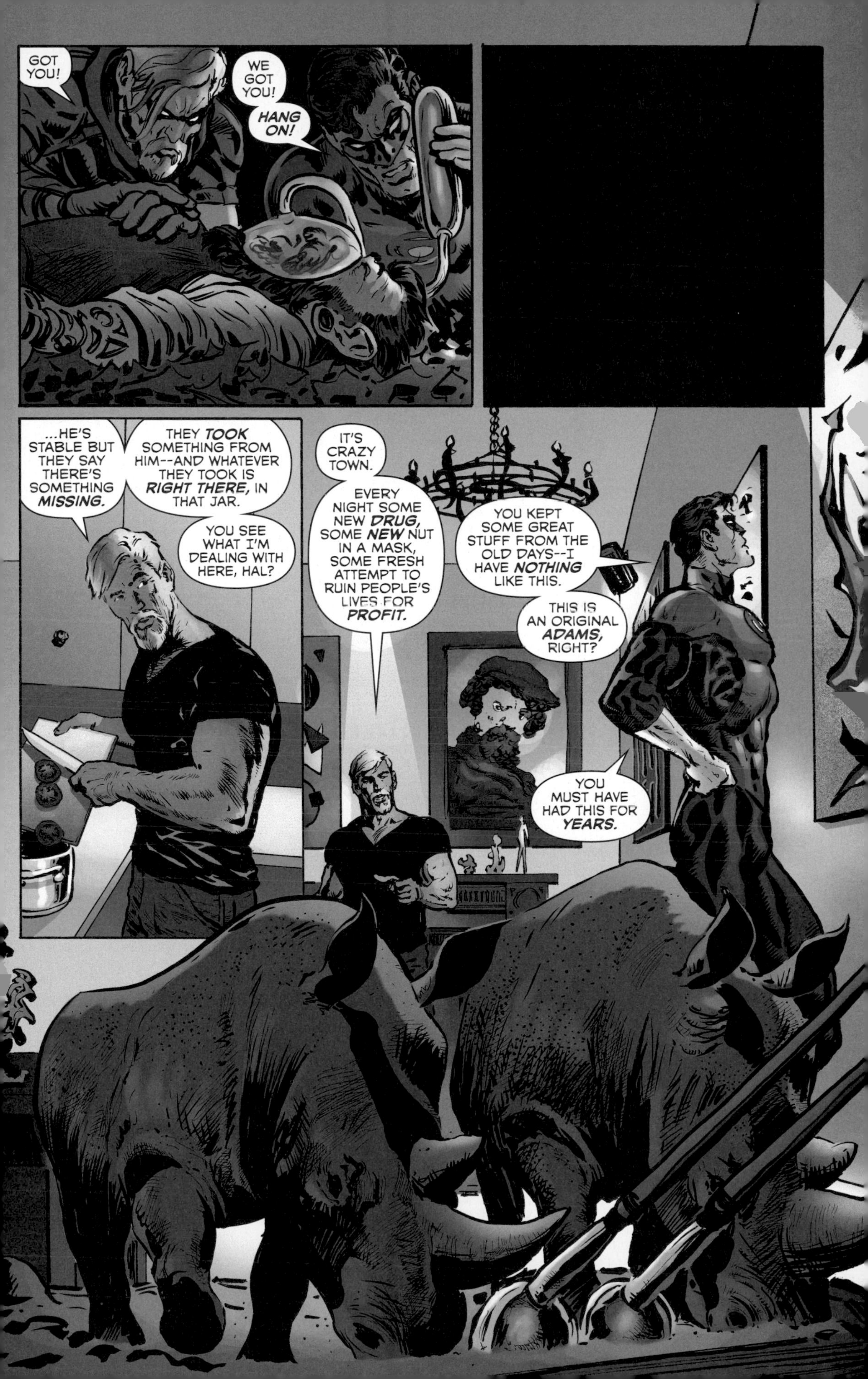
GOT YOU!
WE GOT YOU!
HANG ON!
...HE'S STABLE BUT THEY SAY THERE'S SOMETHING MISSING.
THEY TOOK SOMETHING FROM HIM--AND WHATEVER THEY TOOK IS RIGHT THERE, IN THAT JAR.
YOU SEE WHAT I'M DEALING WITH HERE, HAL?
IT'S CRAZY TOWN.
EVERY NIGHT SOME NEW DRUG, SOME NEW NUT IN A MASK, SOME FRESH ATTEMPT TO RUIN PEOPLE'S LIVES FOR PROFIT.
YOU KEPT SOME GREAT STUFF FROM THE OLD DAYS--I HAVE NOTHING LIKE THIS.
THIS IS AN ORIGINAL ADAMS, RIGHT?
YOU MUST HAVE HAD THIS FOR YEARS.

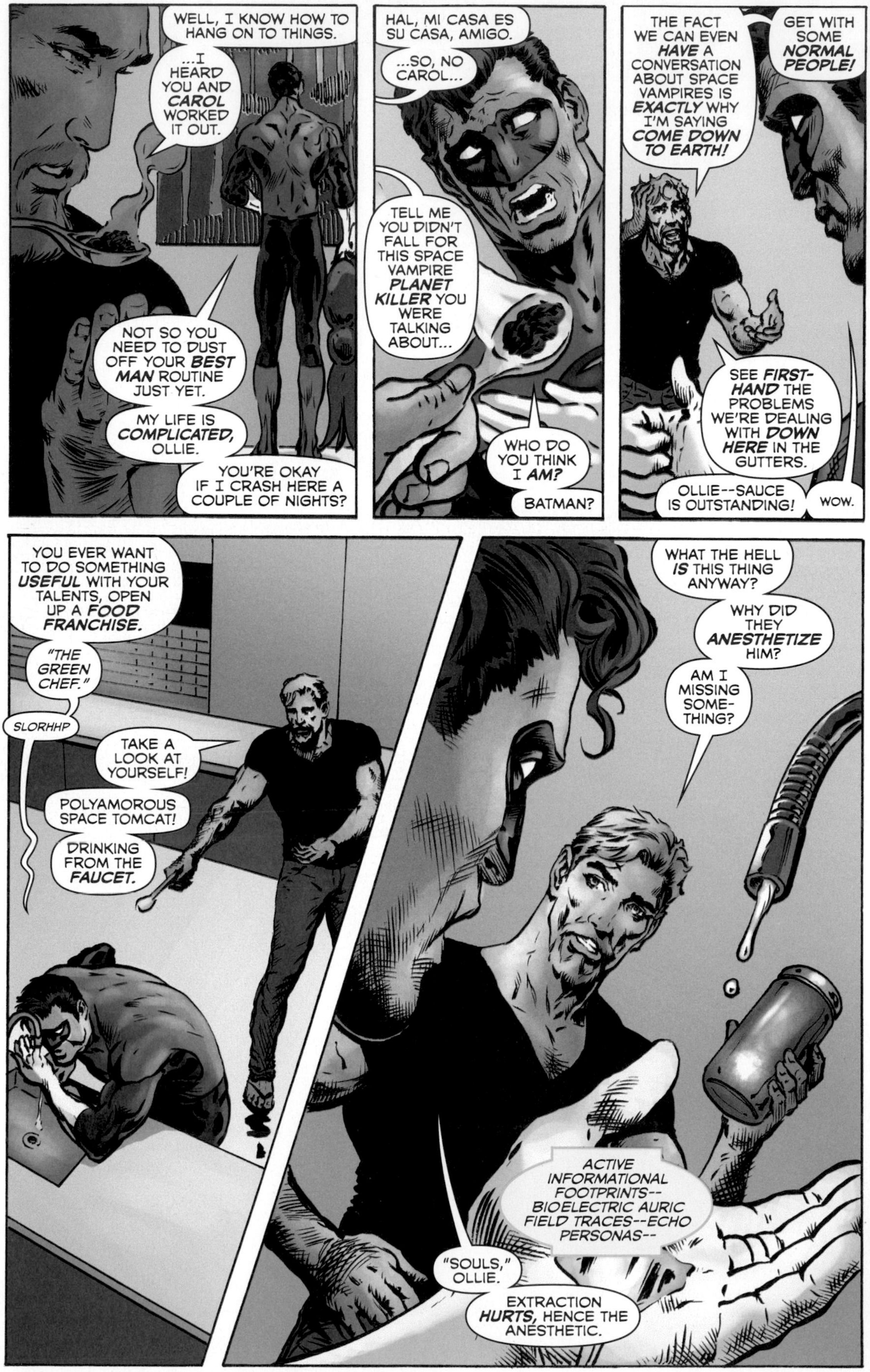
WELL, I KNOW HOW TO HANG ON TO THINGS.
...I HEARD YOU AND CAROL WORKED IT OUT.
NOT SO YOU NEED TO DUST OFF YOUR BEST MAN ROUTINE JUST YET.
MY LIFE IS COMPLICATED, OLLIE.
YOU'RE OKAY IF I CRASH HERE A COUPLE OF NIGHTS?
HAL, MI CASA ES SU CASA, AMIGO.
...SO, NO CAROL...
TELL ME YOU DIDN'T FALL FOR THIS SPACE VAMPIRE PLANET KILLER YOU WERE TALKING ABOUT...
WHO DO YOU THINK I AM?
BATMAN?
THE FACT WE CAN EVEN HAVE A CONVERSATION ABOUT SPACE VAMPIRES IS EXACTLY WHY I'M SAYING COME DOWN TO EARTH!
GET WITH SOME NORMAL PEOPLE!
SEE FIRST-HAND THE PROBLEMS WE'RE DEALING WITH DOWN HERE IN THE GUTTERS.
OLLIE--SAUCE IS OUTSTANDING!
WOW.
YOU EVER WANT TO DO SOMETHING USEFUL WITH YOUR TALENTS, OPEN UP A FOOD FRANCHISE.
"THE GREEN CHEF."
SLORHHP
TAKE A LOOK AT YOURSELF!
POLYAMOROUS SPACE TOMCAT!
DRINKING FROM THE FAUCET.
WHAT THE HELL IS THIS THING ANYWAY?
WHY DID THEY ANESTHETIZE HIM?
AM I MISSING SOME-THING?
ACTIVE INFORMATIONAL FOOTPRINTS--BIOELECTRIC AURIC FIELD TRACES--ECHO PERSONAS--
"SOULS," OLLIE.
EXTRACTION HURTS, HENCE THE ANESTHETIC.

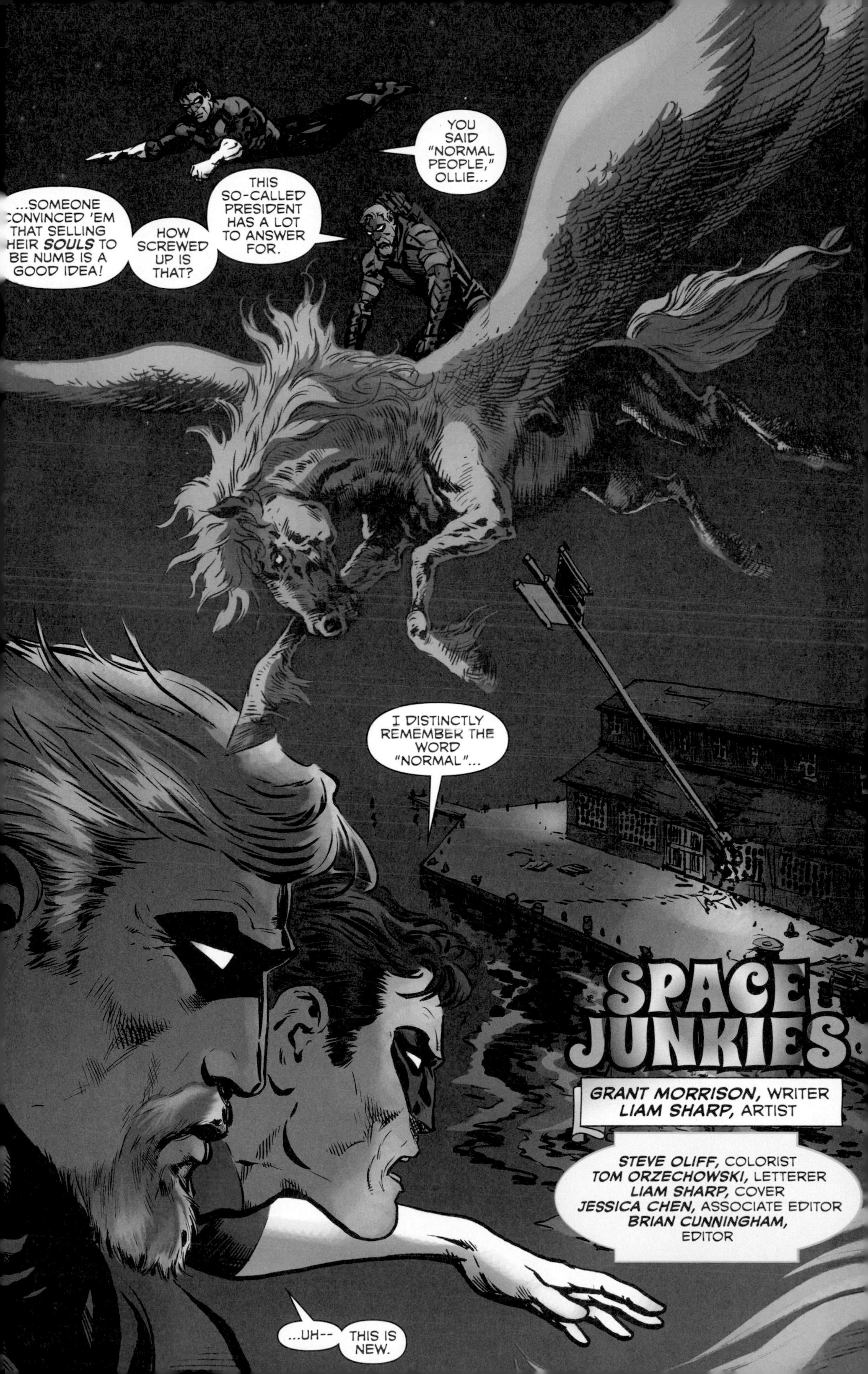
YOU SAID "NORMAL PEOPLE," OLLIE...
THIS SO-CALLED PRESIDENT HAS A LOT TO ANSWER FOR.
HOW SCREWED UP IS THAT?
...SOMEONE CONVINCED 'EM THAT SELLING HEIR SOULS TO BE NUMB IS A GOOD IDEA!
I DISTINCTLY REMEMBER THE WORD "NORMAL"...
SPACE JUNKIES
GRANT MORRISON, WRITER
LIAM SHARP, ARTIST
STEVE OLIFF, COLORIST
TOM ORZECHOWSKI, LETTERER
LIAM SHARP, COVER
JESSICA CHEN, ASSOCIATE EDITOR
BRIAN CUNNINGHAM, EDITOR
...UH--
THIS IS NEW.

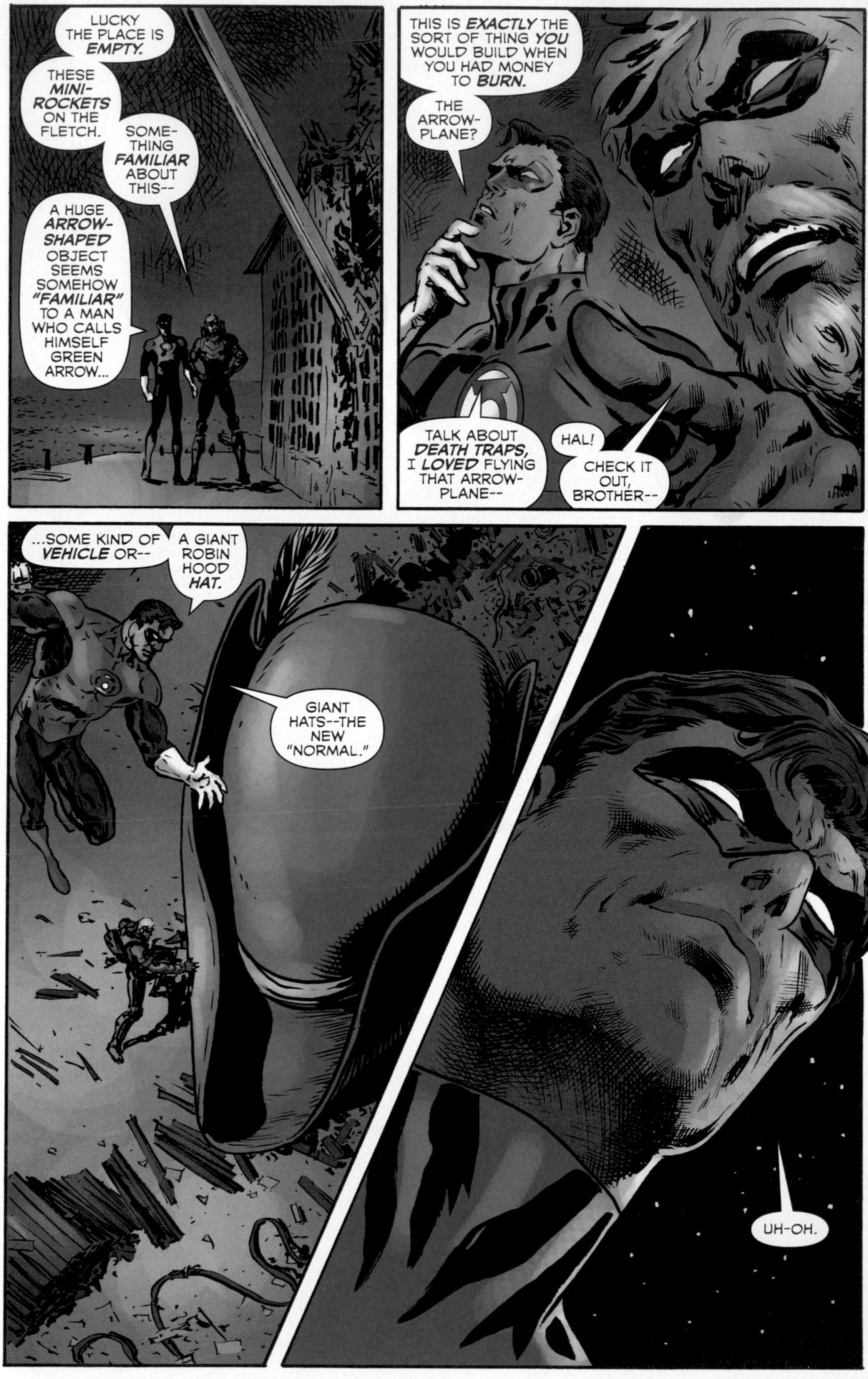
LUCKY THE PLACE IS EMPTY.
THESE MINI-ROCKETS ON THE FLETCH.
SOME-THING FAMILIAR ABOUT THIS--
A HUGE ARROW-SHAPED OBJECT SEEMS SOMEHOW "FAMILIAR" TO A MAN WHO CALLS HIMSELF GREEN ARROW...
THIS IS EXACTLY THE SORT OF THING YOU WOULD BUILD WHEN YOU HAD MONEY TO BURN.
THE ARROW-PLANE?
TALK ABOUT DEATH TRAPS, I LOVED FLYING THAT ARROW-PLANE--
HAL!
CHECK IT OUT, BROTHER--
...SOME KIND OF VEHICLE OR--
A GIANT ROBIN HOOD HAT.
GIANT HATS--THE NEW "NORMAL."
UH-OH.

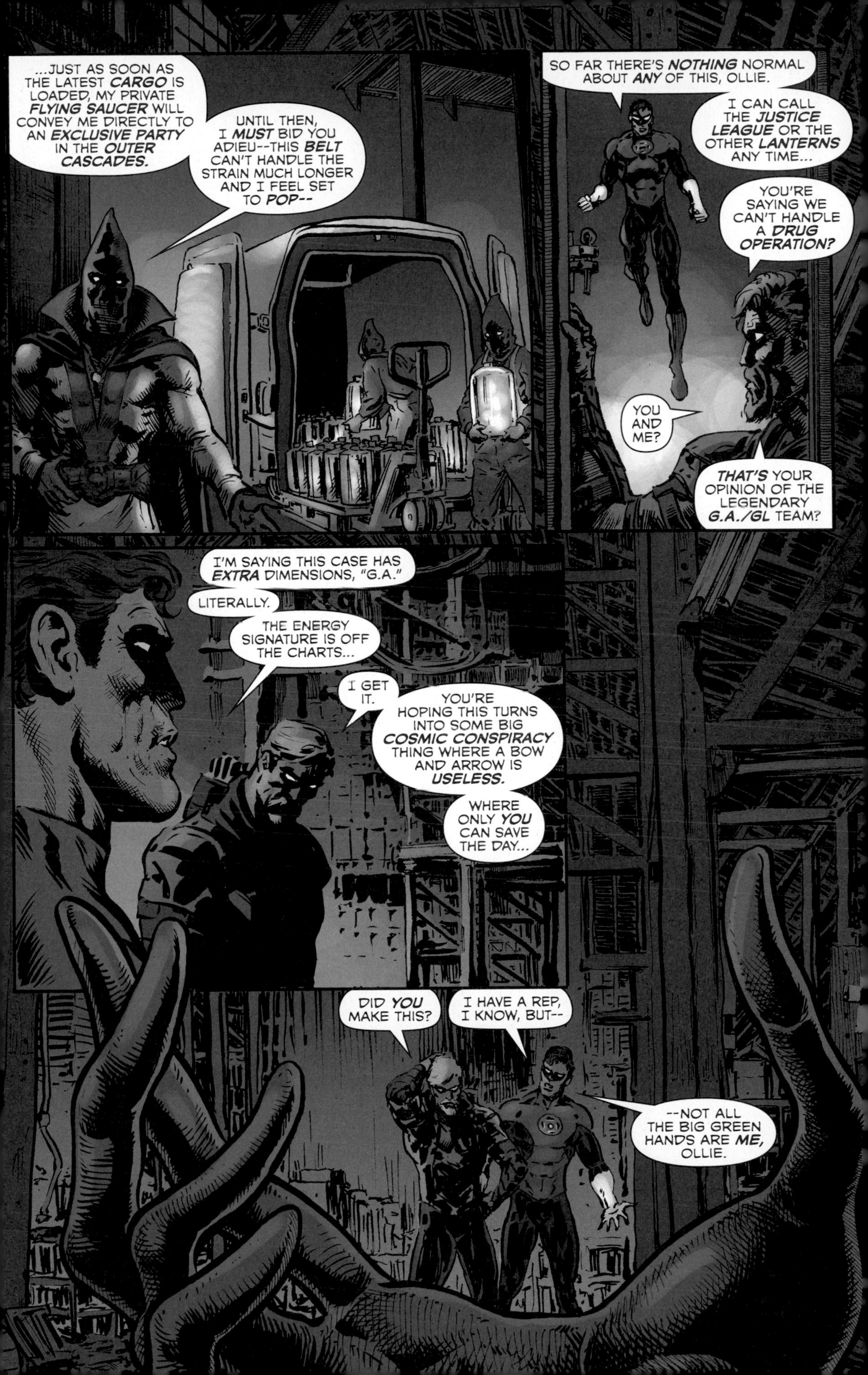
...JUST AS SOON AS THE LATEST CARGO IS LOADED, MY PRIVATE FLYING SAUCER WILL CONVEY ME DIRECTLY TO AN EXCLUSIVE PARTY IN THE OUTER CASCADES.
UNTIL THEN, I MUST BID YOU ADIEU--THIS BELT CAN'T HANDLE THE STRAIN MUCH LONGER AND I FEEL SET TO POP--
SO FAR THERE'S NOTHING NORMAL ABOUT ANY OF THIS, OLLIE.
I CAN CALL THE JUSTICE LEAGUE OR THE OTHER LANTERNS ANY TIME...
YOU'RE SAYING WE CAN'T HANDLE A DRUG OPERATION?
YOU AND ME?
THAT'S YOUR OPINION OF THE LEGENDARY G.A./GL TEAM?
I'M SAYING THIS CASE HAS EXTRA DIMENSIONS, "G.A."
LITERALLY.
THE ENERGY SIGNATURE IS OFF THE CHARTS...
I GET IT.
YOU'RE HOPING THIS TURNS INTO SOME BIG COSMIC CONSPIRACY THING WHERE A BOW AND ARROW IS USELESS.
WHERE ONLY YOU CAN SAVE THE DAY...
DID YOU MAKE THIS?
I HAVE A REP, I KNOW, BUT--
--NOT ALL THE BIG GREEN HANDS ARE ME, OLLIE.

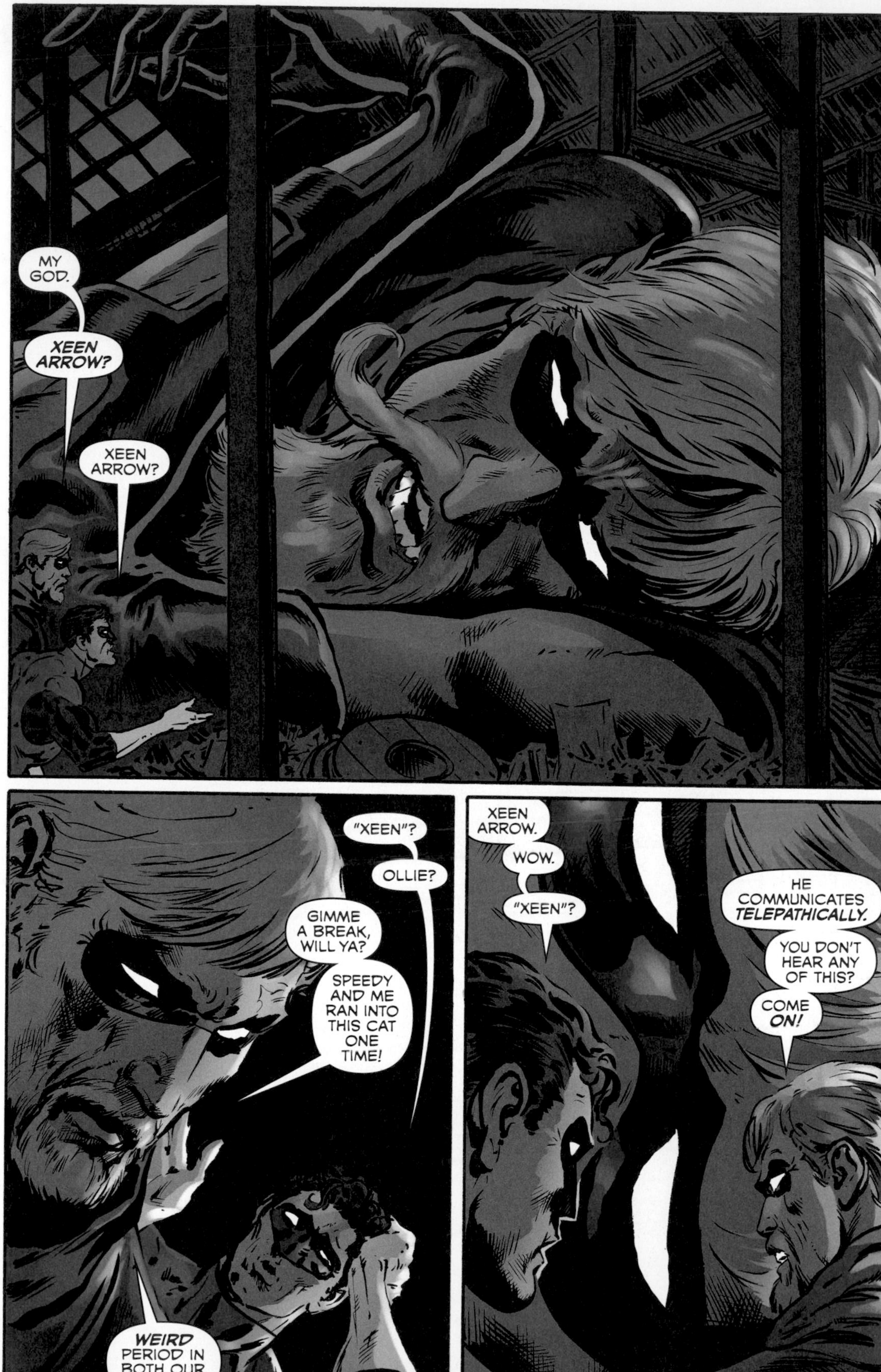
MY GOD.
XEEN ARROW?
XEEN ARROW?
"XEEN"?
OLLIE?
GIMME A BREAK, WILL YA?
SPEEDY AND ME RAN INTO THIS CAT ONE TIME!
WEIRD PERIOD IN BOTH OUR LIVES.
XEEN ARROW.
WOW.
"XEEN"?
HE COMMUNICATES TELEPATHICALLY.
YOU DON'T HEAR ANY OF THIS?
COME ON!

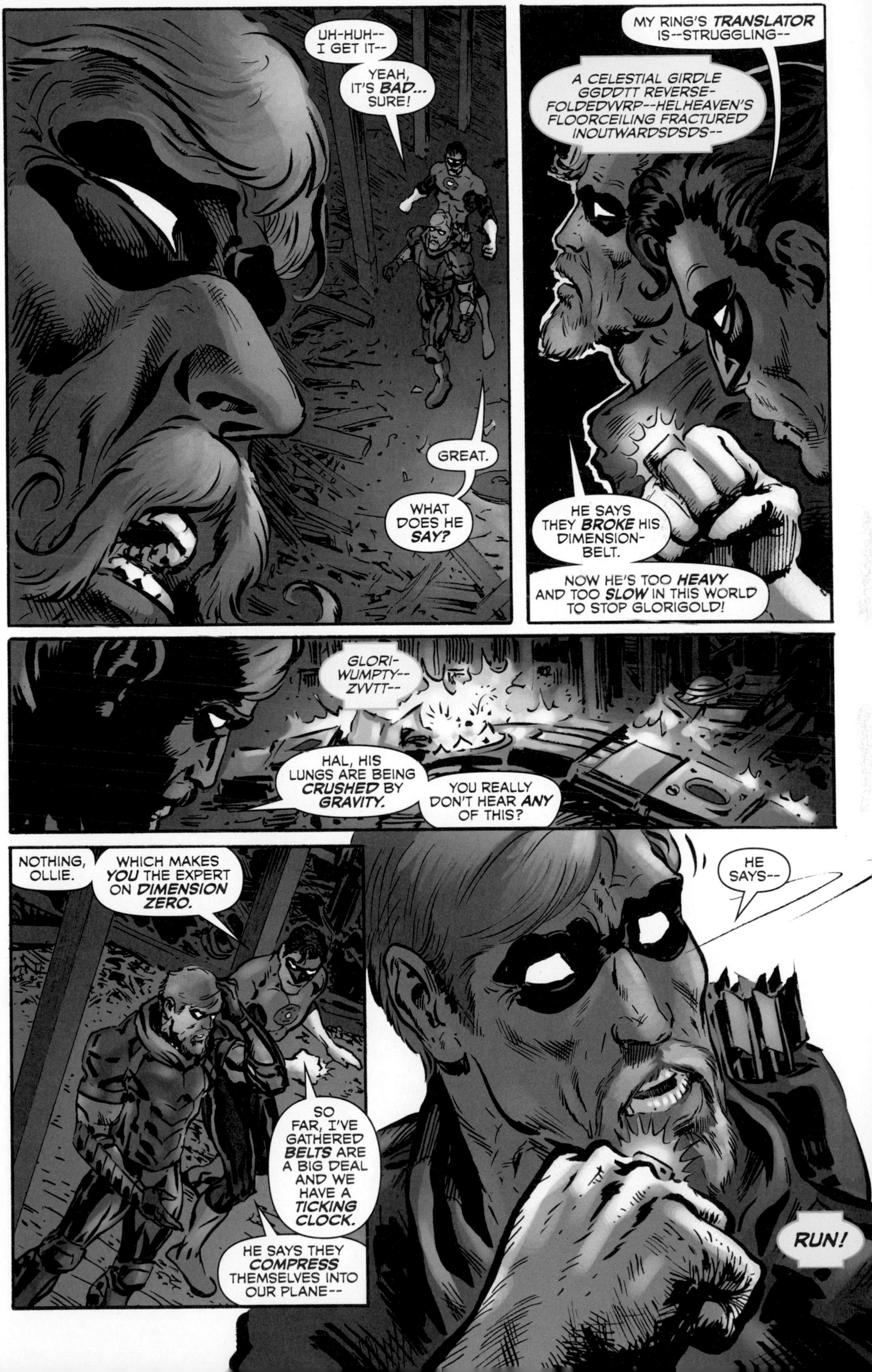
UH-HUH--
I GET IT--
YEAH, IT'S BAD... SURE!
GREAT.
WHAT DOES HE SAY?
MY RING'S TRANSLATOR IS--STRUGGLING--
A CELESTIAL GIRDLE GGDDTT REVERSE-FOLDEDWRP--HELHEAVEN'S FLOORCEILING FRACTURED INOUTWARDSDSDS--
HE SAYS THEY BROKE HIS DIMENSION-BELT.
NOW HE'S TOO HEAVY AND TOO SLOW IN THIS WORLD TO STOP GLORIGOLD!
GLORI-WUMPTY--ZWTT--
HAL, HIS LUNGS ARE BEING CRUSHED BY GRAVITY.
YOU REALLY DON'T HEAR ANY OF THIS?
NOTHING, OLLIE.
WHICH MAKES YOU THE EXPERT ON DIMENSION ZERO.
SO FAR, I'VE GATHERED BELTS ARE A BIG DEAL AND WE HAVE A TICKING CLOCK.
HE SAYS THEY COMPRESS THEMSELVES INTO OUR PLANE--
HE SAYS--
RUN!

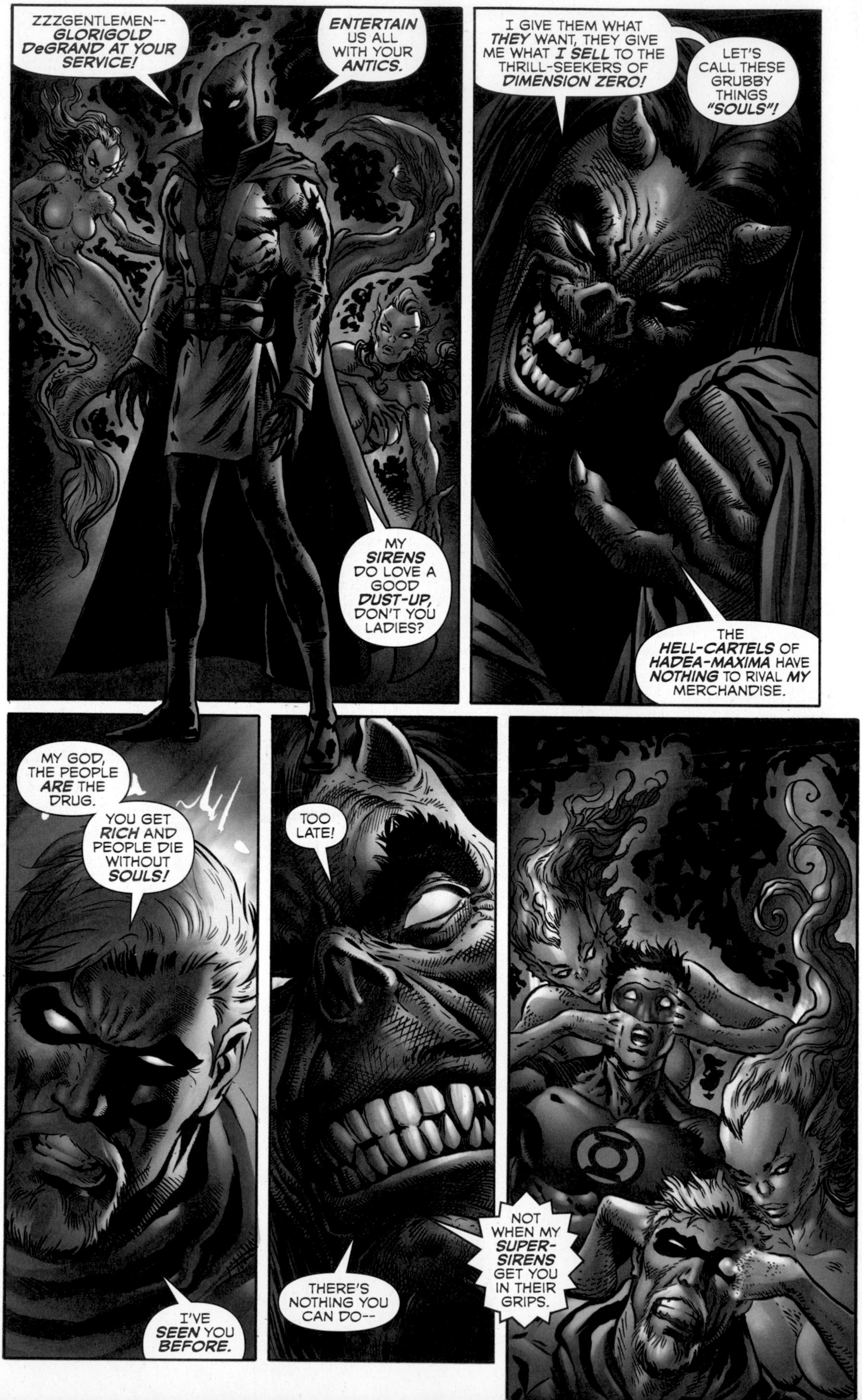
ZZZGENTLEMEN-- GLORIGOLD DeGRAND AT YOUR SERVICE!
ENTERTAIN US ALL WITH YOUR ANTICS.
MY SIRENS DO LOVE A GOOD DUST-UP, DON'T YOU LADIES?
I GIVE THEM WHAT THEY WANT, THEY GIVE ME WHAT I SELL TO THE THRILL-SEEKERS OF DIMENSION ZERO!
LET'S CALL THESE GRUBBY THINGS "SOULS"!
THE HELL-CARTELS OF HADEA-MAXIMA HAVE NOTHING TO RIVAL MY MERCHANDISE.
MY GOD, THE PEOPLE ARE THE DRUG.
YOU GET RICH AND PEOPLE DIE WITHOUT SOULS!
I'VE SEEN YOU BEFORE.
TOO LATE!
THERE'S NOTHING YOU CAN DO--
NOT WHEN MY SUPER-SIRENS GET YOU IN THEIR GRIPS.

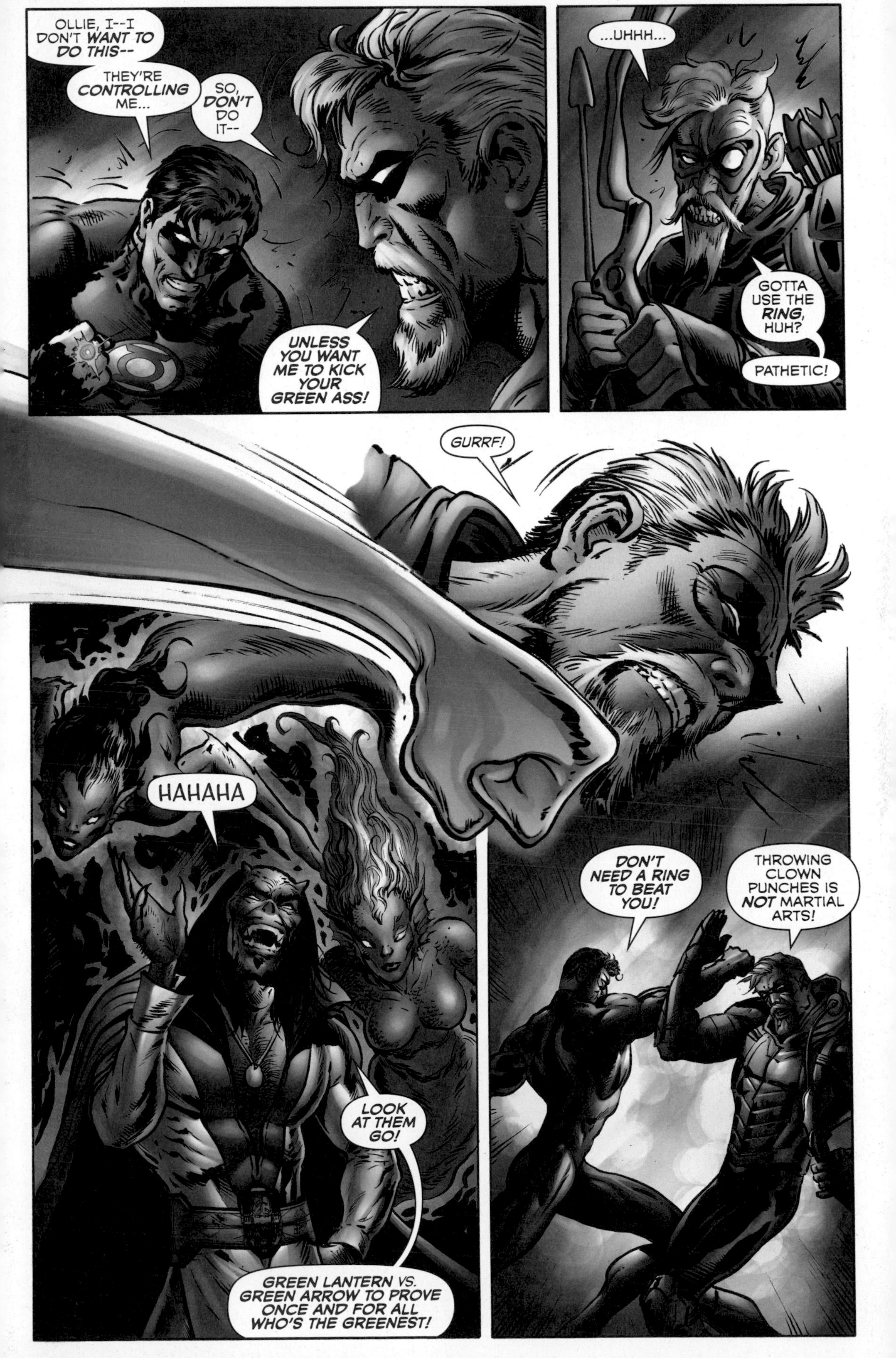
OLLIE, I--I DON'T WANT TO DO THIS--
THEY'RE CONTROLLING ME...
SO, DON'T DO IT--
UNLESS YOU WANT ME TO KICK YOUR GREEN ASS!
...UHHH...
GOTTA USE THE RING, HUH?
PATHETIC!
GURRF!
HAHAHA
LOOK AT THEM GO!
GREEN LANTERN VS. GREEN ARROW TO PROVE ONCE AND FOR ALL WHO'S THE GREENEST!
DON'T NEED A RING TO BEAT YOU!
THROWING CLOWN PUNCHES IS NOT MARTIAL ARTS!

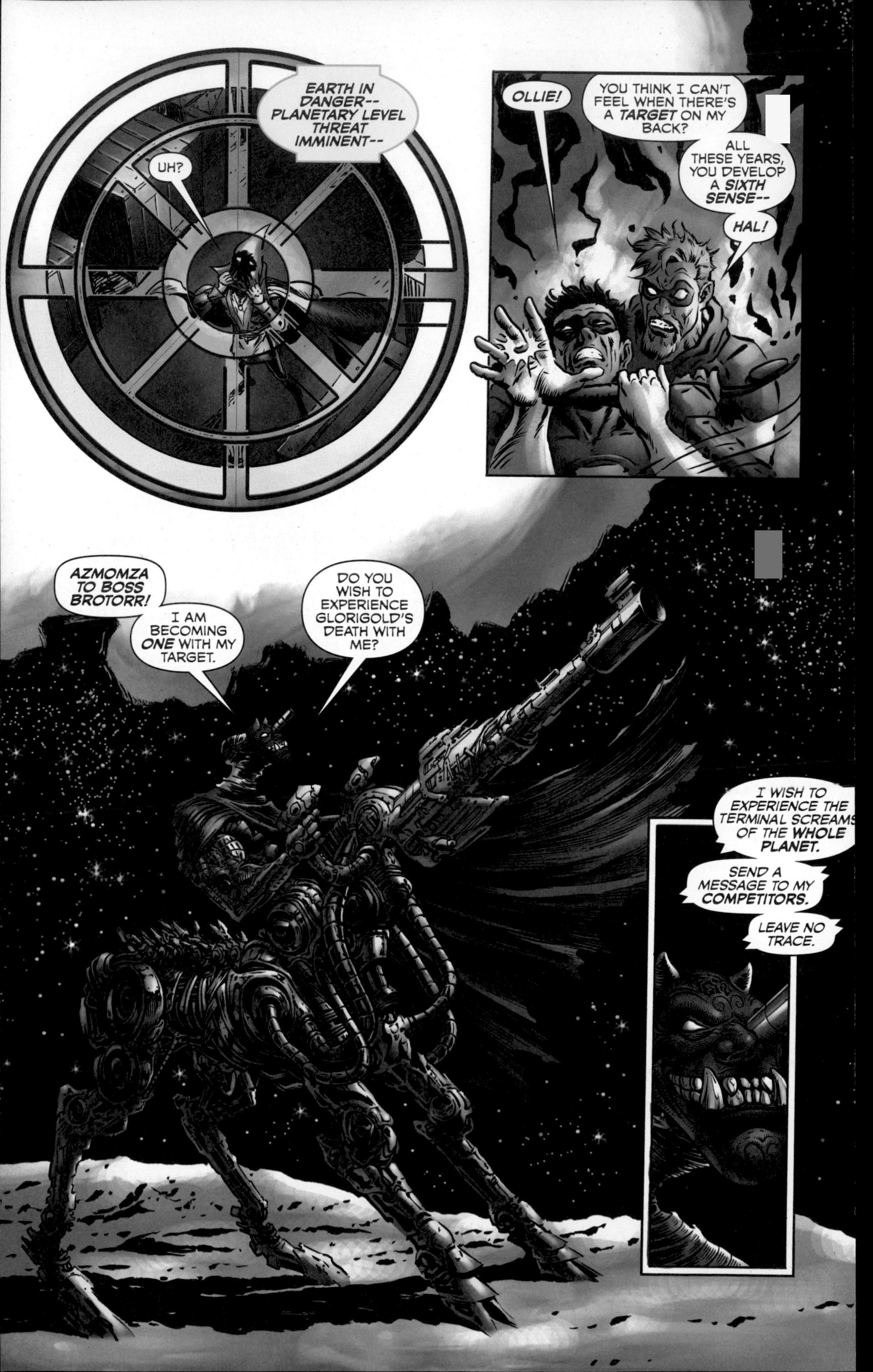
EARTH IN DANGER-- PLANETARY LEVEL THREAT IMMINENT--
UH?
OLLIE!
YOU THINK I CAN'T FEEL WHEN THERE'S A TARGET ON MY BACK?
ALL THESE YEARS, YOU DEVELOP A SIXTH SENSE--
HAL!
AZMOMZA TO BOSS BROTORR!
I AM BECOMING ONE WITH MY TARGET.
DO YOU WISH TO EXPERIENCE GLORIGOLD'S DEATH WITH ME?
I WISH TO EXPERIENCE THE TERMINAL SCREAMS OF THE WHOLE PLANET.
SEND A MESSAGE TO MY COMPETITORS.
LEAVE NO TRACE.

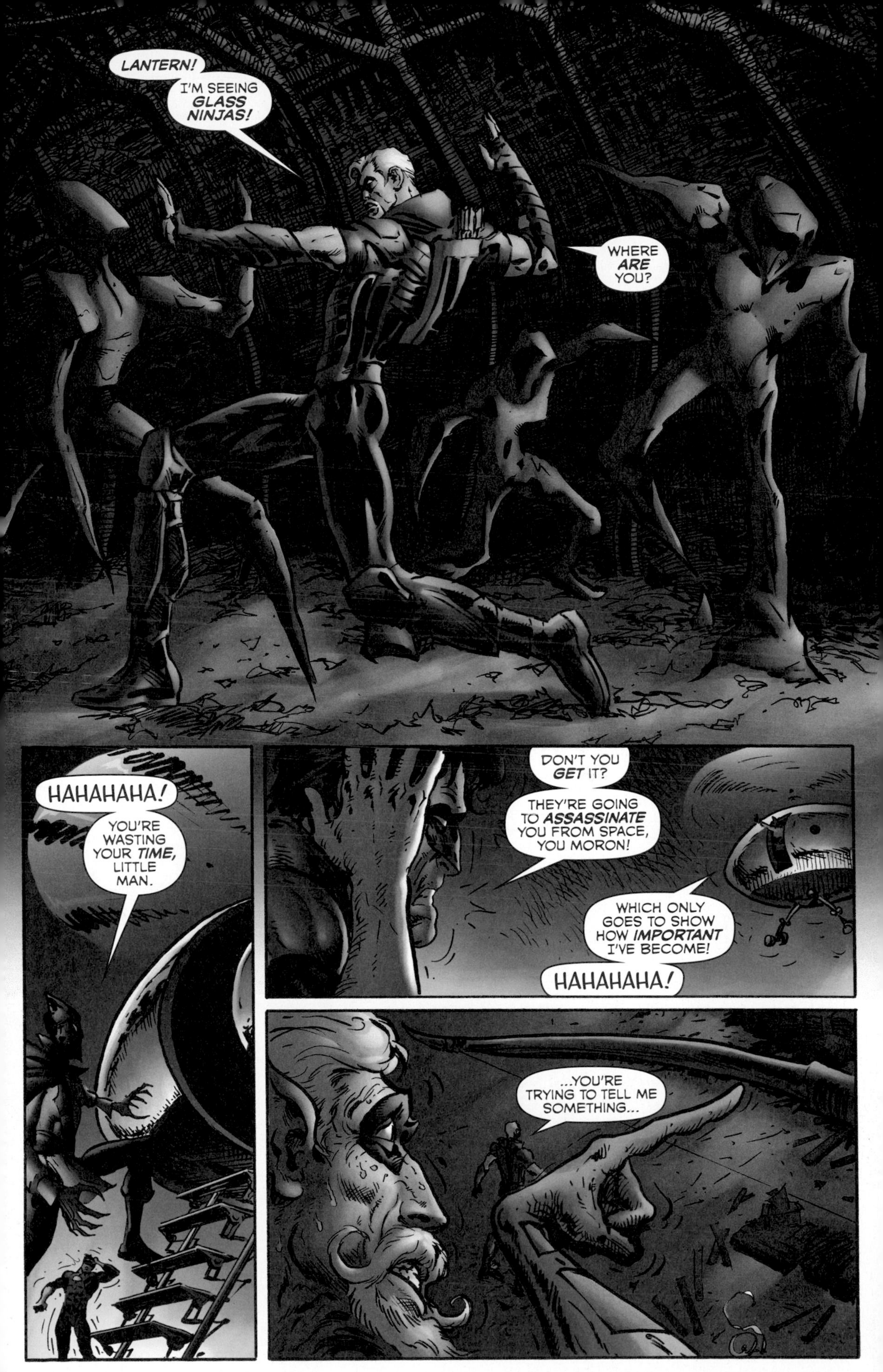
LANTERN!
I'M SEEING GLASS NINJAS!
WHERE ARE YOU?
HAHAHAHA!
YOU'RE WASTING YOUR TIME, LITTLE MAN.
DON'T YOU GET IT?
THEY'RE GOING TO ASSASSINATE YOU FROM SPACE, YOU MORON!
WHICH ONLY GOES TO SHOW HOW IMPORTANT I'VE BECOME!
HAHAHAHA!
...YOU'RE TRYING TO TELL ME SOMETHING...

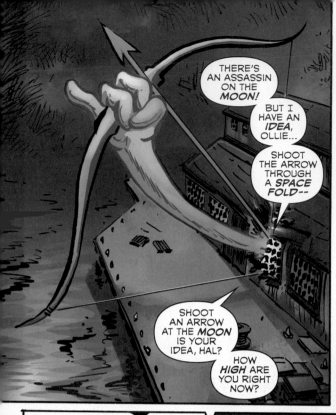

THERE'S AN ASSASSIN ON THE *MOON!*

BUT I HAVE AN *IDEA*, OLLIE...

SHOOT THE ARROW THROUGH A *SPACE FOLD*--

SHOOT AN ARROW AT THE *MOON* IS YOUR IDEA, HAL?

HOW *HIGH* ARE YOU RIGHT NOW?

EXTREMELY--

BUT I'M FOCUSED ON THE *MISSION.*

CREATIVE THINKING-- OUTSIDE THE BOX--

BACK ME UP, OLLIE-- I'M HALF-*BLIND.*

MY RING CAN INTERFACE WITH THE ARROW'S *A.I.*--

OH, LIKE IT DID WITH *XEEN?*

FORGET IT.

IT'S *INTUITIVELY* GUIDED-- *TELEPATHIC*, LIKE HIM.

SHOW ME!

THE ARROW HAS *ROCKET THRUSTERS.*

THE RING CAN PLACE A *TARGET* ON THE MOON-- SPACE-FOLD STRAIGHT *TO* IT.

ADJUSTING FOR DISTANCE--

--NO, LEFT! LEFT!!

DOWN!

NAH, NAH, RIGHT!

YOU *SURE* ABOUT THIS?

NOW I'M FEELING IT!

SHOOT.

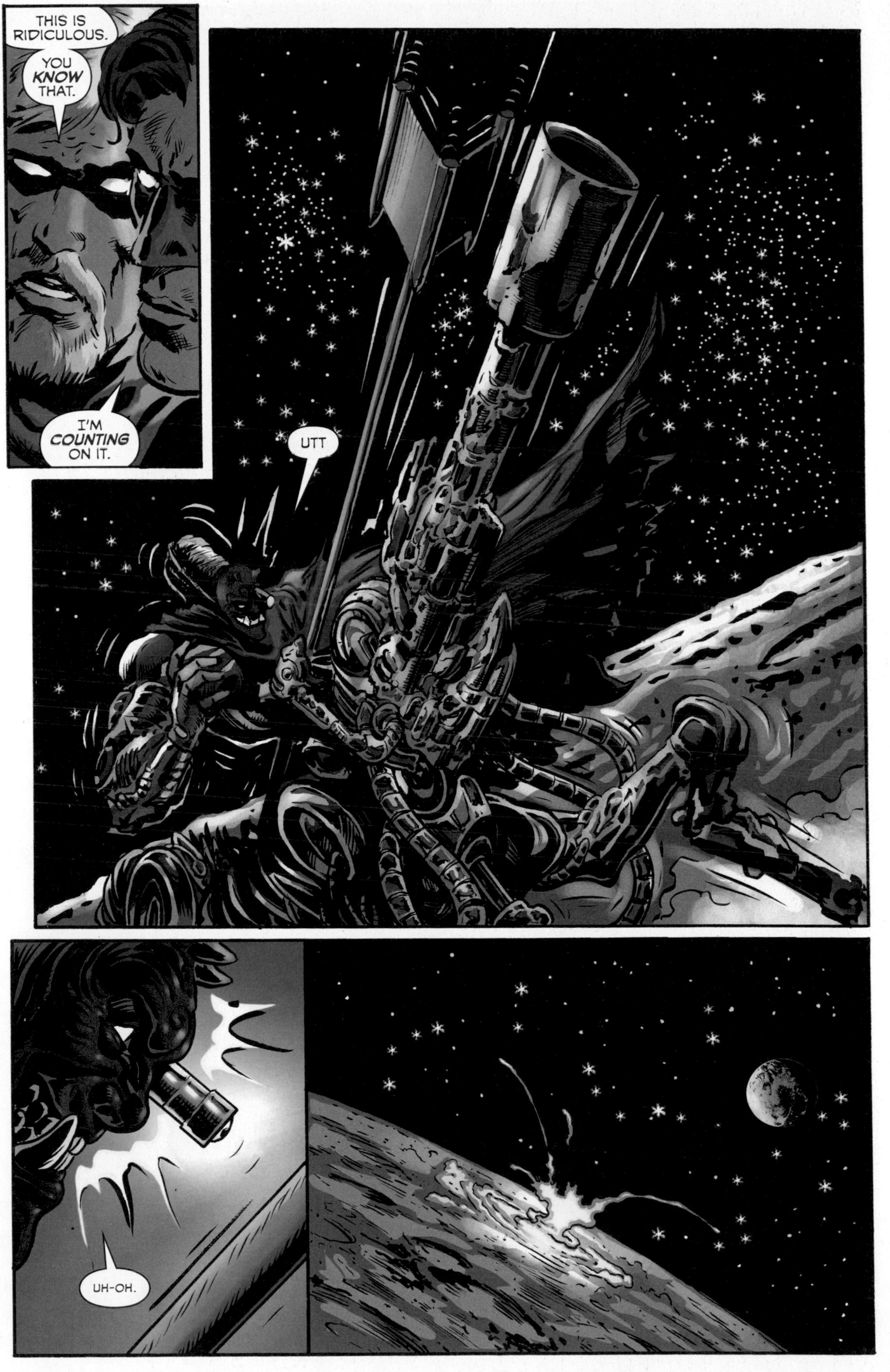
THIS IS RIDICULOUS.
YOU **KNOW** THAT.
I'M ***COUNTING*** ON IT.
UTT
UH-OH.

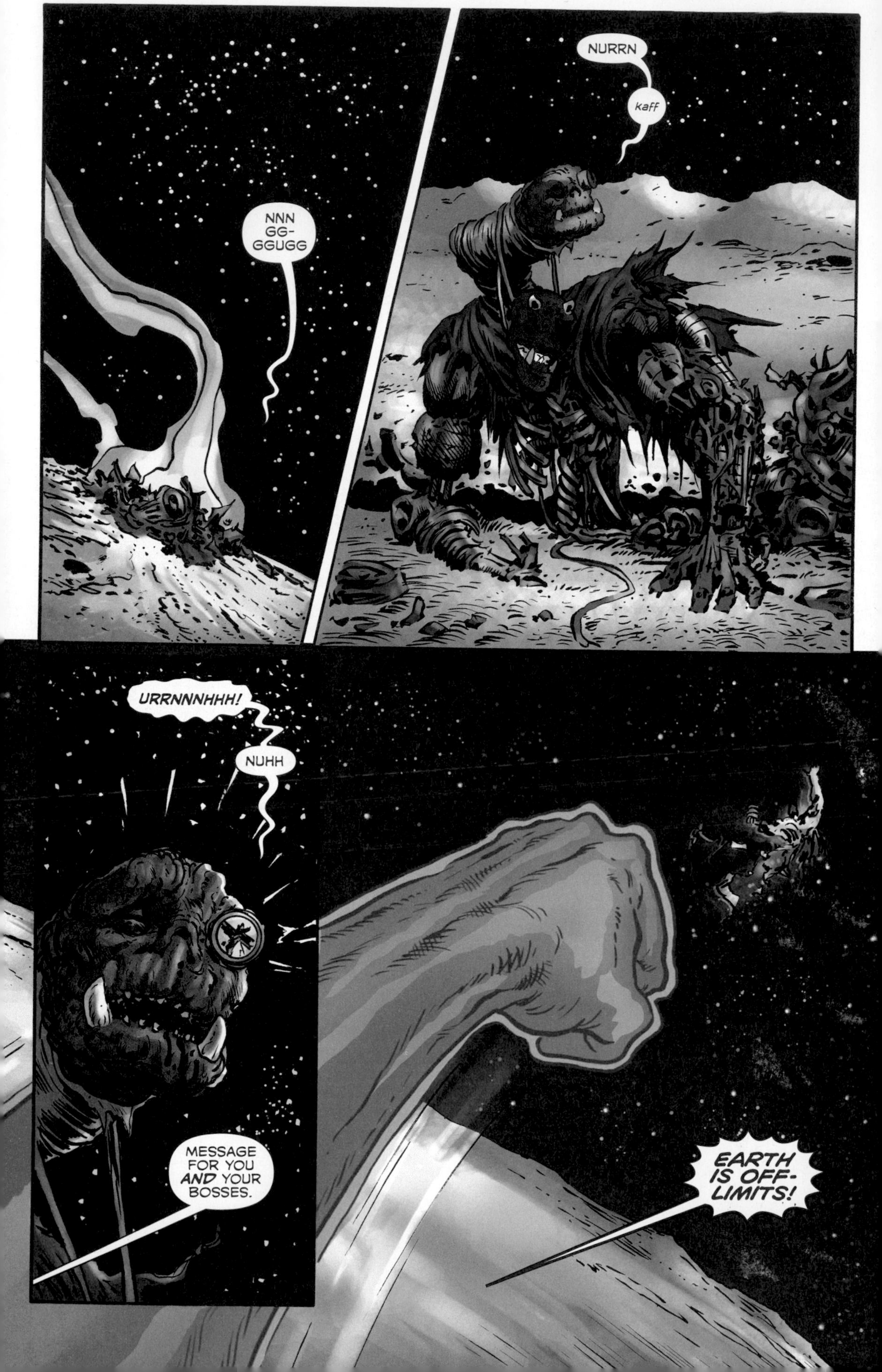
NNN GG-GGUGG
NURRN
kaff
URRNNNHHH!
NUHH
MESSAGE FOR YOU AND YOUR BOSSES.
EARTH IS OFF-LIMITS!

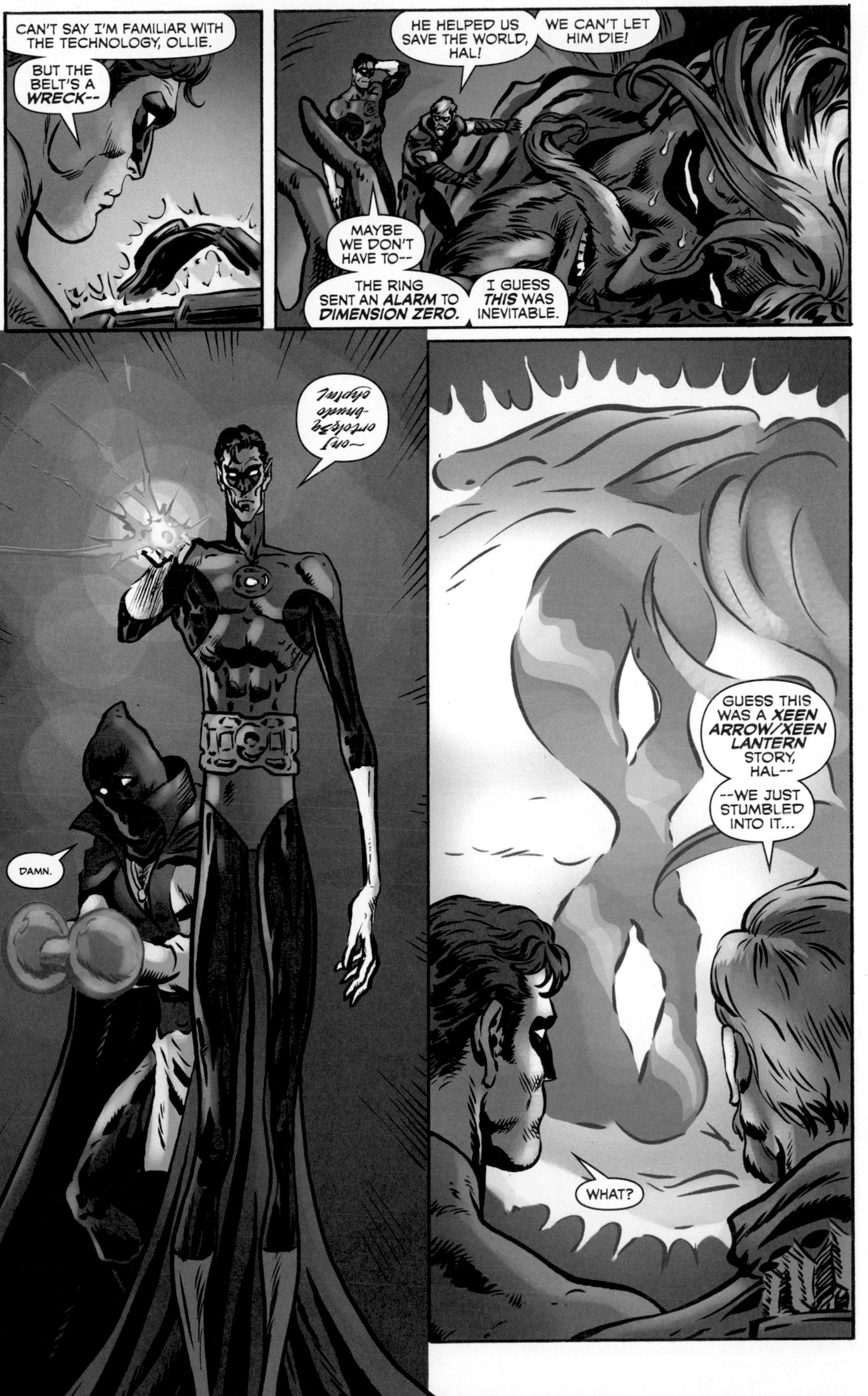
CAN'T SAY I'M FAMILIAR WITH THE TECHNOLOGY, OLLIE.
BUT THE BELT'S A ***WRECK--***
HE HELPED US SAVE THE WORLD, HAL!
WE CAN'T LET HIM DIE!
MAYBE WE DON'T HAVE TO--
THE RING SENT AN ***ALARM*** TO ***DIMENSION ZERO.***
I GUESS ***THIS*** WAS INEVITABLE.
DAMN.
GUESS THIS WAS A ***XEEN ARROW/XEEN LANTERN*** STORY, HAL--
--WE JUST STUMBLED INTO IT...
WHAT?

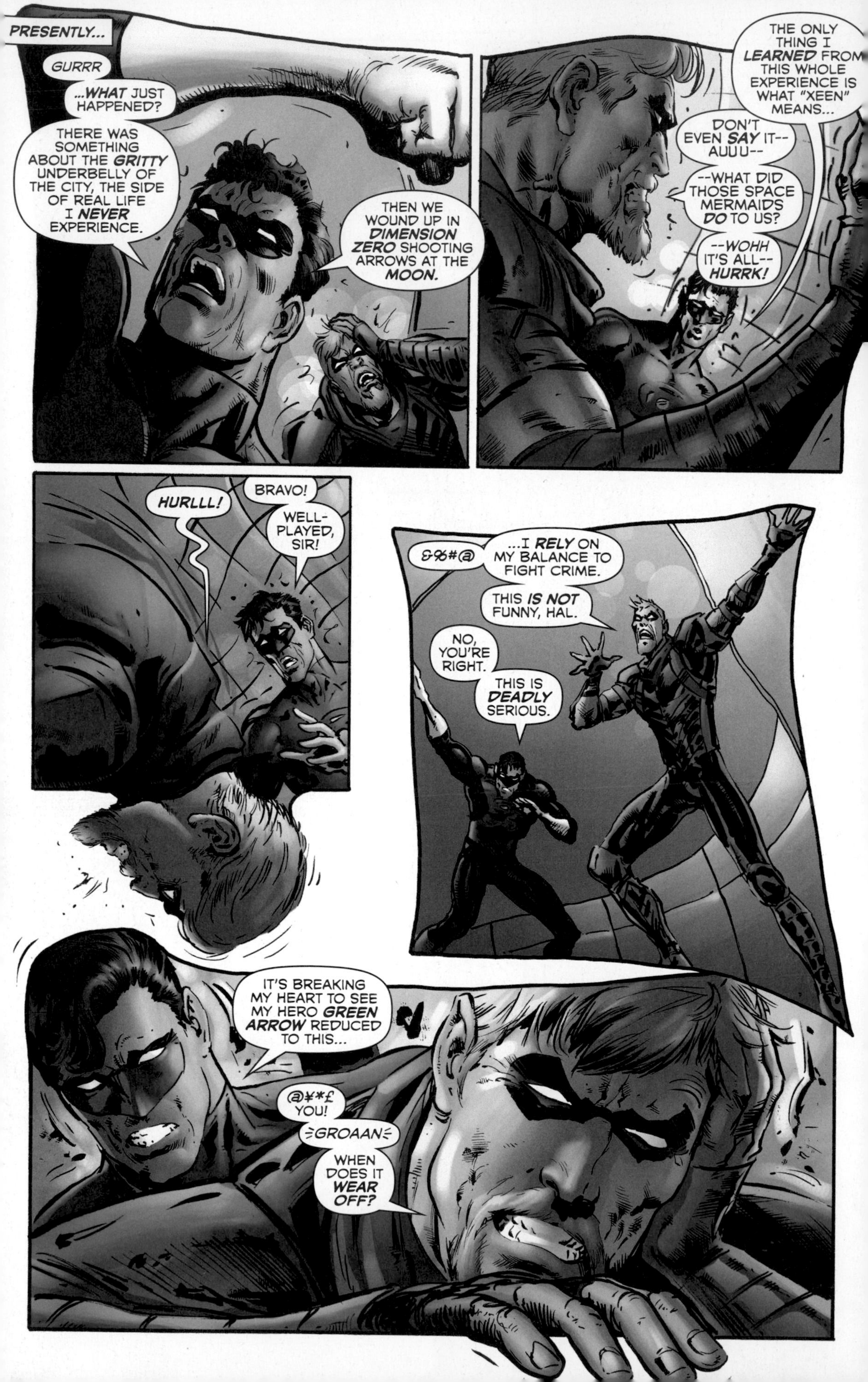
PRESENTLY...
GURRR
...WHAT JUST HAPPENED?
THERE WAS SOMETHING ABOUT THE GRITTY UNDERBELLY OF THE CITY, THE SIDE OF REAL LIFE I NEVER EXPERIENCE.
THEN WE WOUND UP IN DIMENSION ZERO SHOOTING ARROWS AT THE MOON.
THE ONLY THING I LEARNED FROM THIS WHOLE EXPERIENCE IS WHAT "XEEN" MEANS...
DON'T EVEN SAY IT-- AUUU--
--WHAT DID THOSE SPACE MERMAIDS DO TO US?
--WOHH IT'S ALL-- HURRK!
HURLLL!
BRAVO!
WELL-PLAYED, SIR!
&%#@
...I RELY ON MY BALANCE TO FIGHT CRIME.
THIS IS NOT FUNNY, HAL.
NO, YOU'RE RIGHT.
THIS IS DEADLY SERIOUS.
IT'S BREAKING MY HEART TO SEE MY HERO GREEN ARROW REDUCED TO THIS...
@¥*£ YOU!
GROAAN
WHEN DOES IT WEAR OFF?

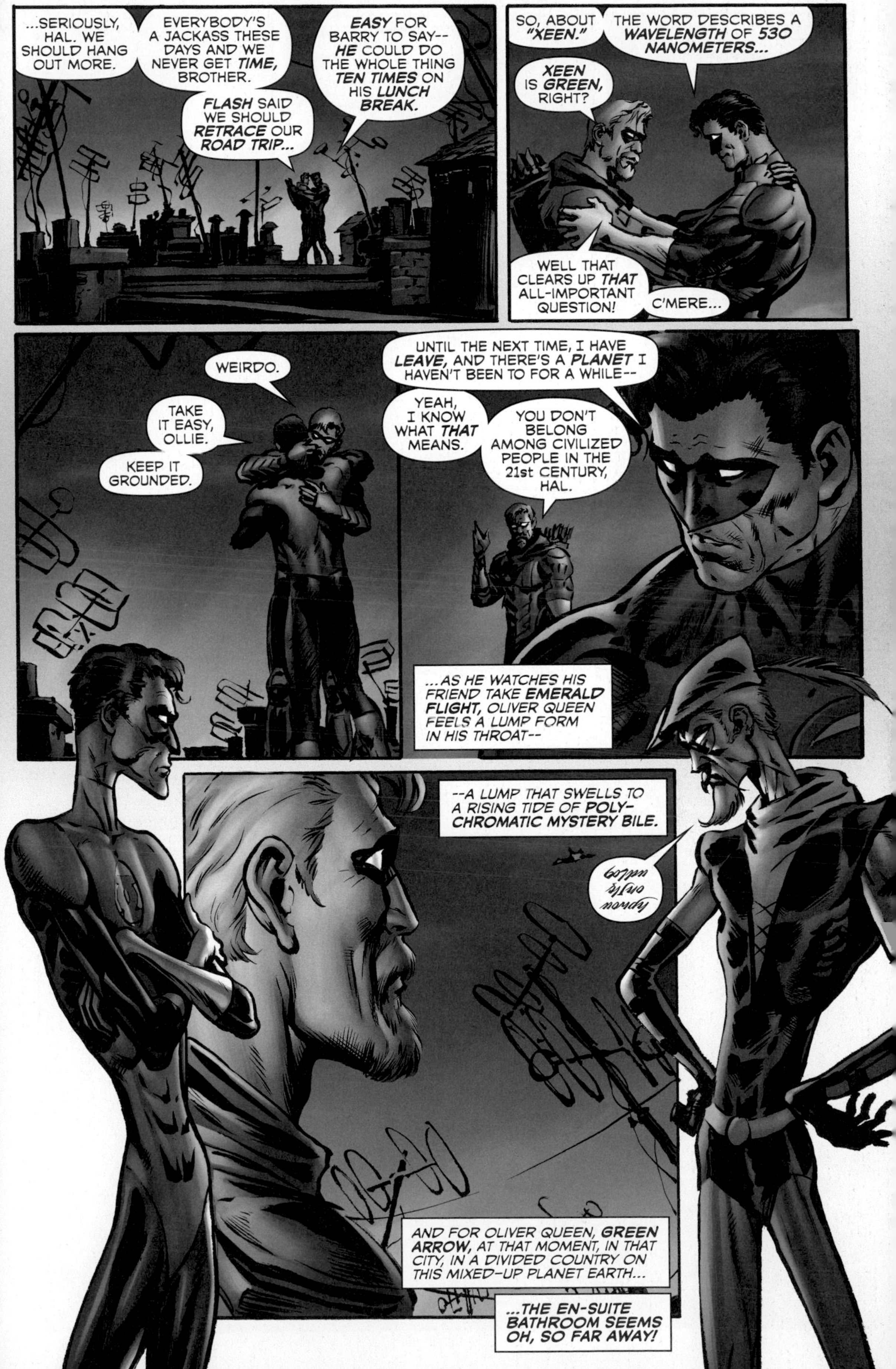
...SERIOUSLY, HAL. WE SHOULD HANG OUT MORE.
EVERYBODY'S A JACKASS THESE DAYS AND WE NEVER GET *TIME,* BROTHER.
FLASH SAID WE SHOULD ***RETRACE*** OUR ***ROAD TRIP...***
EASY FOR BARRY TO SAY-- ***HE*** COULD DO THE WHOLE THING ***TEN TIMES*** ON HIS ***LUNCH BREAK.***
SO, ABOUT ***"XEEN."***
THE WORD DESCRIBES A ***WAVELENGTH*** OF ***530 NANOMETERS...***
XEEN IS ***GREEN,*** RIGHT?
WELL THAT CLEARS UP ***THAT*** ALL-IMPORTANT QUESTION!
C'MERE...
WEIRDO.
TAKE IT EASY, OLLIE.
KEEP IT GROUNDED.
UNTIL THE NEXT TIME, I HAVE ***LEAVE,*** AND THERE'S A ***PLANET*** I HAVEN'T BEEN TO FOR A WHILE--
YEAH, I KNOW WHAT ***THAT*** MEANS.
YOU DON'T BELONG AMONG CIVILIZED PEOPLE IN THE 21st CENTURY, HAL.
...AS HE WATCHES HIS FRIEND TAKE ***EMERALD FLIGHT,*** *OLIVER QUEEN FEELS A LUMP FORM IN HIS THROAT--*
--A LUMP THAT SWELLS TO A RISING TIDE OF ***POLY-CHROMATIC MYSTERY BILE.***
AND FOR OLIVER QUEEN, ***GREEN ARROW,*** *AT THAT MOMENT, IN THAT CITY, IN A DIVIDED COUNTRY ON THIS MIXED-UP PLANET EARTH...*
...THE EN-SUITE BATHROOM SEEMS OH, SO FAR AWAY!

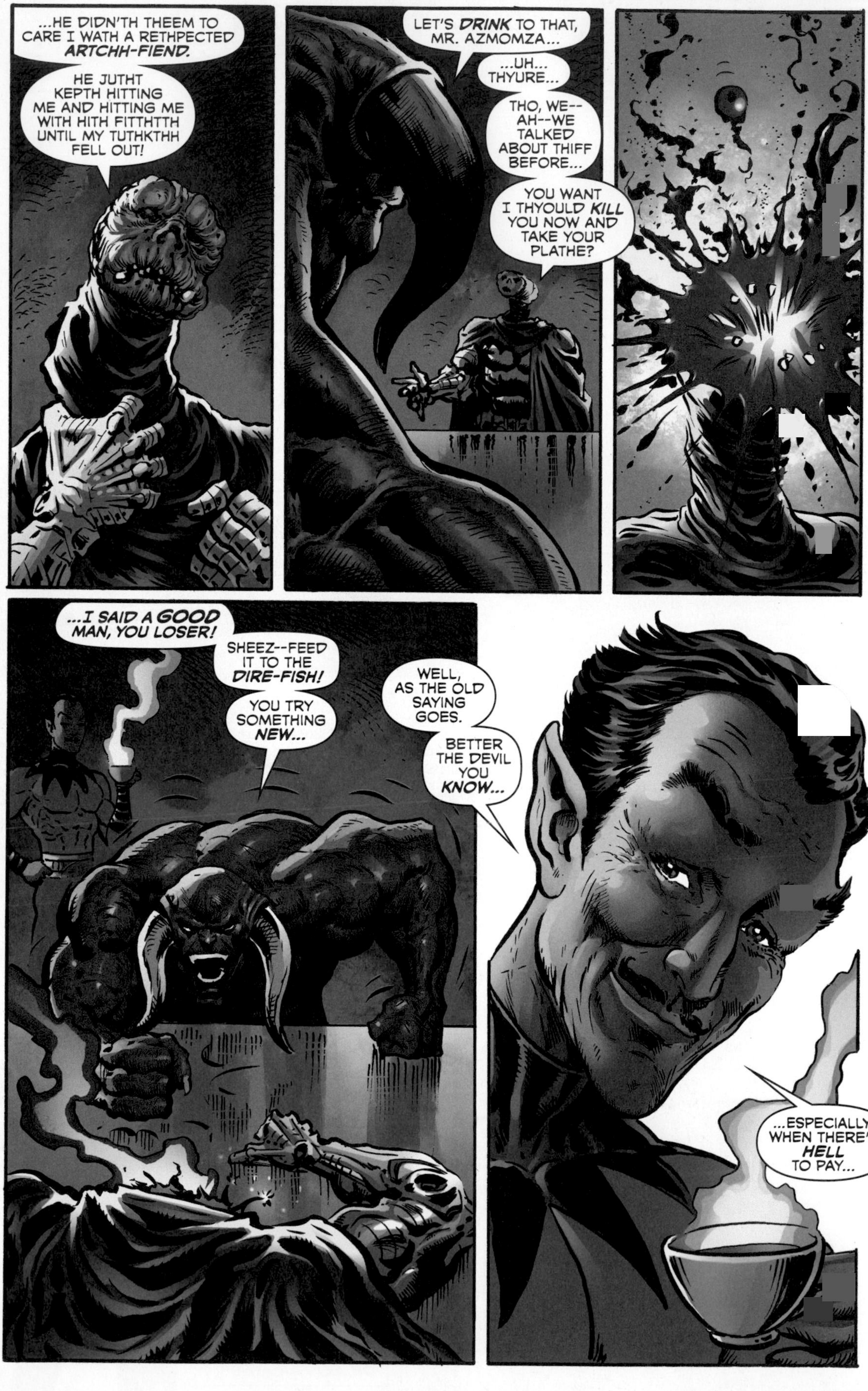
...HE DIDN'TH THEEM TO CARE I WATH A RETHPECTED ARTCHH-FIEND.
HE JUTHT KEPTH HITTING ME AND HITTING ME WITH HITH FITTHTTH UNTIL MY TUTHKTHH FELL OUT!
LET'S DRINK TO THAT, MR. AZMOMZA...
...UH... THYURE...
THO, WE-- AH--WE TALKED ABOUT THIFF BEFORE...
YOU WANT I THYOULD KILL YOU NOW AND TAKE YOUR PLATHE?
...I SAID A GOOD MAN, YOU LOSER!
SHEEZ--FEED IT TO THE DIRE-FISH!
YOU TRY SOMETHING NEW...
WELL, AS THE OLD SAYING GOES.
BETTER THE DEVIL YOU KNOW...
...ESPECIALLY WHEN THERE'S HELL TO PAY...

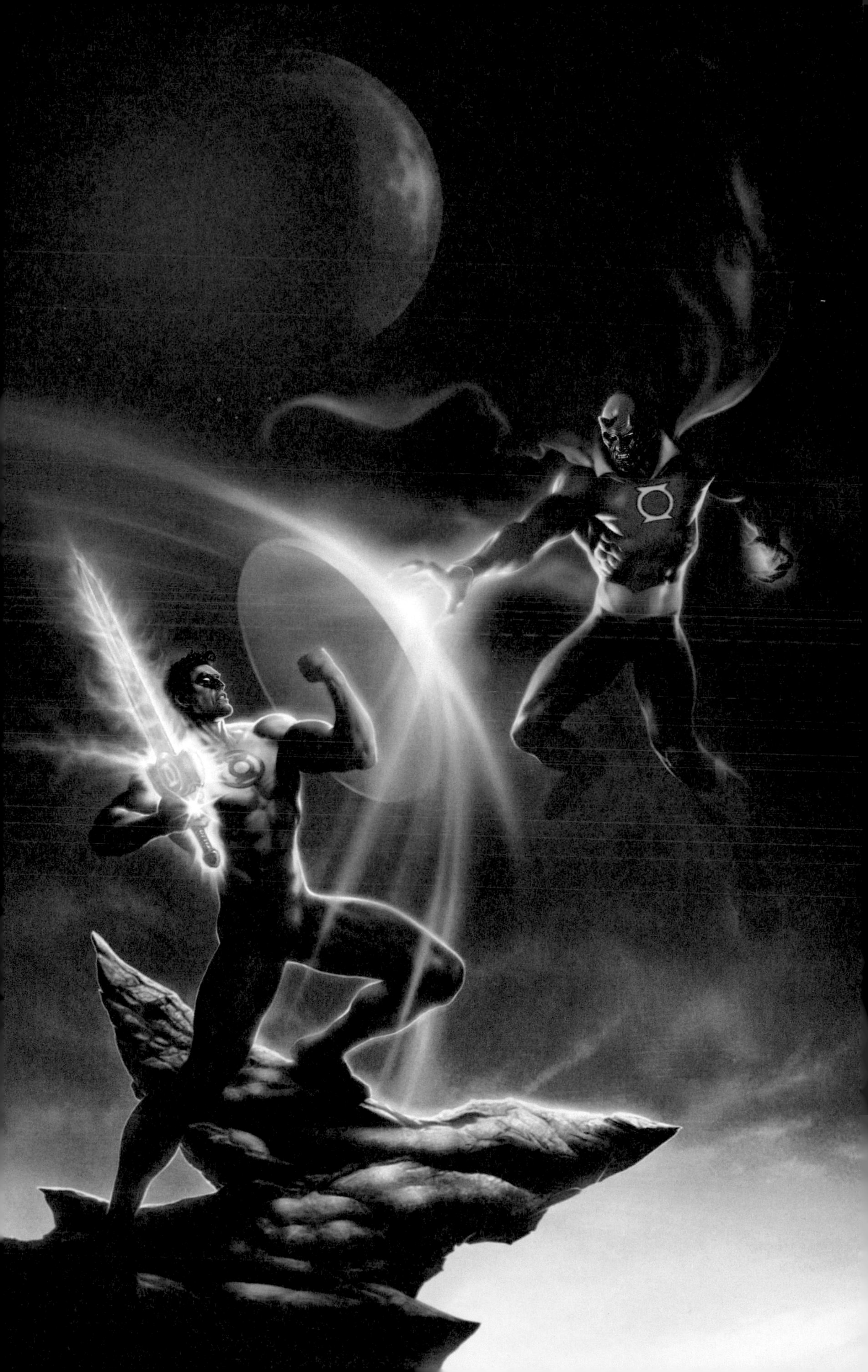

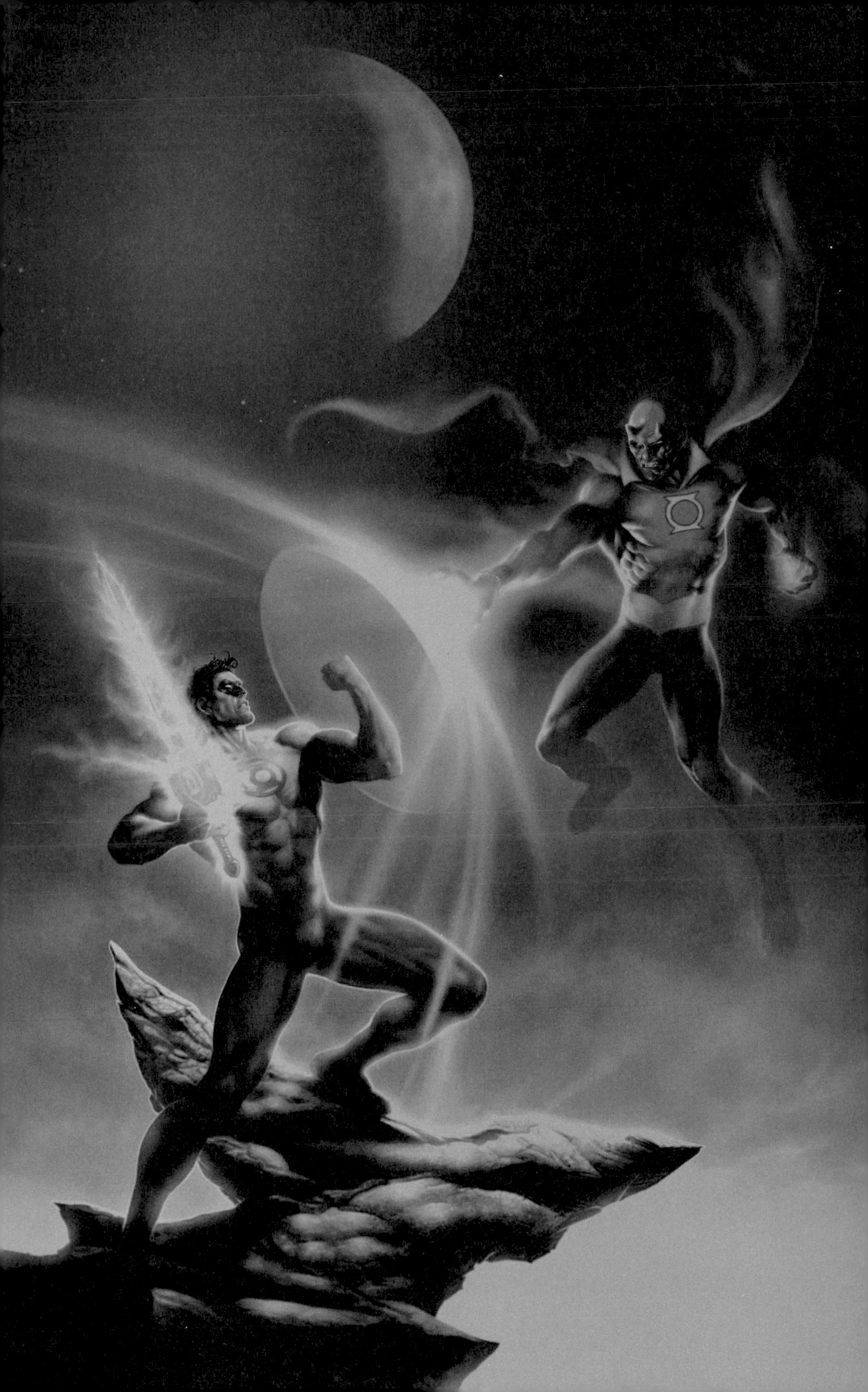

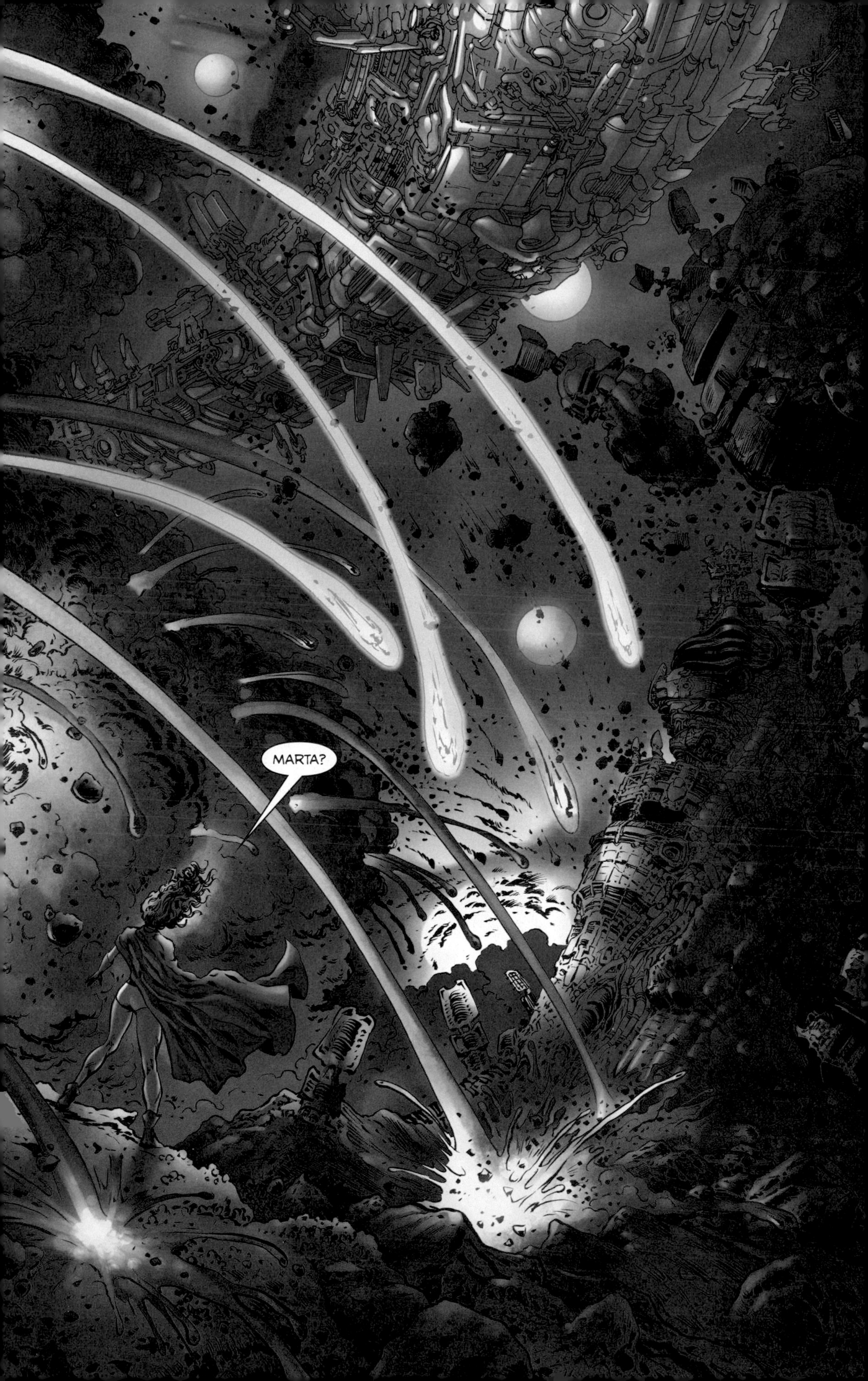
MARTA?

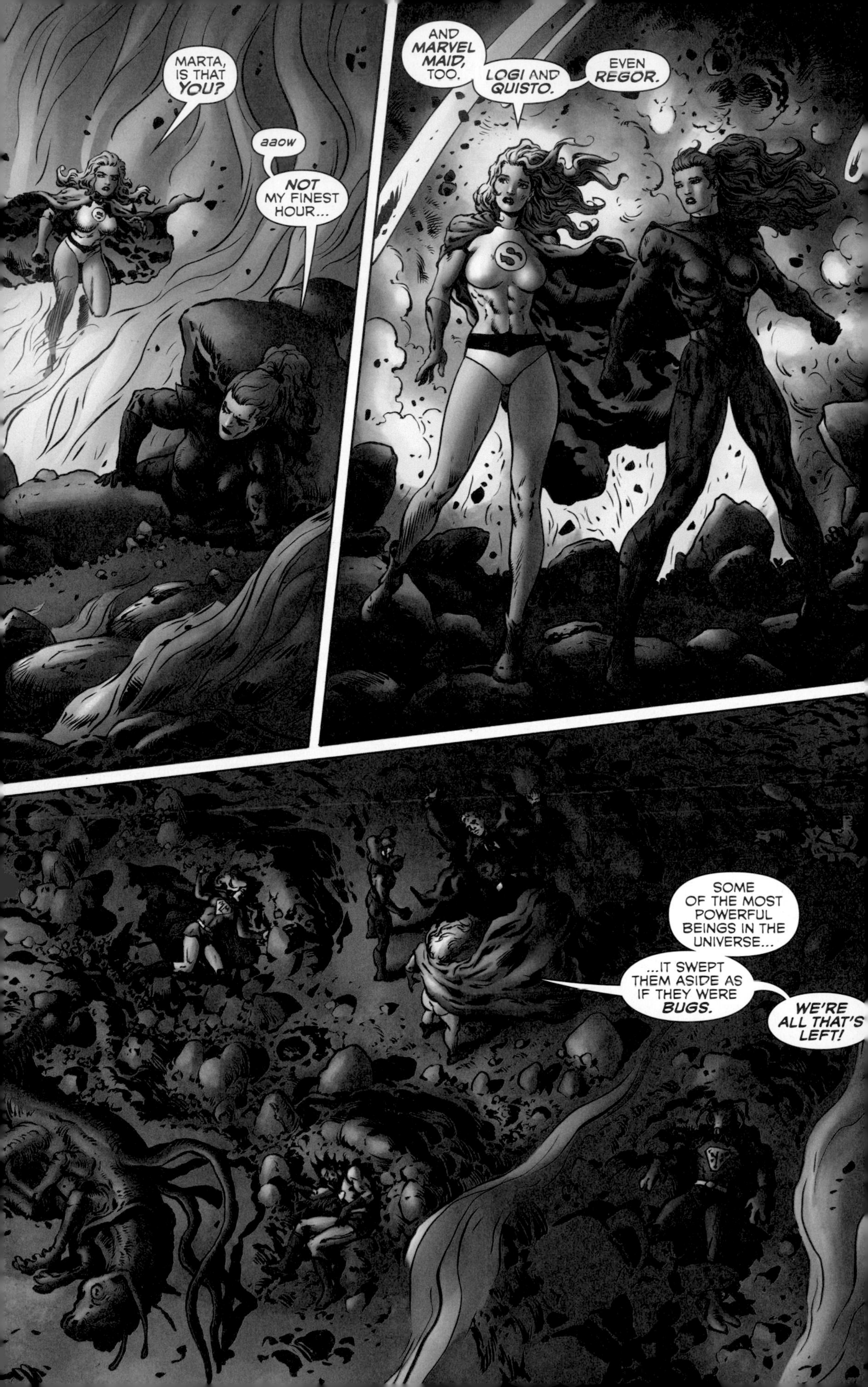
MARTA, IS THAT YOU?
aaow
NOT MY FINEST HOUR...
AND MARVEL MAID, TOO.
LOGI AND QUISTO.
EVEN REGOR.
SOME OF THE MOST POWERFUL BEINGS IN THE UNIVERSE...
...IT SWEPT THEM ASIDE AS IF THEY WERE BUGS.
WE'RE ALL THAT'S LEFT!

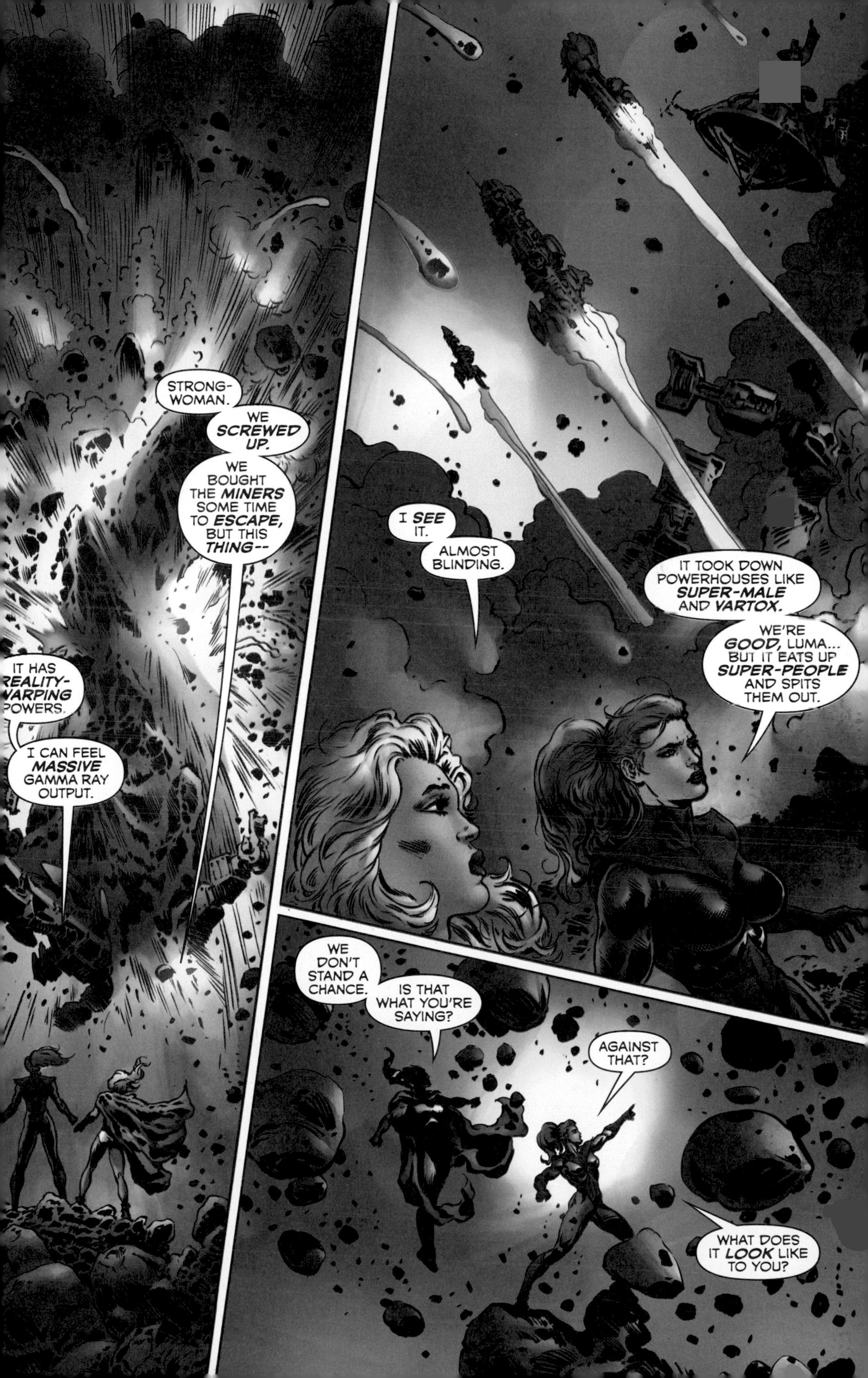
STRONG-WOMAN.
WE SCREWED UP.
WE BOUGHT THE MINERS SOME TIME TO ESCAPE, BUT THIS THING--
IT HAS REALITY-WARPING POWERS.
I CAN FEEL MASSIVE GAMMA RAY OUTPUT.
I SEE IT.
ALMOST BLINDING.
IT TOOK DOWN POWERHOUSES LIKE SUPER-MALE AND VARTOX.
WE'RE GOOD, LUMA... BUT IT EATS UP SUPER-PEOPLE AND SPITS THEM OUT.
WE DON'T STAND A CHANCE.
IS THAT WHAT YOU'RE SAYING?
AGAINST THAT?
WHAT DOES IT LOOK LIKE TO YOU?

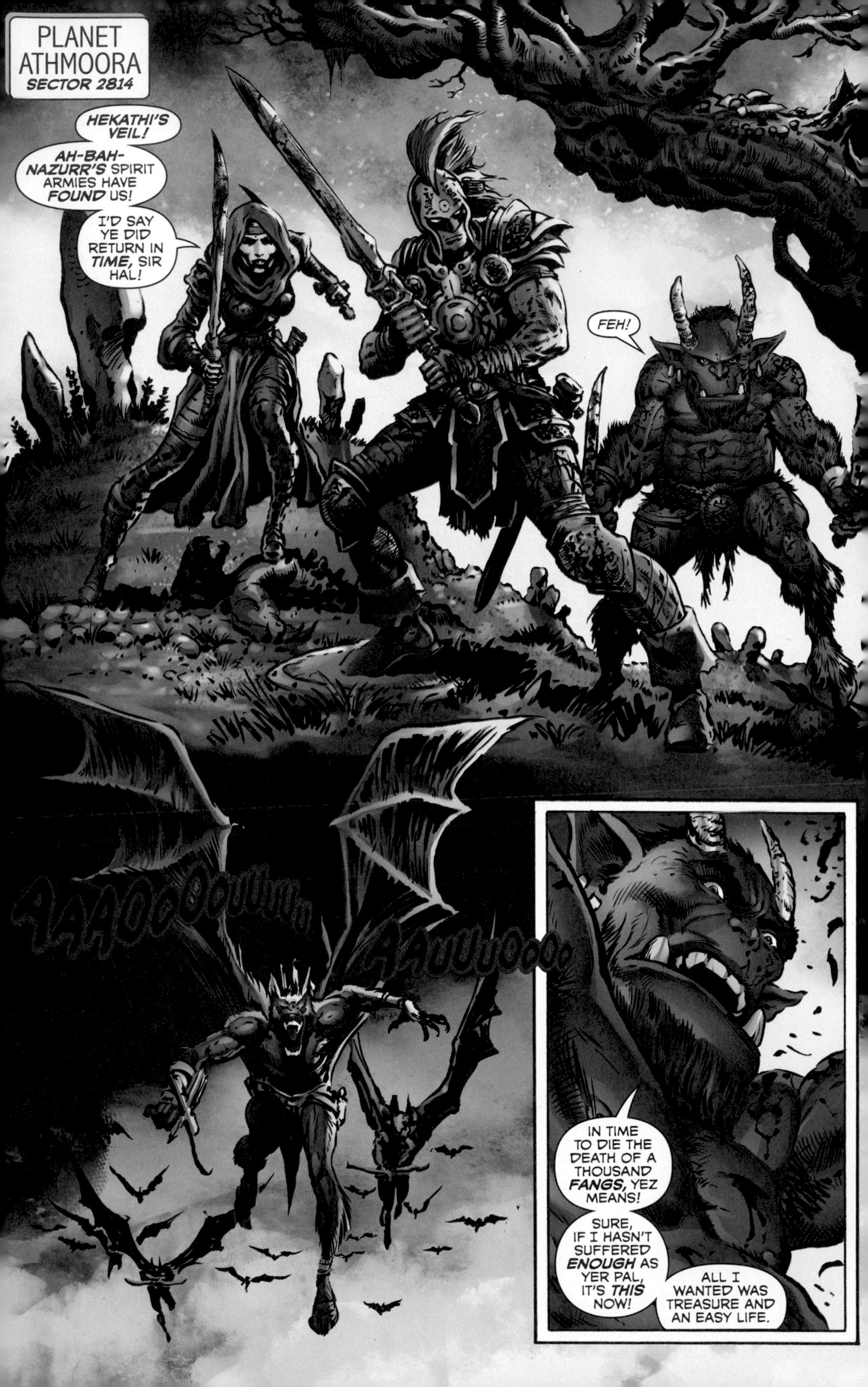
PLANET ATHMOORA SECTOR 2814
HEKATHI'S VEIL!
AH-BAH-NAZURR'S SPIRIT ARMIES HAVE FOUND US!
I'D SAY YE DID RETURN IN TIME, SIR HAL!
FEH!
AAAOOOOUUUUU
AAUUUOOOO
IN TIME TO DIE THE DEATH OF A THOUSAND FANGS, YEZ MEANS!
SURE, IF I HASN'T SUFFERED ENOUGH AS YER PAL, IT'S THIS NOW!
ALL I WANTED WAS TREASURE AND AN EASY LIFE.

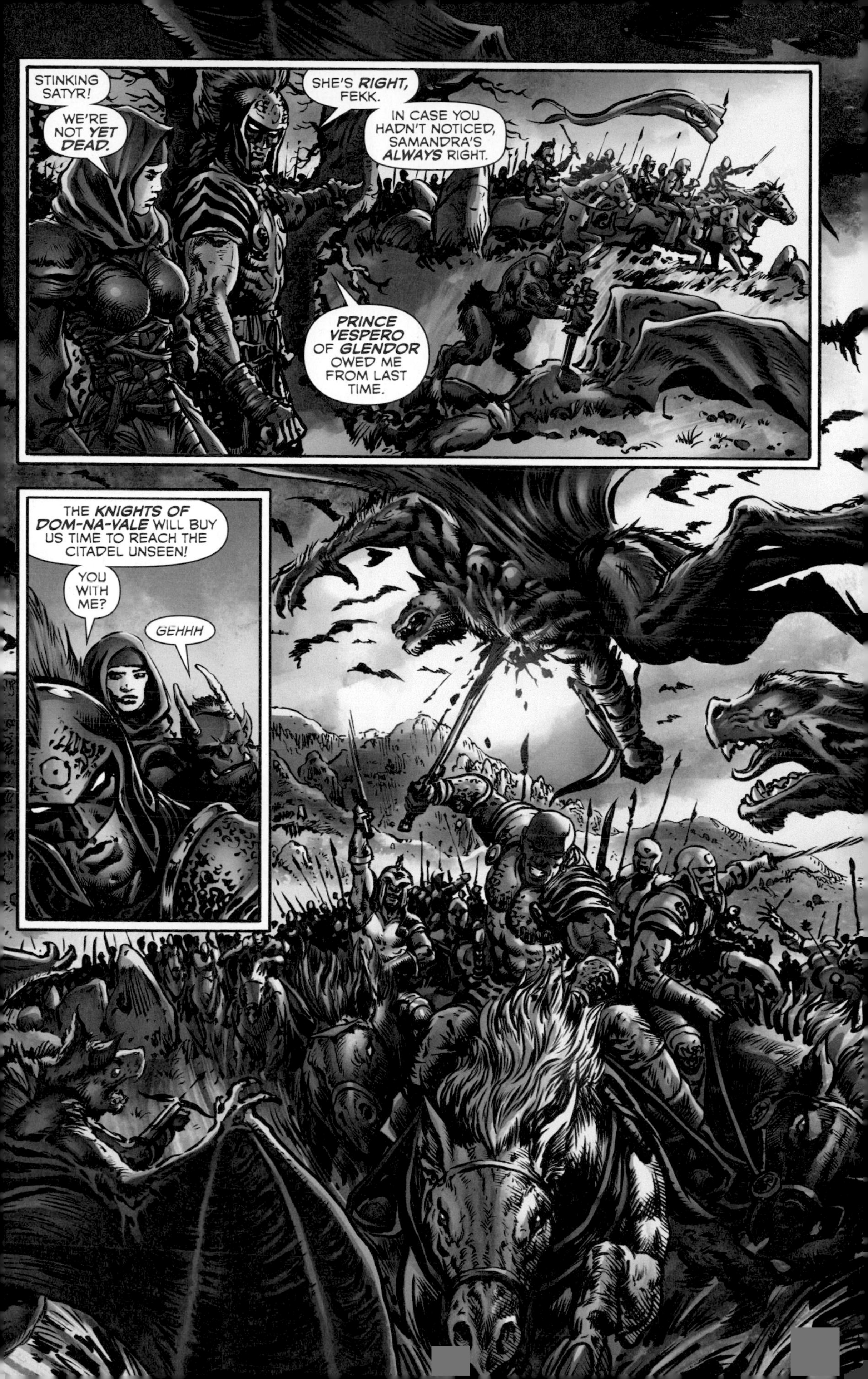
STINKING SATYR!
WE'RE NOT YET DEAD.
SHE'S RIGHT, FEKK.
IN CASE YOU HADN'T NOTICED, SAMANDRA'S ALWAYS RIGHT.
PRINCE VESPERO OF GLENDOR OWED ME FROM LAST TIME.
THE KNIGHTS OF DOM-NA-VALE WILL BUY US TIME TO REACH THE CITADEL UNSEEN!
YOU WITH ME?
GEHHH

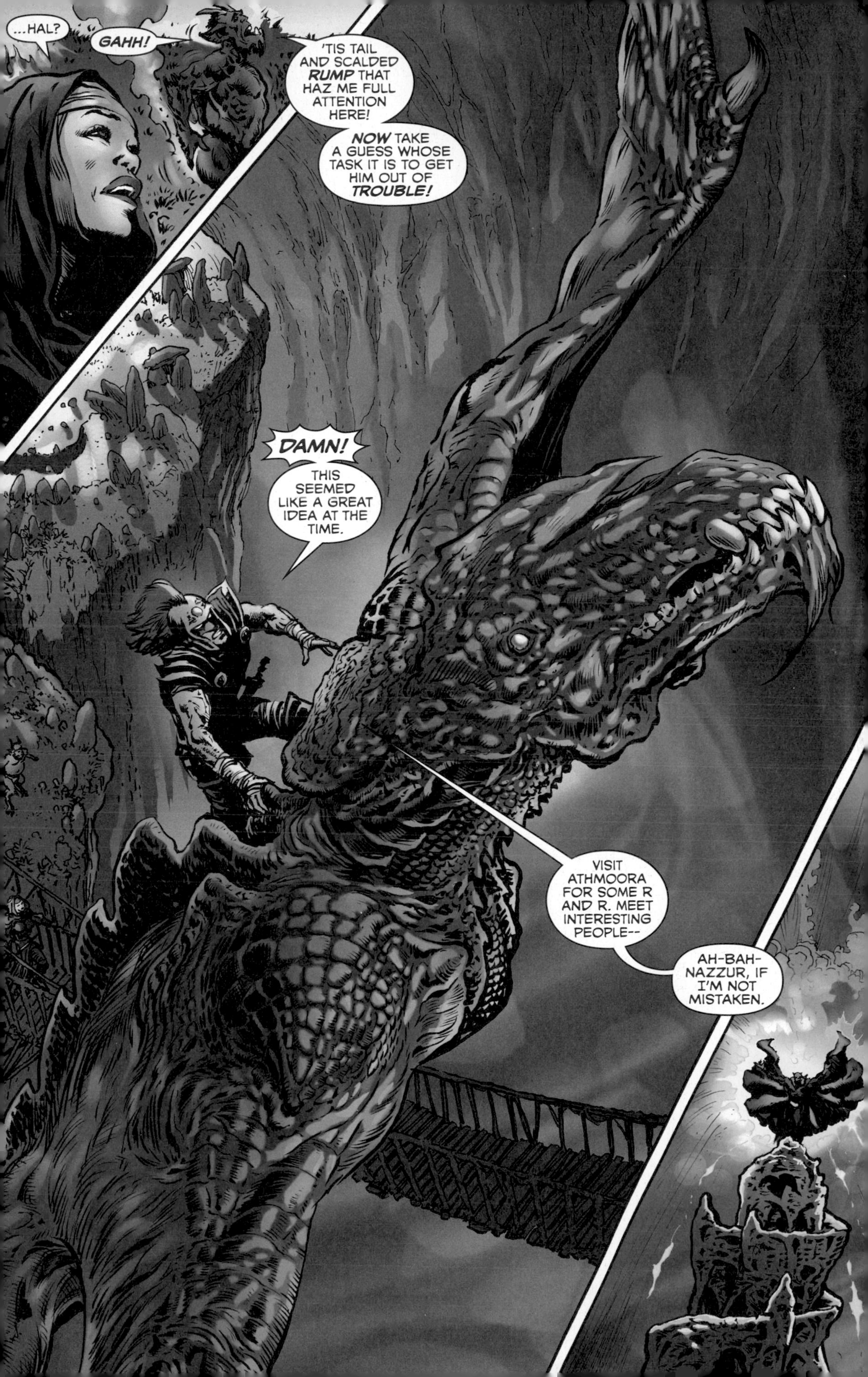
...HAL?
GAHH!
'TIS TAIL AND SCALDED RUMP THAT HAZ ME FULL ATTENTION HERE!
NOW TAKE A GUESS WHOSE TASK IT IS TO GET HIM OUT OF TROUBLE!
DAMN!
THIS SEEMED LIKE A GREAT IDEA AT THE TIME.
VISIT ATHMOORA FOR SOME R AND R. MEET INTERESTING PEOPLE--
AH-BAH-NAZZUR, IF I'M NOT MISTAKEN.

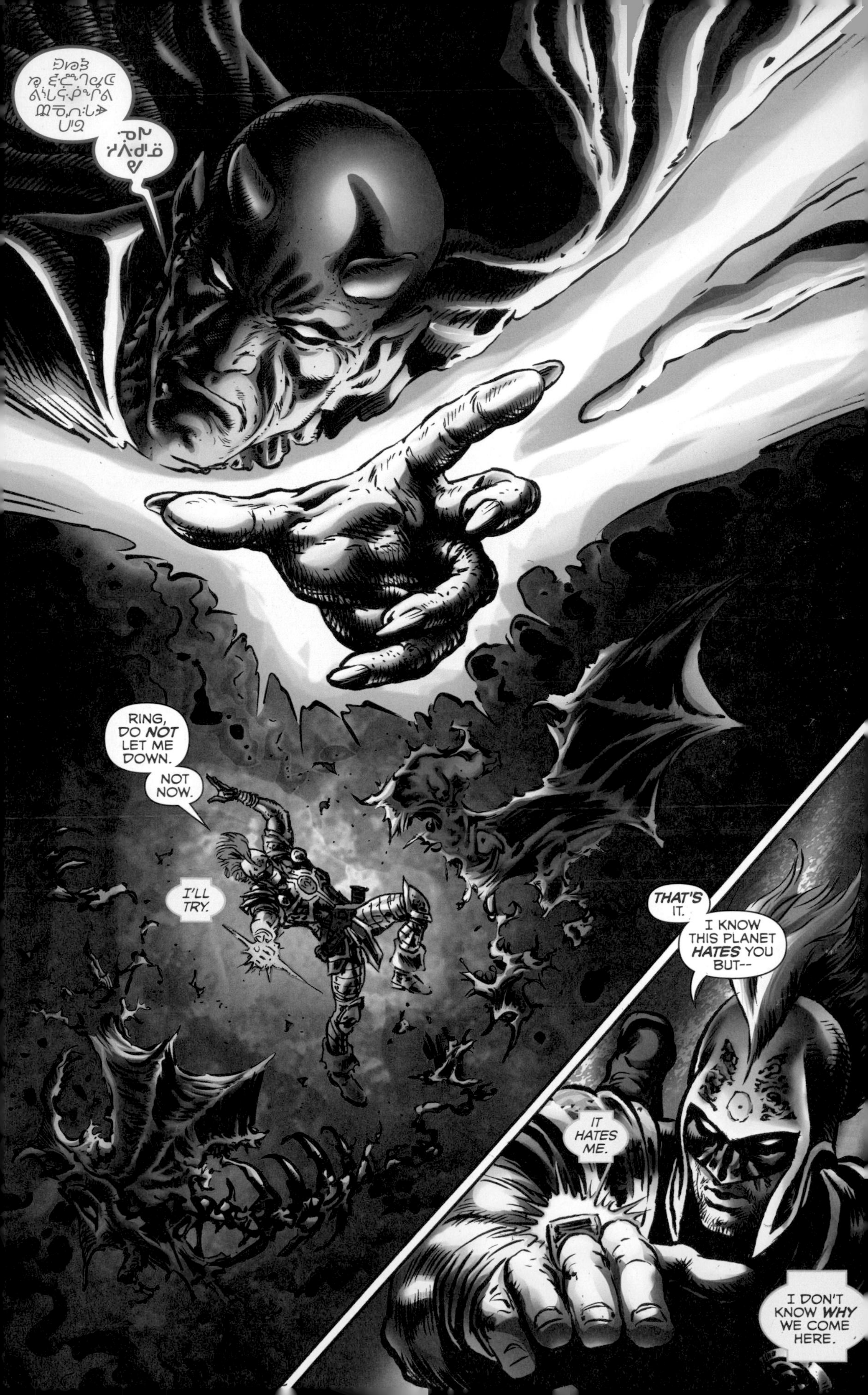
RING, DO NOT LET ME DOWN.
NOT NOW.
I'LL TRY.
THAT'S IT.
I KNOW THIS PLANET HATES YOU BUT--
IT HATES ME.
I DON'T KNOW WHY WE COME HERE.

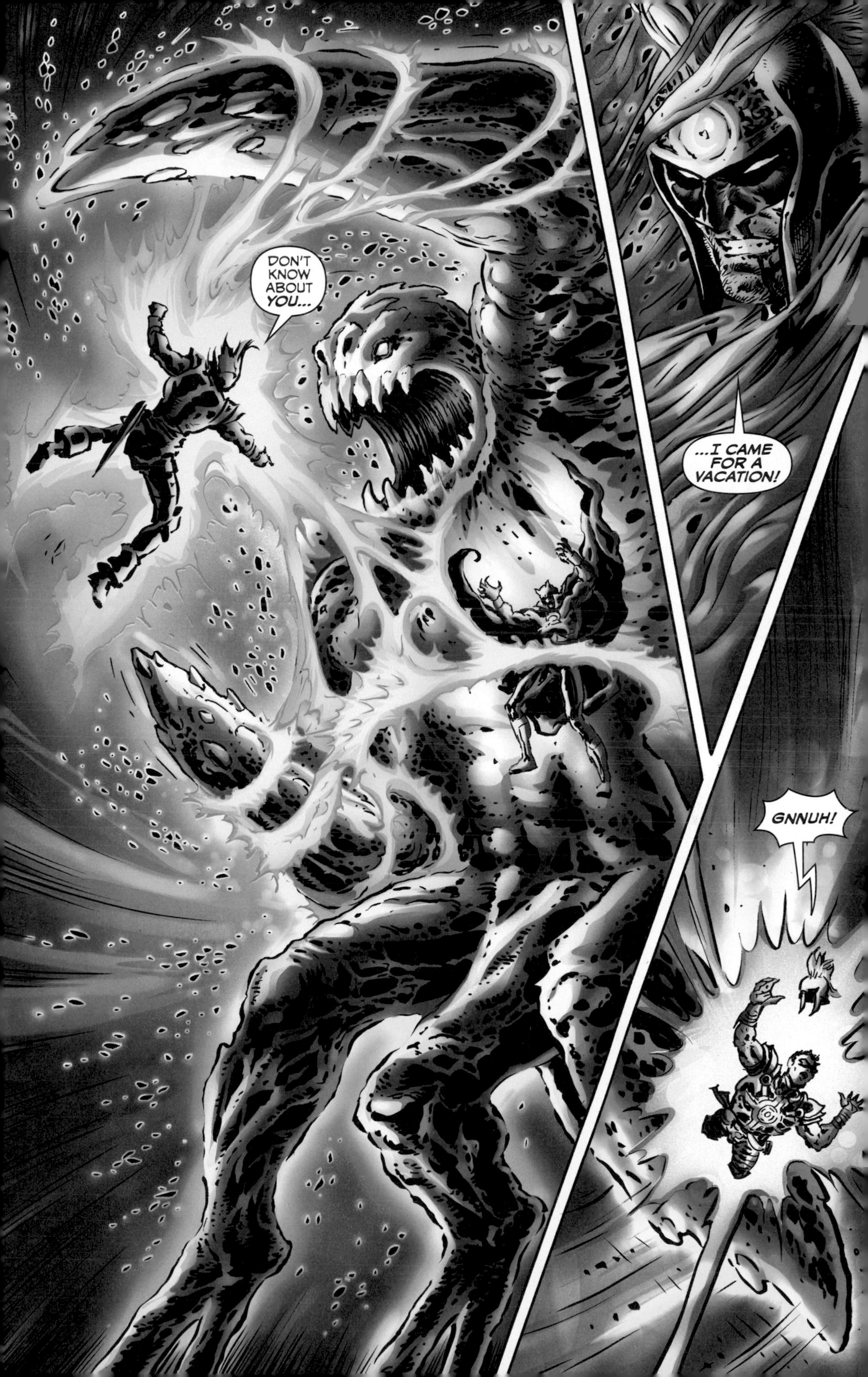
DON'T KNOW ABOUT YOU...
...I CAME FOR A VACATION!
GNNUH!

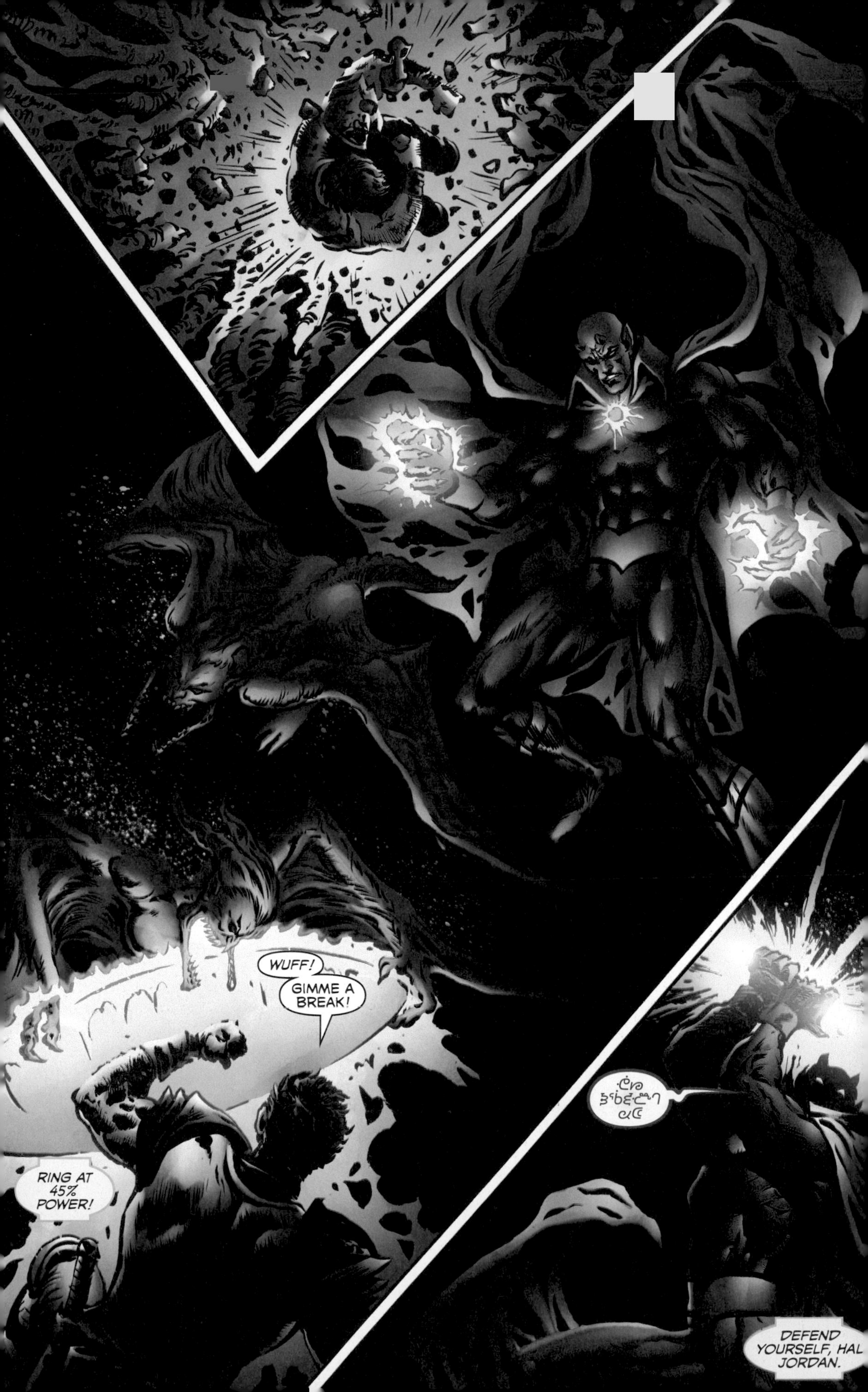
WUFF!
GIMME A BREAK!
RING AT 45% POWER!
DEFEND YOURSELF, HAL JORDAN.

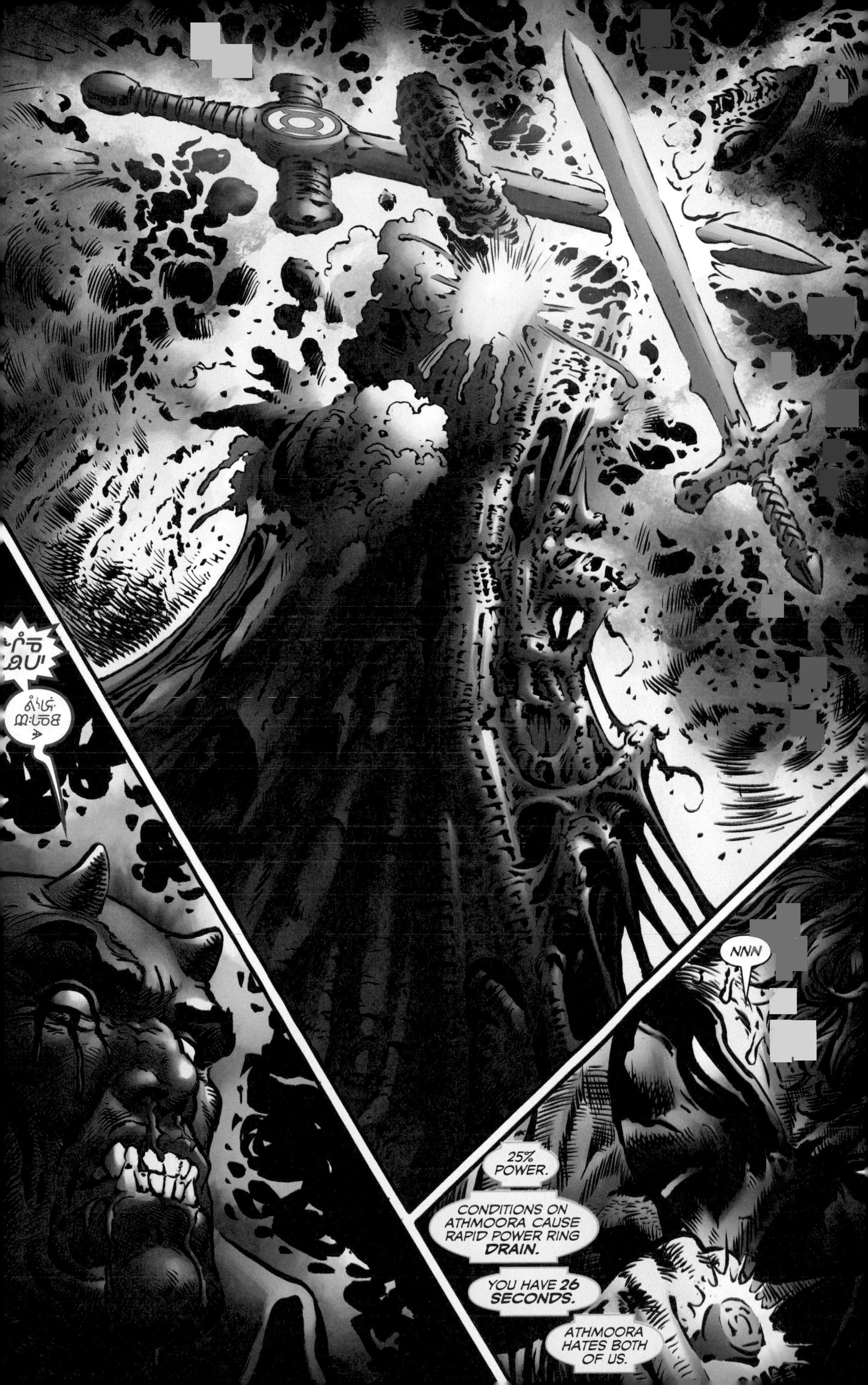
NNN
25% POWER.
CONDITIONS ON ATHMOORA CAUSE RAPID POWER RING DRAIN.
YOU HAVE 26 SECONDS.
ATHMOORA HATES BOTH OF US.

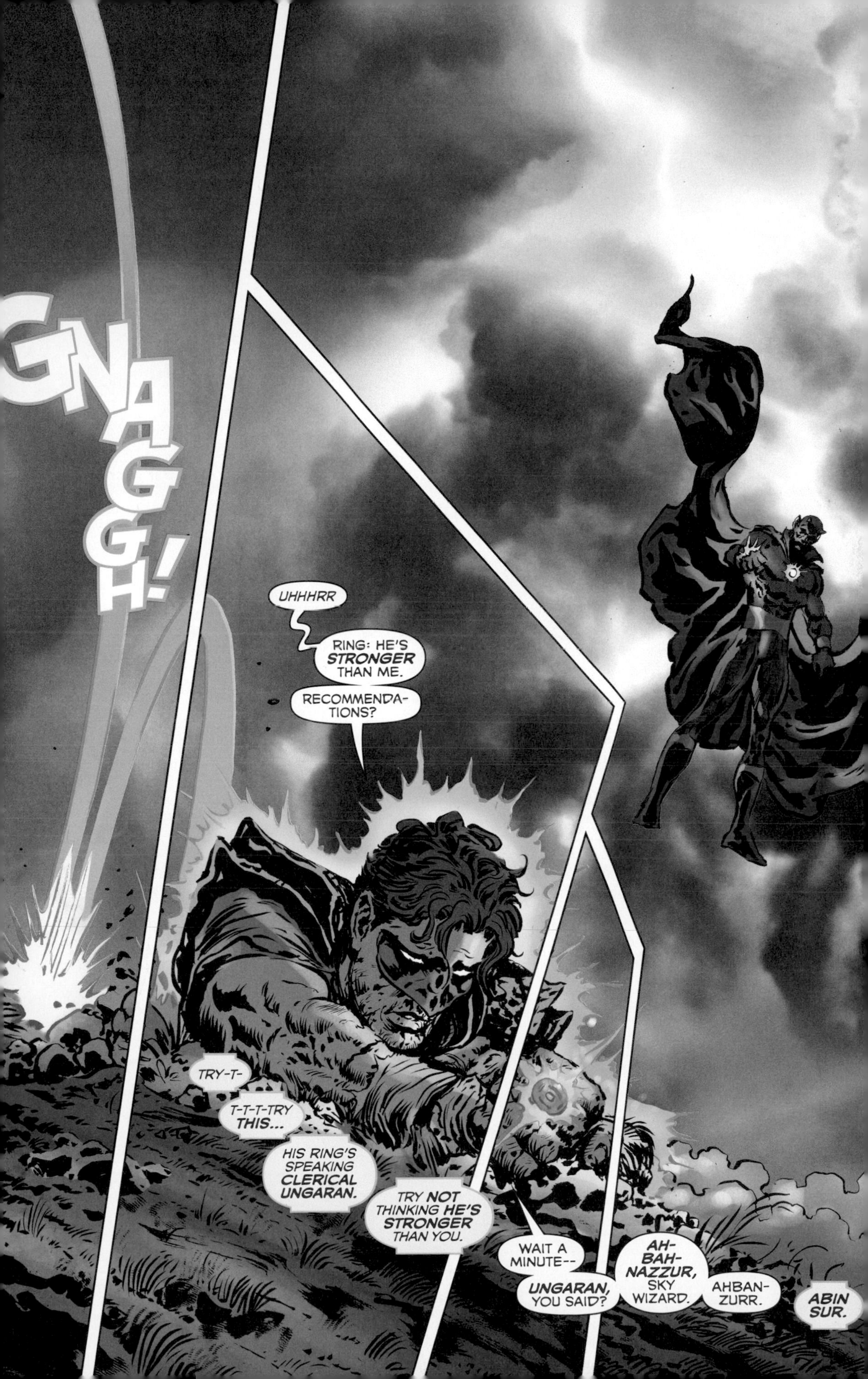
GNAGGH!
UHHHRR
RING: HE'S STRONGER THAN ME.
RECOMMENDA-TIONS?
TRY-T-
T-T-T-TRY THIS...
HIS RING'S SPEAKING CLERICAL UNGARAN.
TRY NOT THINKING HE'S STRONGER THAN YOU.
WAIT A MINUTE--
UNGARAN, YOU SAID?
AH-BAH-NAZZUR, SKY WIZARD.
AHBAN-ZURR.
ABIN SUR.

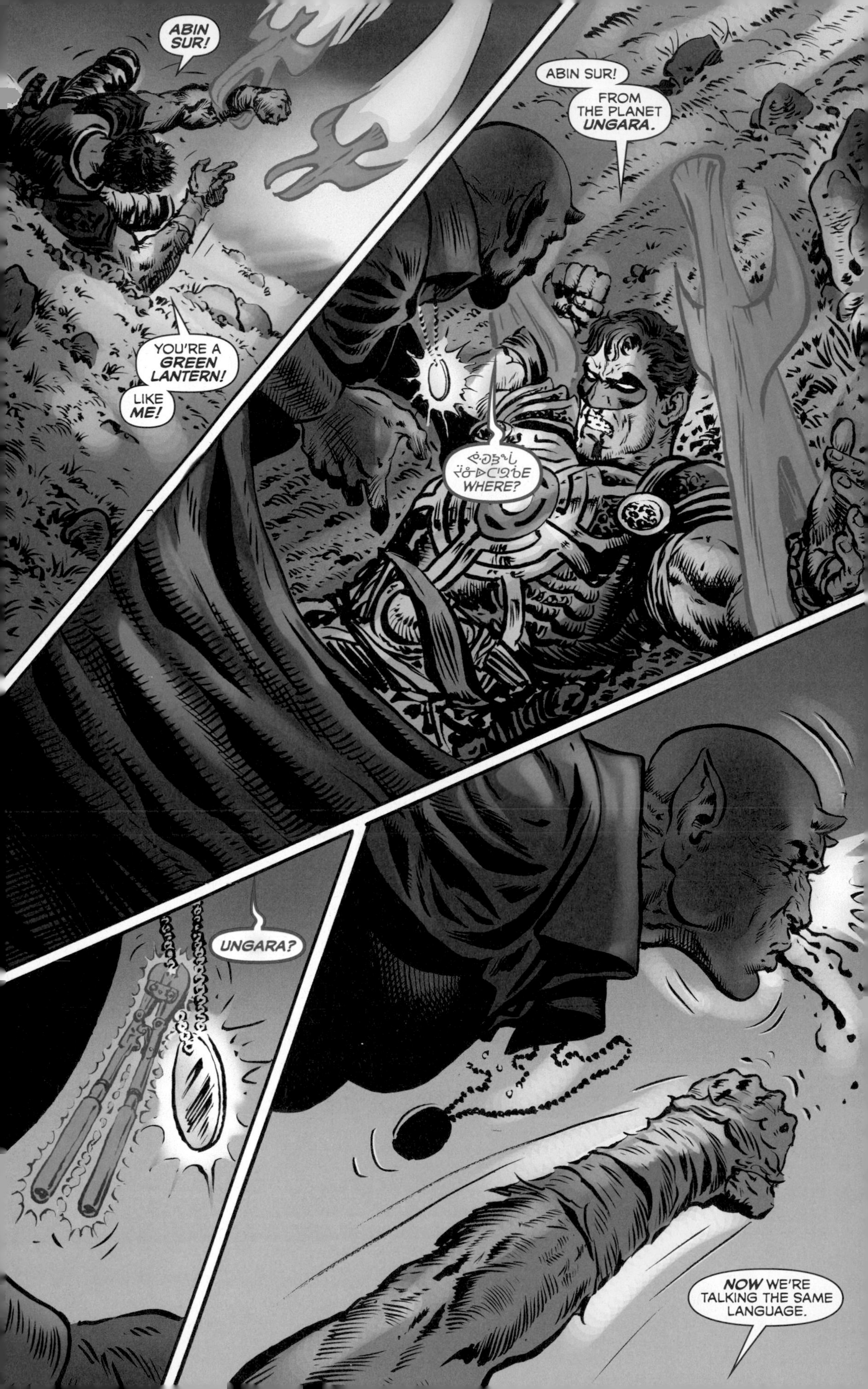
ABIN SUR!
YOU'RE A GREEN LANTERN!
LIKE ME!
ABIN SUR!
FROM THE PLANET UNGARA.
WHERE?
UNGARA?
NOW WE'RE TALKING THE SAME LANGUAGE.

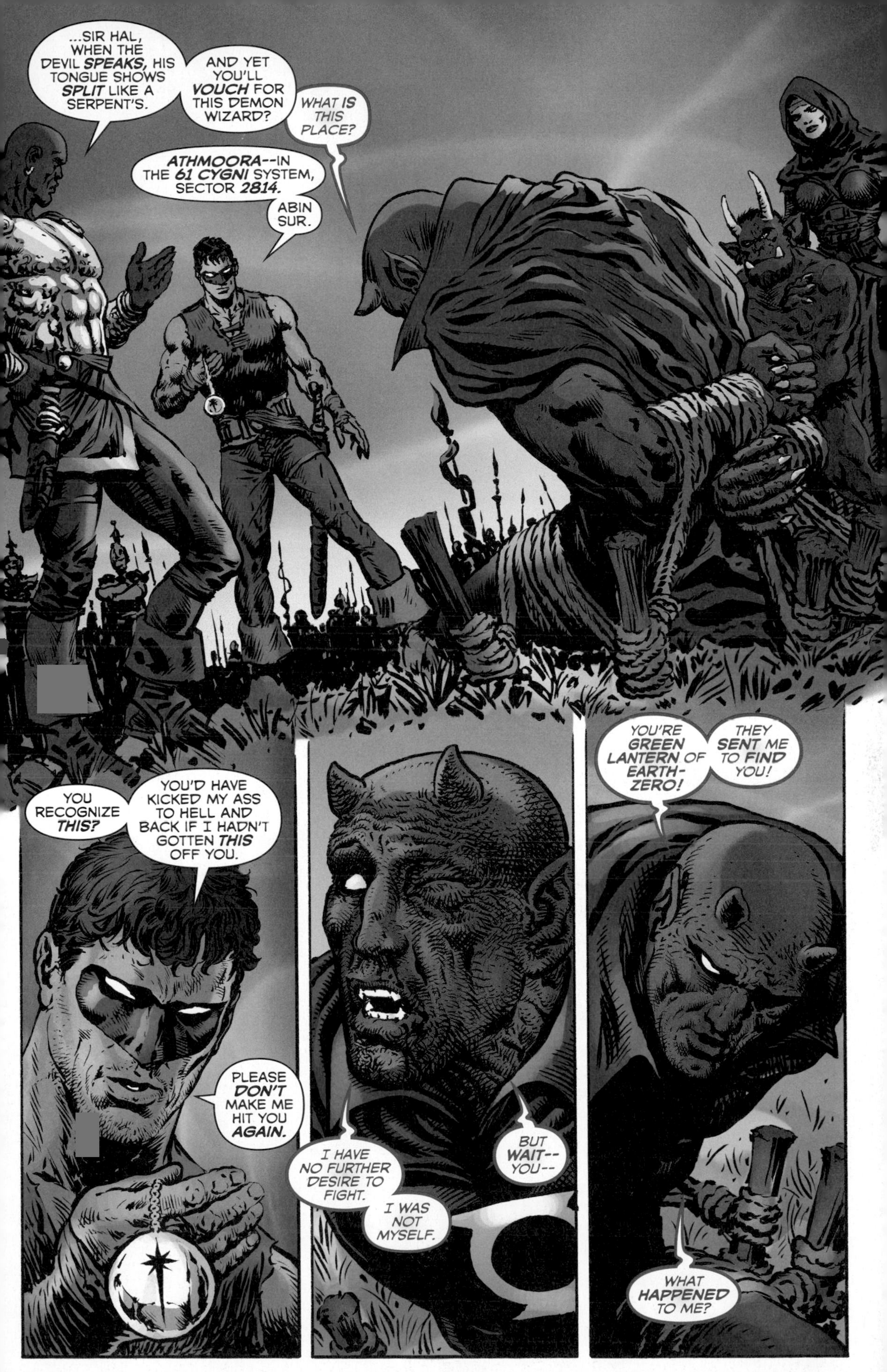
...SIR HAL, WHEN THE DEVIL SPEAKS, HIS TONGUE SHOWS SPLIT LIKE A SERPENT'S.
AND YET YOU'LL VOUCH FOR THIS DEMON WIZARD?
WHAT IS THIS PLACE?
ATHMOORA--IN THE 61 CYGNI SYSTEM, SECTOR 2814.
ABIN SUR.
YOU RECOGNIZE THIS?
YOU'D HAVE KICKED MY ASS TO HELL AND BACK IF I HADN'T GOTTEN THIS OFF YOU.
PLEASE DON'T MAKE ME HIT YOU AGAIN.
I HAVE NO FURTHER DESIRE TO FIGHT.
I WAS NOT MYSELF.
BUT WAIT-- YOU--
YOU'RE GREEN LANTERN OF EARTH-ZERO!
THEY SENT ME TO FIND YOU!
WHAT HAPPENED TO ME?

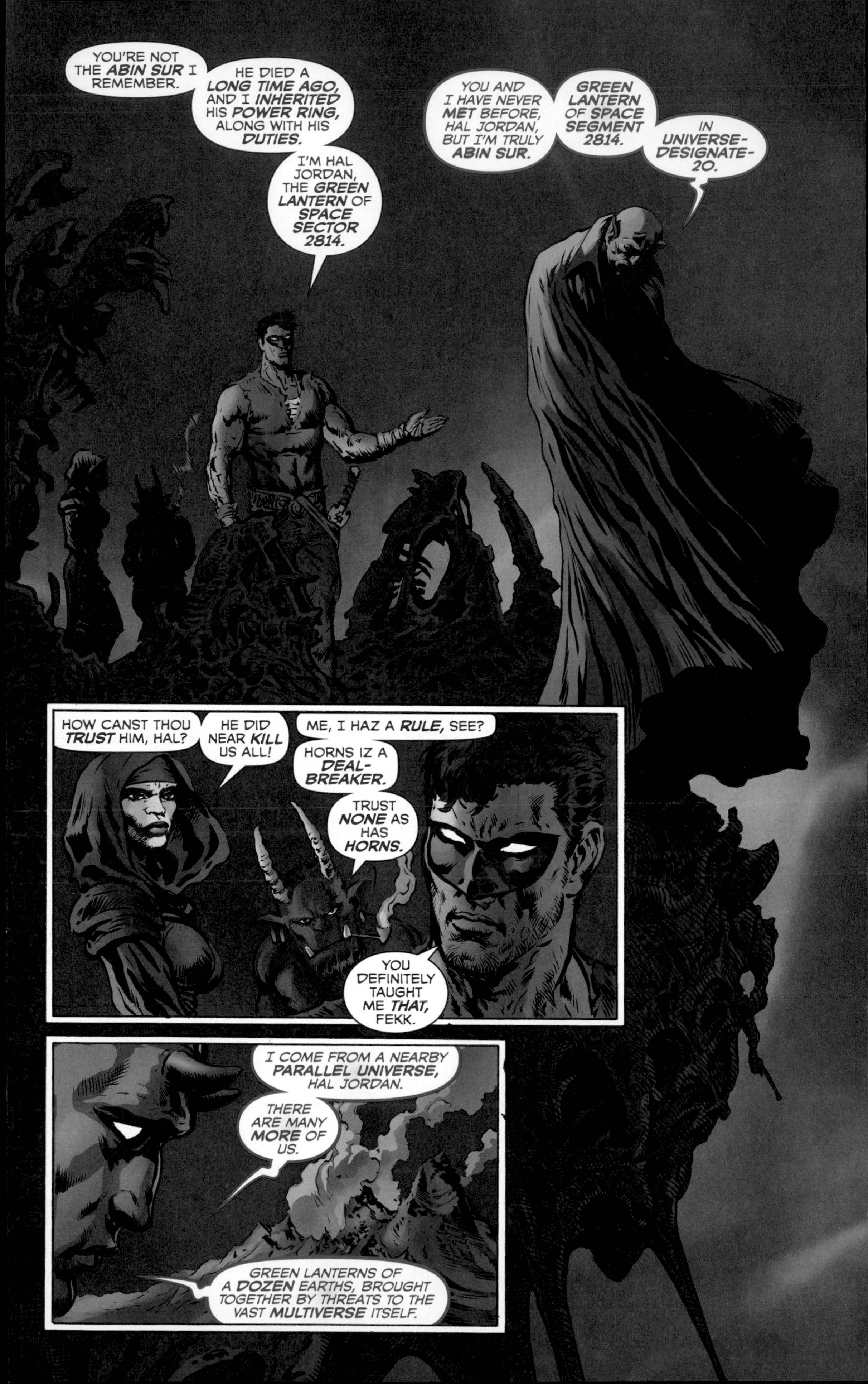
YOU'RE NOT THE ABIN SUR I REMEMBER.
HE DIED A LONG TIME AGO, AND I INHERITED HIS POWER RING, ALONG WITH HIS DUTIES.
I'M HAL JORDAN, THE GREEN LANTERN OF SPACE SECTOR 2814.
YOU AND I HAVE NEVER MET BEFORE, HAL JORDAN, BUT I'M TRULY ABIN SUR.
GREEN LANTERN OF SPACE SEGMENT 2814.
IN UNIVERSE-DESIGNATE-20.
HOW CANST THOU TRUST HIM, HAL?
HE DID NEAR KILL US ALL!
ME, I HAZ A RULE, SEE?
HORNS IZ A DEAL-BREAKER.
TRUST NONE AS HAS HORNS.
YOU DEFINITELY TAUGHT ME THAT, FEKK.
I COME FROM A NEARBY PARALLEL UNIVERSE, HAL JORDAN.
THERE ARE MANY MORE OF US.
GREEN LANTERNS OF A DOZEN EARTHS, BROUGHT TOGETHER BY THREATS TO THE VAST MULTIVERSE ITSELF.

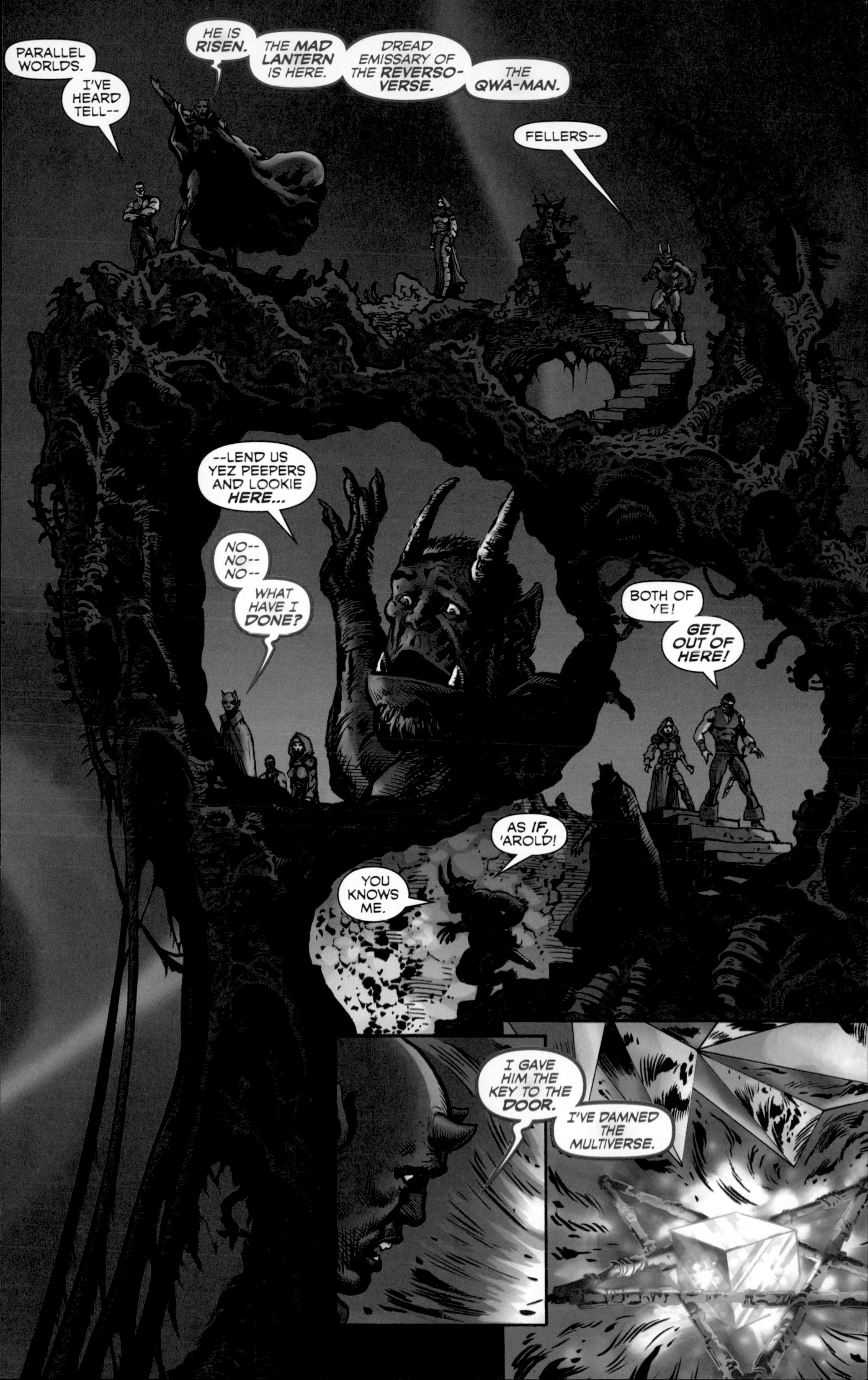
PARALLEL WORLDS.
I'VE HEARD TELL--
HE IS RISEN.
THE MAD LANTERN IS HERE.
DREAD EMISSARY OF THE REVERSO-VERSE.
THE QWA-MAN.
FELLERS--
--LEND US YEZ PEEPERS AND LOOKIE HERE...
NO-- NO-- NO--
WHAT HAVE I DONE?
BOTH OF YE!
GET OUT OF HERE!
AS IF, 'AROLD!
YOU KNOWS ME.
I GAVE HIM THE KEY TO THE DOOR.
I'VE DAMNED THE MULTIVERSE.

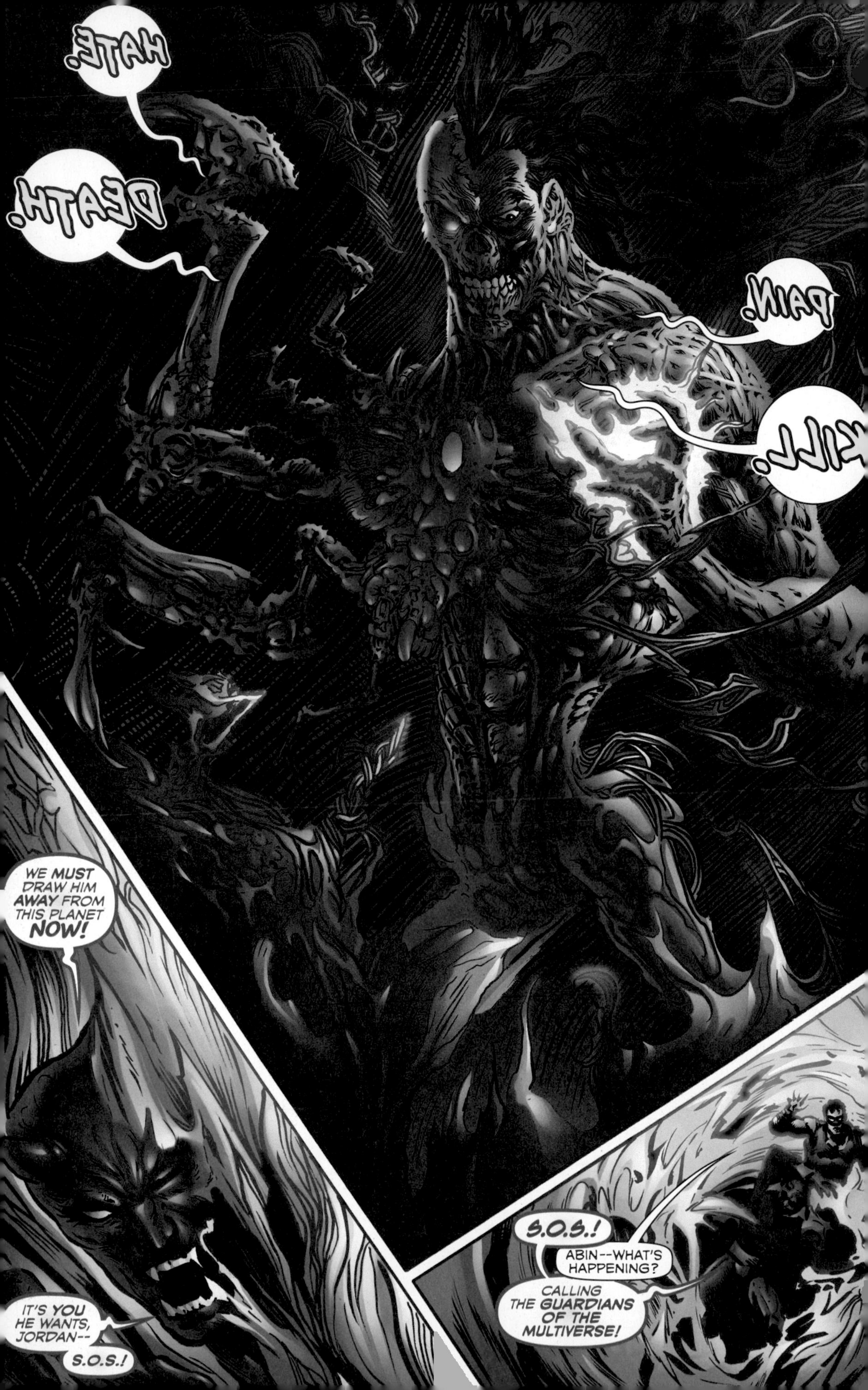
HATE.
DEATH.
PAIN.
KILL.
WE MUST DRAW HIM AWAY FROM THIS PLANET NOW!
IT'S YOU HE WANTS, JORDAN--
S.O.S.!
S.O.S.!
ABIN--WHAT'S HAPPENING?
CALLING THE GUARDIANS OF THE MULTIVERSE!

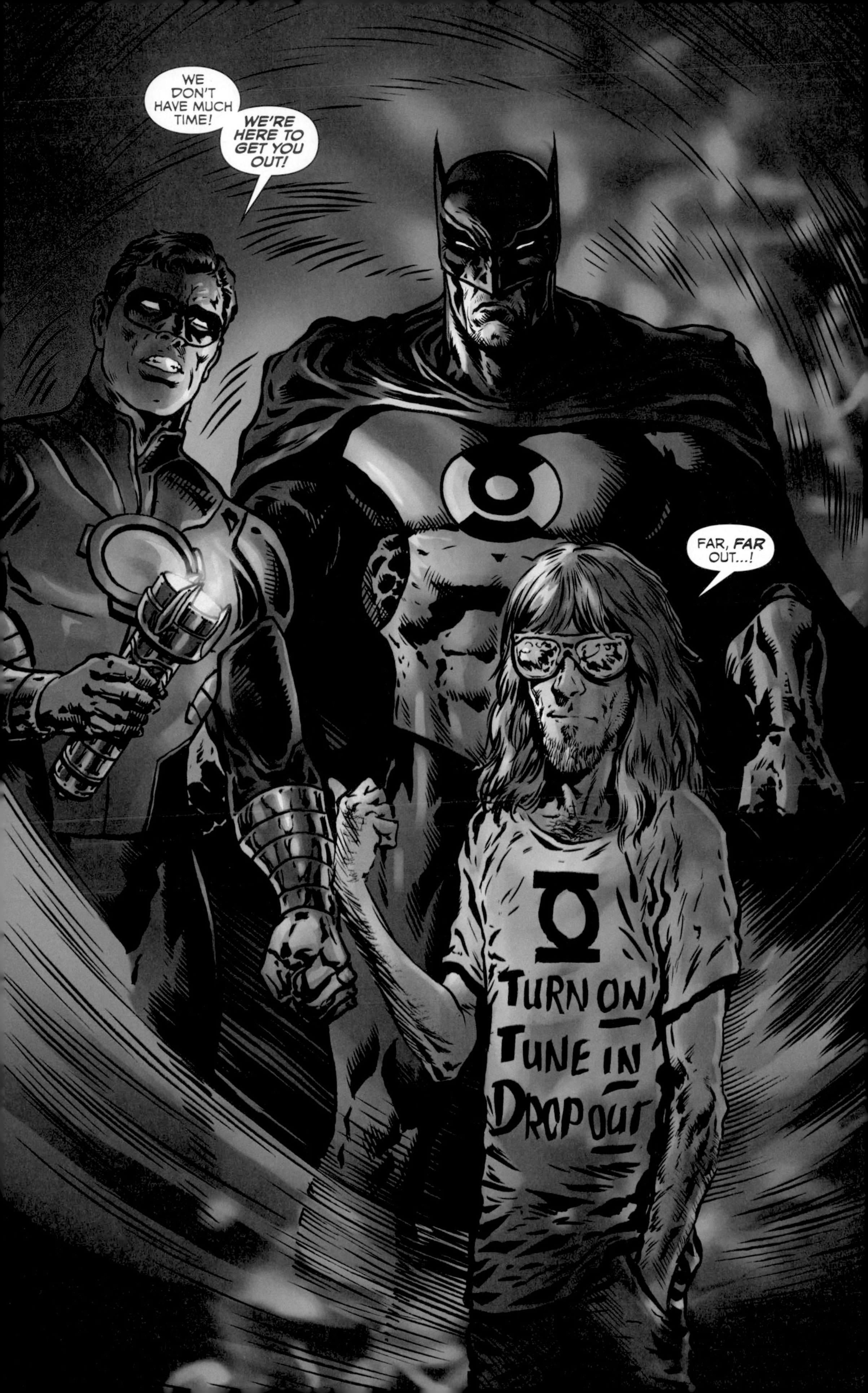
WE DON'T HAVE MUCH TIME!
WE'RE HERE TO GET YOU OUT!
FAR, FAR OUT...!
TURN ON TUNE IN DROP OUT

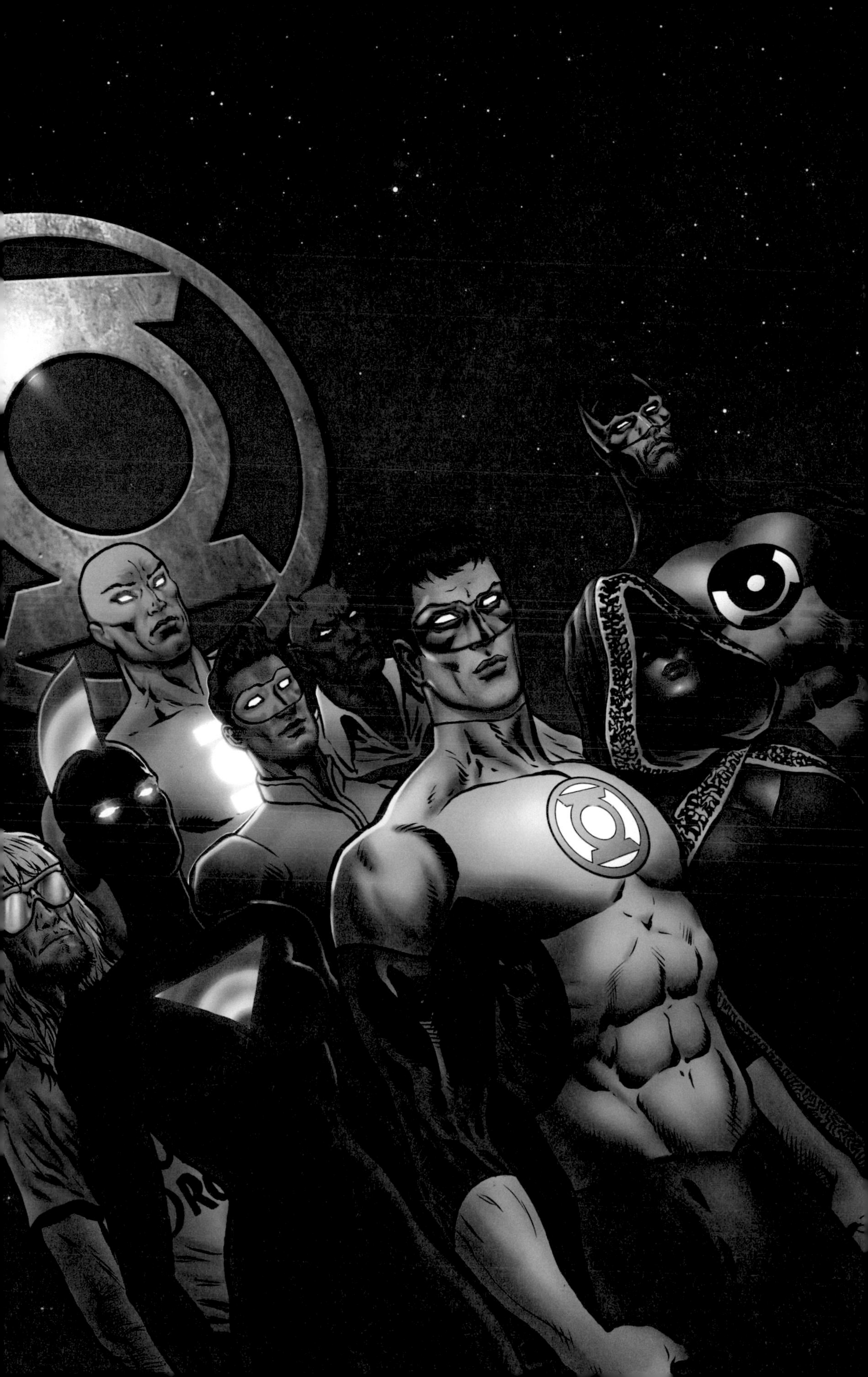

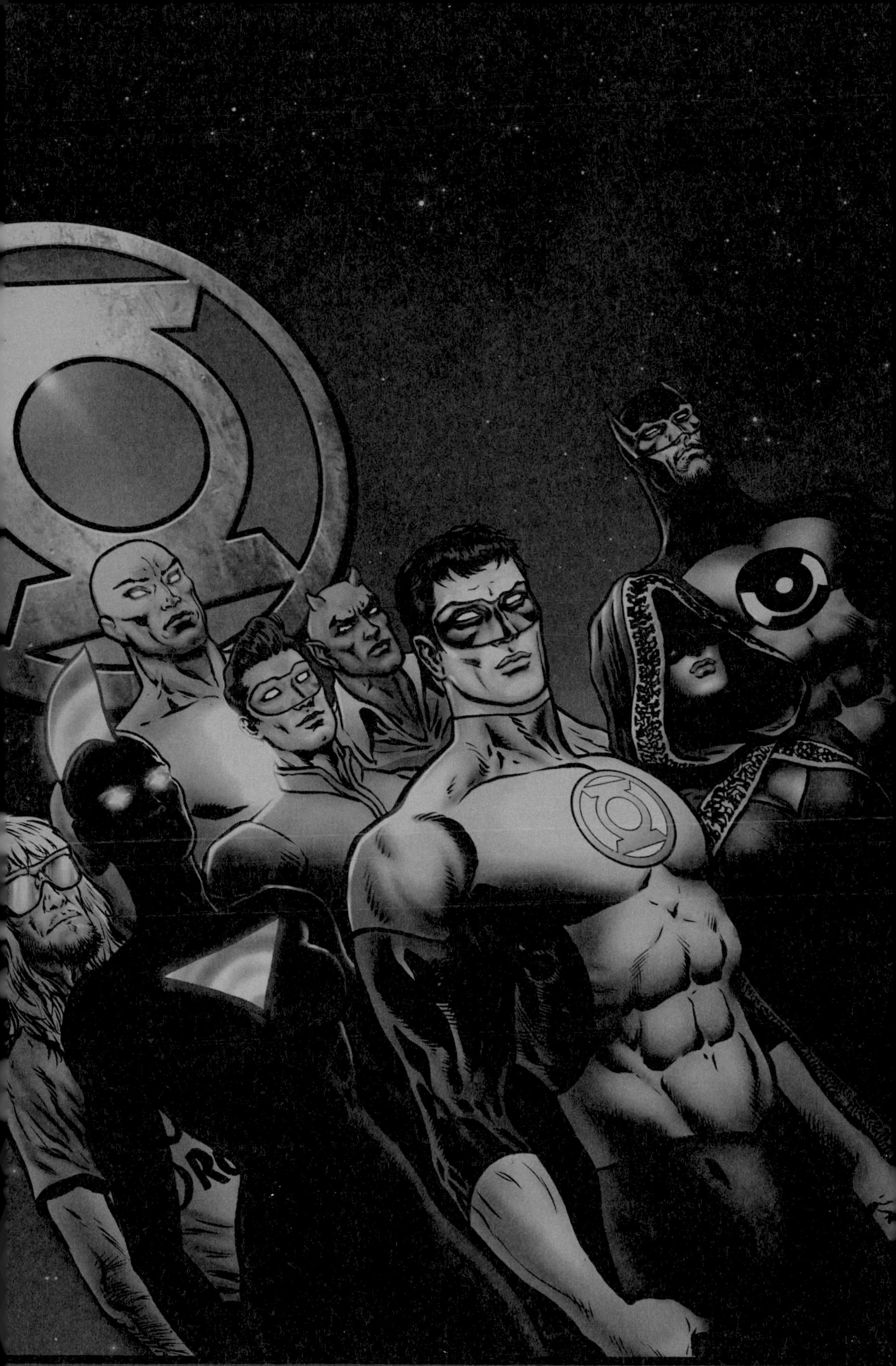

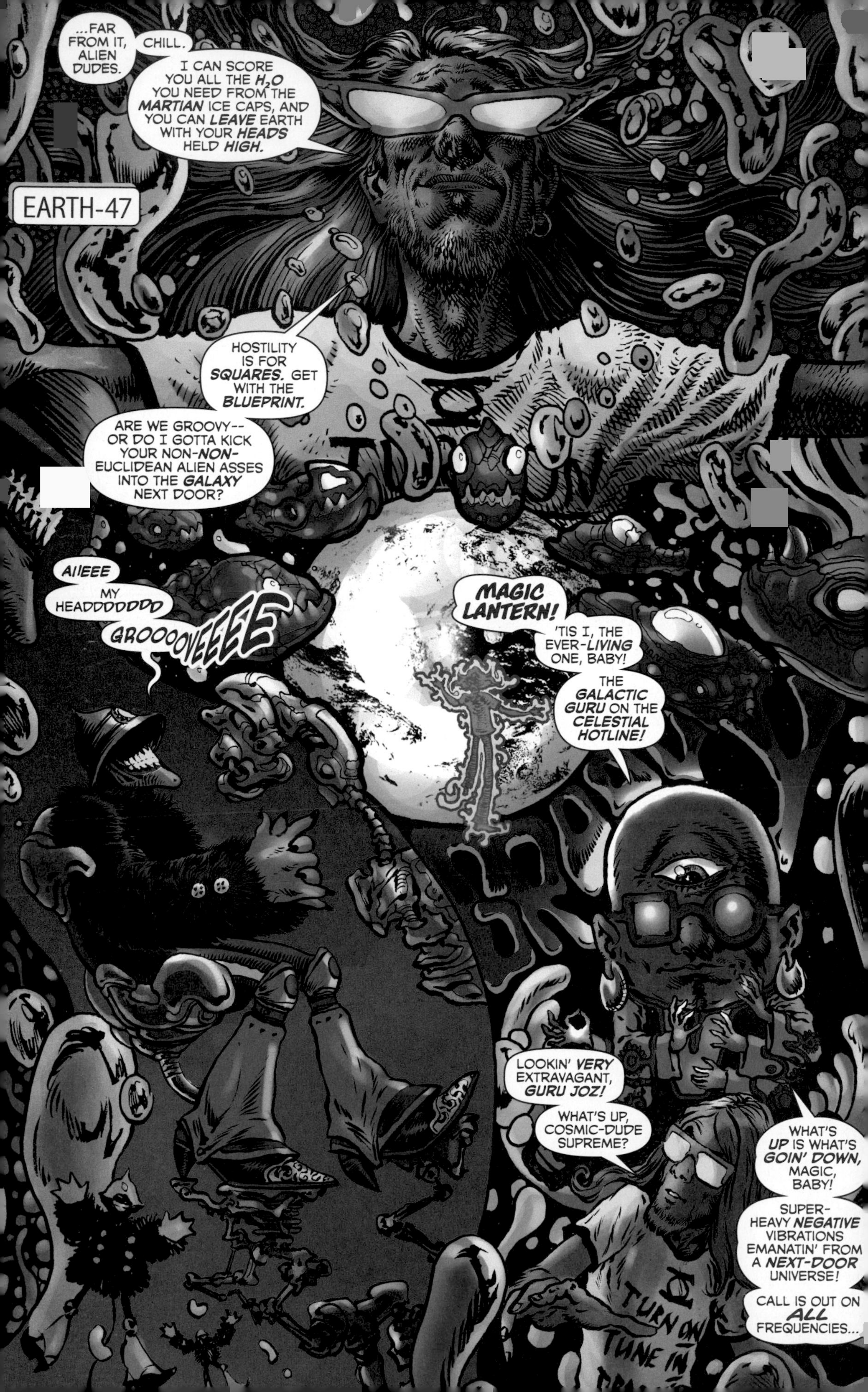

...FAR FROM IT, ALIEN DUDES.
CHILL.
I CAN SCORE YOU ALL THE H_2O YOU NEED FROM THE MARTIAN ICE CAPS, AND YOU CAN LEAVE EARTH WITH YOUR HEADS HELD HIGH.
EARTH-47
HOSTILITY IS FOR SQUARES. GET WITH THE BLUEPRINT.
ARE WE GROOVY-- OR DO I GOTTA KICK YOUR NON-NON-EUCLIDEAN ALIEN ASSES INTO THE GALAXY NEXT DOOR?
AIIEEE MY HEADDDDDDD
GROOOOVEEEEE
MAGIC LANTERN!
'TIS I, THE EVER-LIVING ONE, BABY!
THE GALACTIC GURU ON THE CELESTIAL HOTLINE!
LOOKIN' VERY EXTRAVAGANT, GURU JOZ!
WHAT'S UP, COSMIC-DUDE SUPREME?
WHAT'S UP IS WHAT'S GOIN' DOWN, MAGIC, BABY!
SUPER-HEAVY NEGATIVE VIBRATIONS EMANATIN' FROM A NEXT-DOOR UNIVERSE!
CALL IS OUT ON ALL FREQUENCIES...

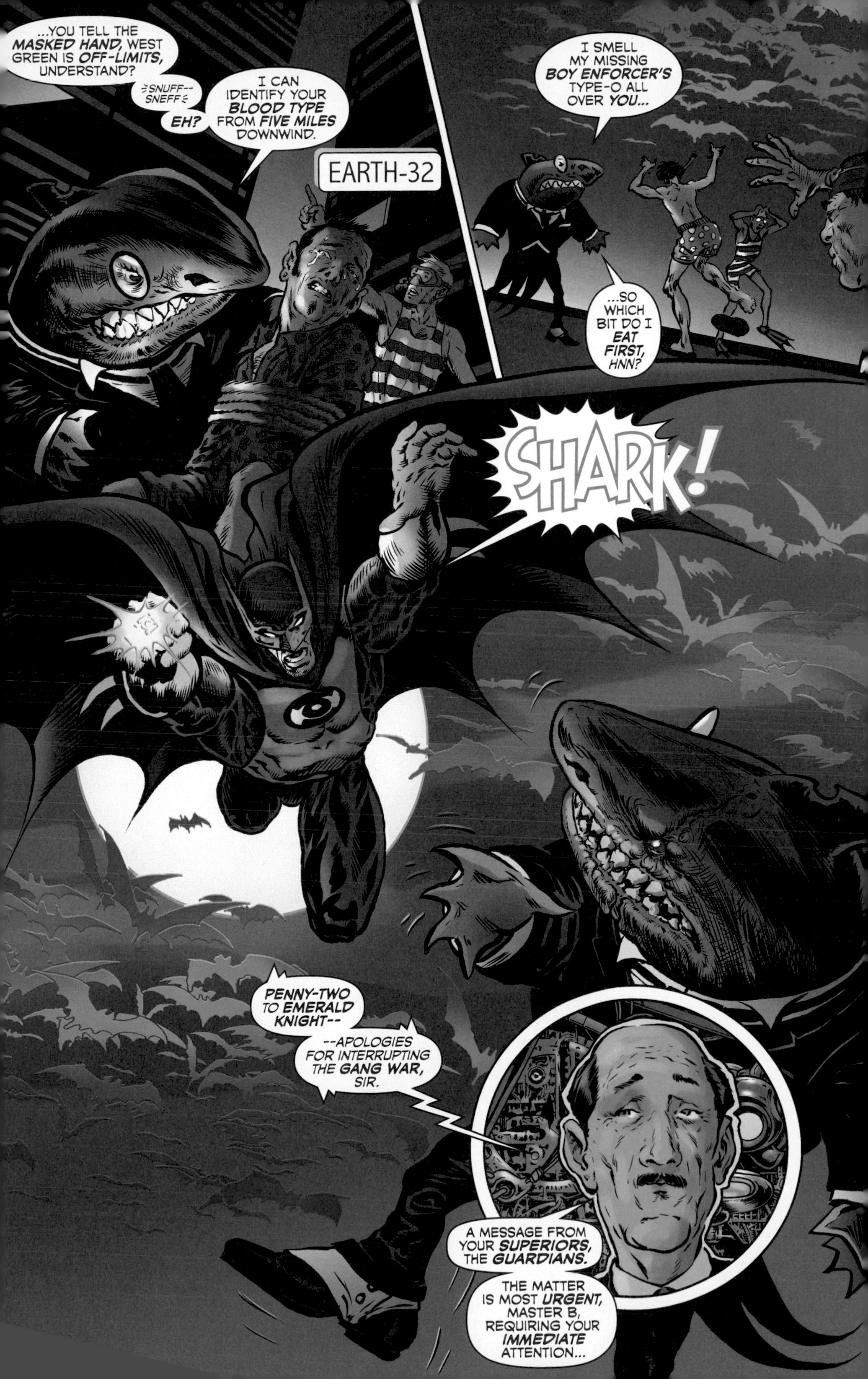
...YOU TELL THE MASKED HAND, WEST GREEN IS OFF-LIMITS, UNDERSTAND?
SNUFF-- SNEFF
EH?
I CAN IDENTIFY YOUR BLOOD TYPE FROM FIVE MILES DOWNWIND.
EARTH-32
I SMELL MY MISSING BOY ENFORCER'S TYPE-O ALL OVER YOU...
...SO WHICH BIT DO I EAT FIRST, HNN?
SHARK!
PENNY-TWO TO EMERALD KNIGHT--
--APOLOGIES FOR INTERRUPTING THE GANG WAR, SIR.
A MESSAGE FROM YOUR SUPERIORS, THE GUARDIANS.
THE MATTER IS MOST URGENT, MASTER B, REQUIRING YOUR IMMEDIATE ATTENTION...

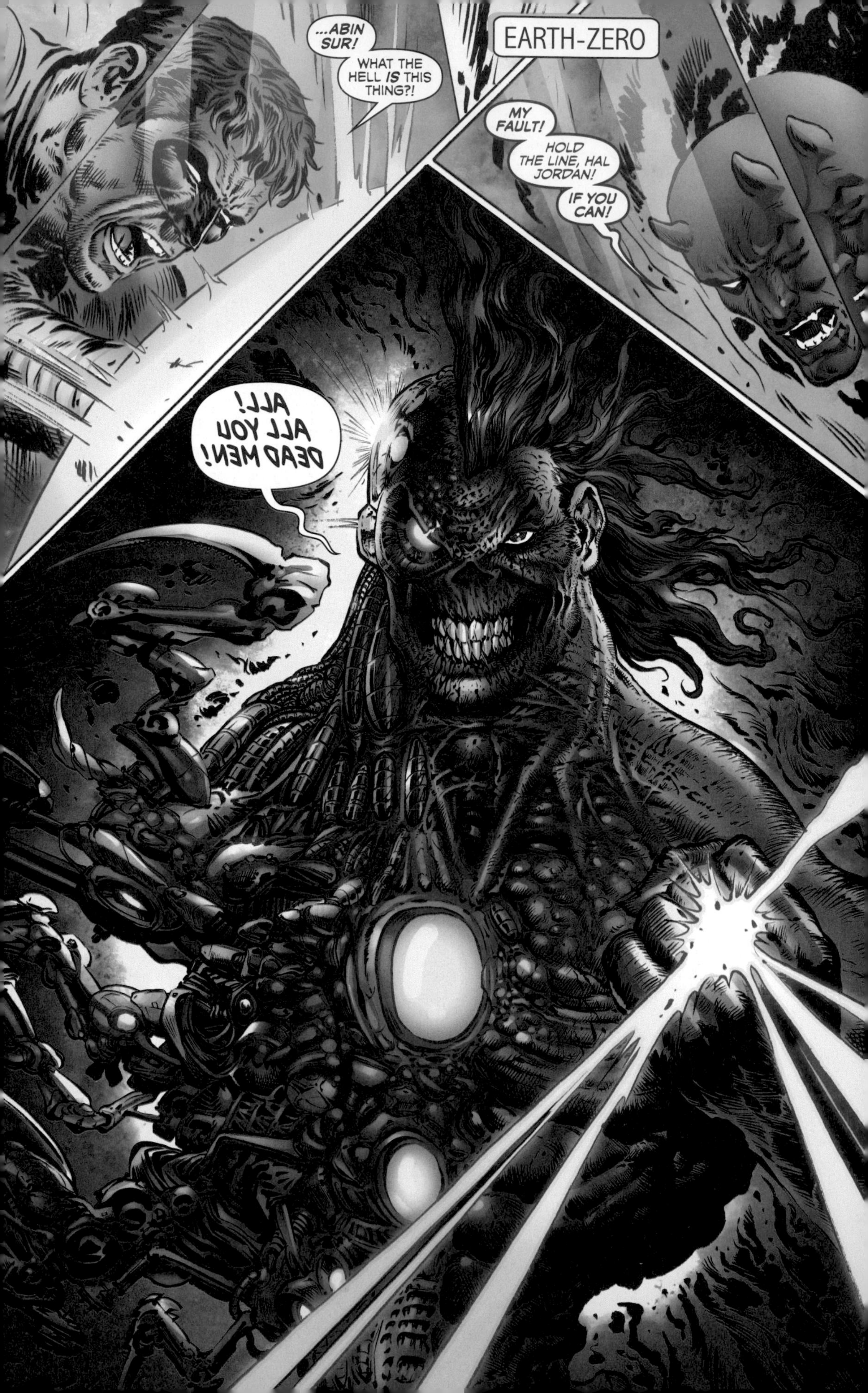
...ABIN SUR!
WHAT THE HELL IS THIS THING?!
EARTH-ZERO
MY FAULT!
HOLD THE LINE, HAL JORDAN!
IF YOU CAN!
ALL! ALL YOU DEAD MEN!

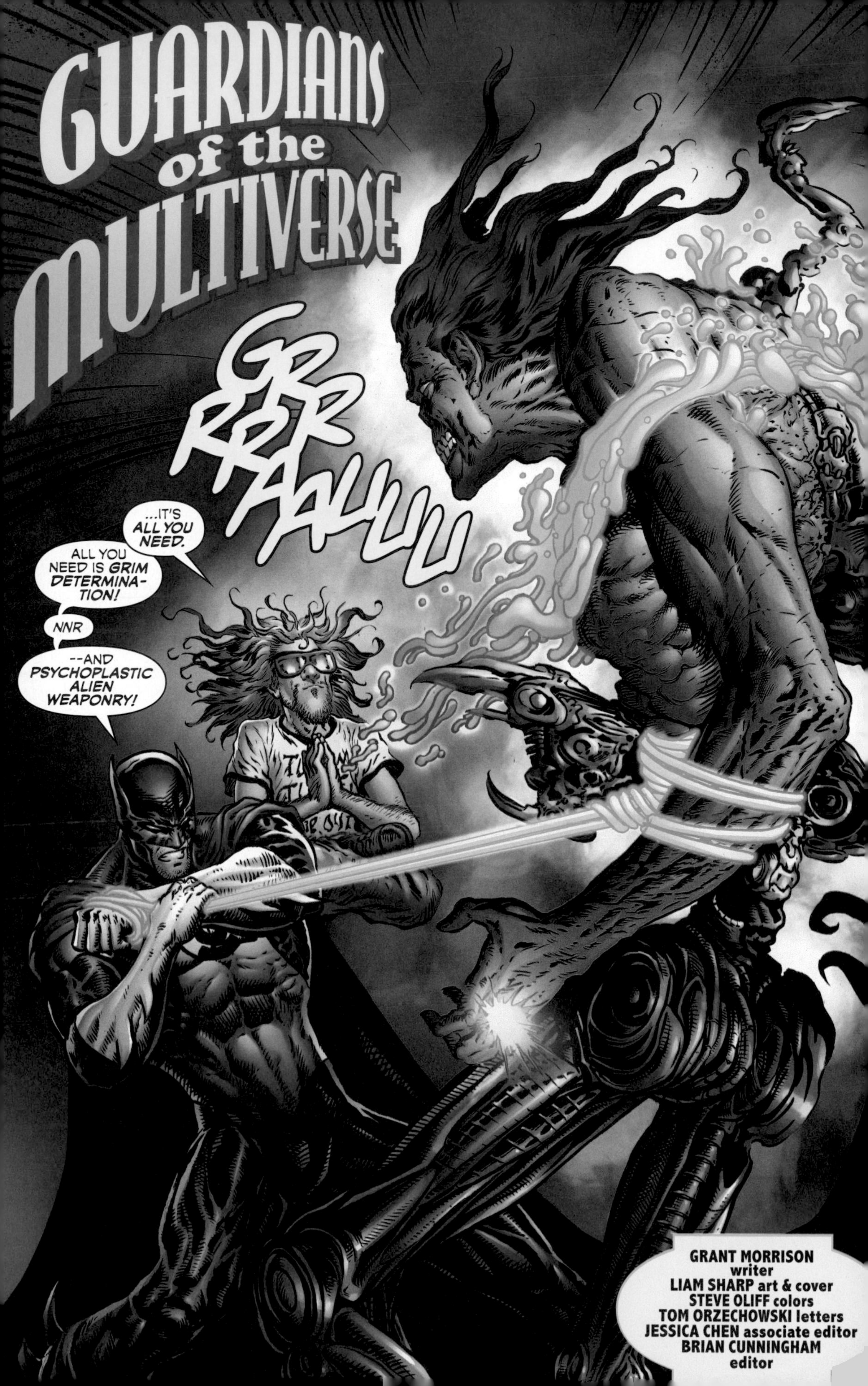
GUARDIANS of the MULTIVERSE
GRRRRAAUUU
...IT'S ALL YOU NEED.
ALL YOU NEED IS GRIM DETERMINA-TION!
NNR
--AND PSYCHOPLASTIC ALIEN WEAPONRY!
GRANT MORRISON writer
LIAM SHARP art & cover
STEVE OLIFF colors
TOM ORZECHOWSKI letters
JESSICA CHEN associate editor
BRIAN CUNNINGHAM editor

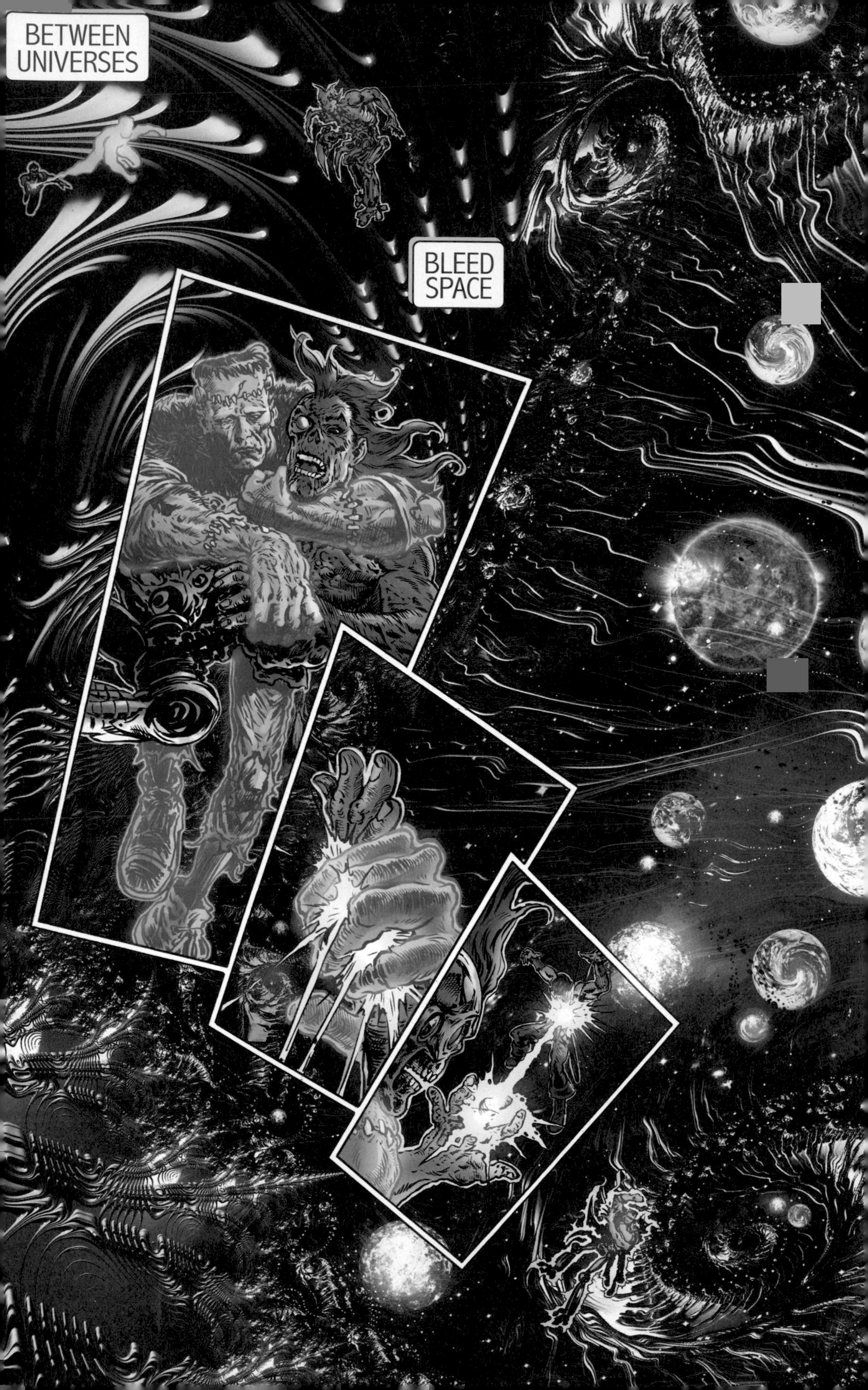
BETWEEN UNIVERSES
BLEED SPACE

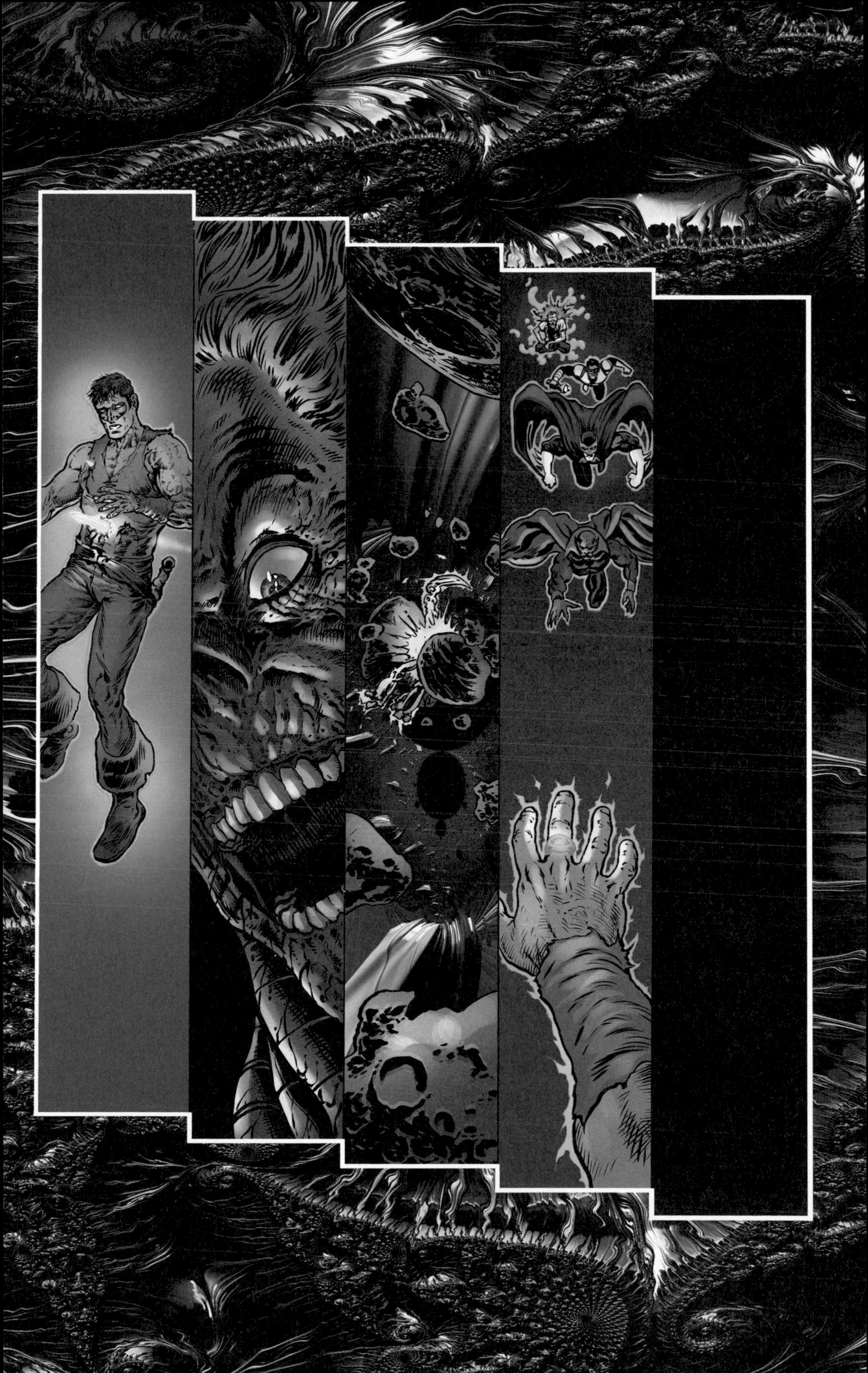

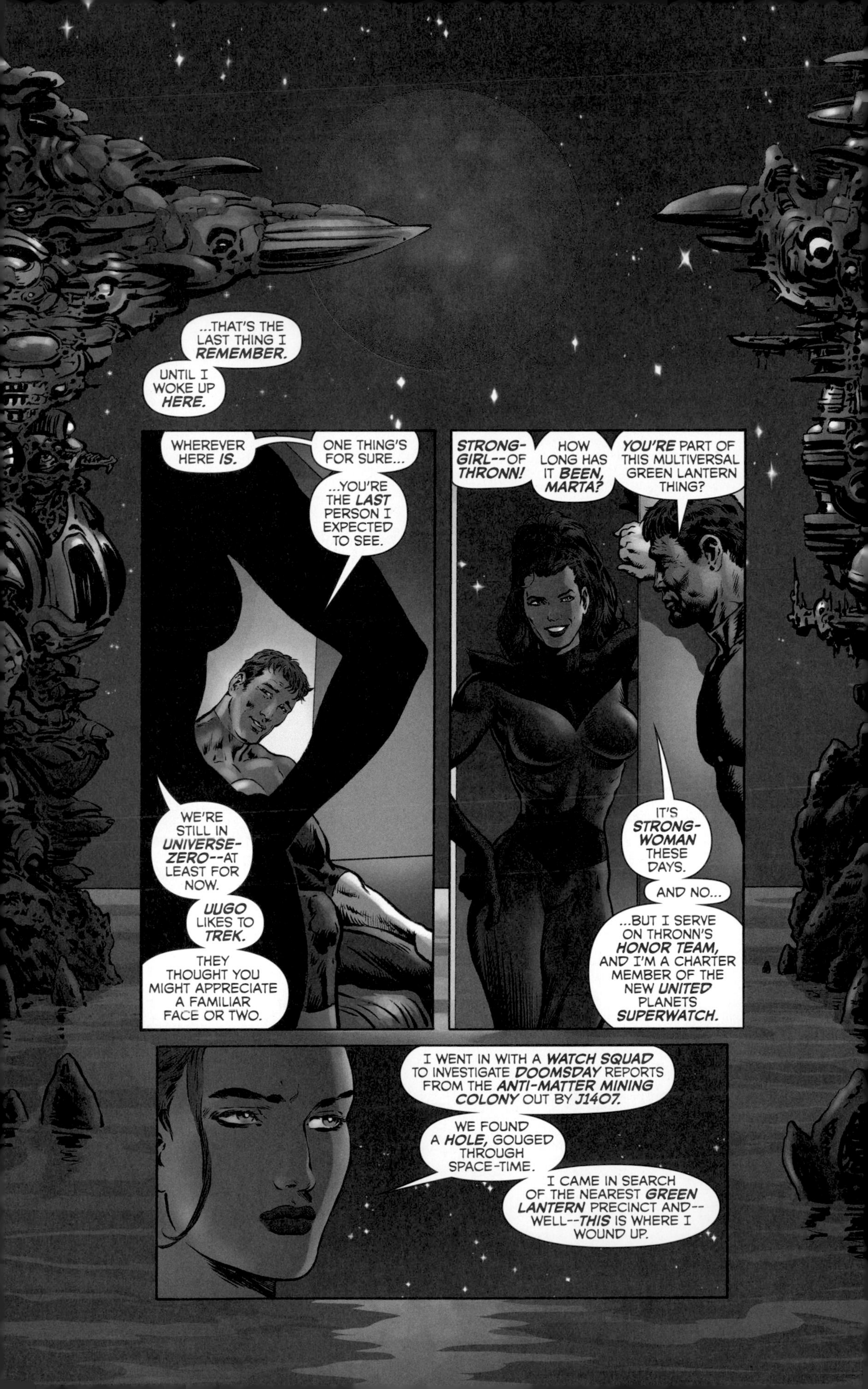
...THAT'S THE LAST THING I REMEMBER.
UNTIL I WOKE UP HERE.
WHEREVER HERE IS.
ONE THING'S FOR SURE...
...YOU'RE THE LAST PERSON I EXPECTED TO SEE.
WE'RE STILL IN UNIVERSE-ZERO--AT LEAST FOR NOW.
UUGO LIKES TO TREK.
THEY THOUGHT YOU MIGHT APPRECIATE A FAMILIAR FACE OR TWO.
STRONG-GIRL--OF THRONN!
HOW LONG HAS IT BEEN, MARTA?
YOU'RE PART OF THIS MULTIVERSAL GREEN LANTERN THING?
IT'S STRONG-WOMAN THESE DAYS.
AND NO...
...BUT I SERVE ON THRONN'S HONOR TEAM, AND I'M A CHARTER MEMBER OF THE NEW UNITED PLANETS SUPERWATCH.
I WENT IN WITH A WATCH SQUAD TO INVESTIGATE DOOMSDAY REPORTS FROM THE ANTI-MATTER MINING COLONY OUT BY J1407.
WE FOUND A HOLE, GOUGED THROUGH SPACE-TIME.
I CAME IN SEARCH OF THE NEAREST GREEN LANTERN PRECINCT AND--WELL--THIS IS WHERE I WOUND UP.

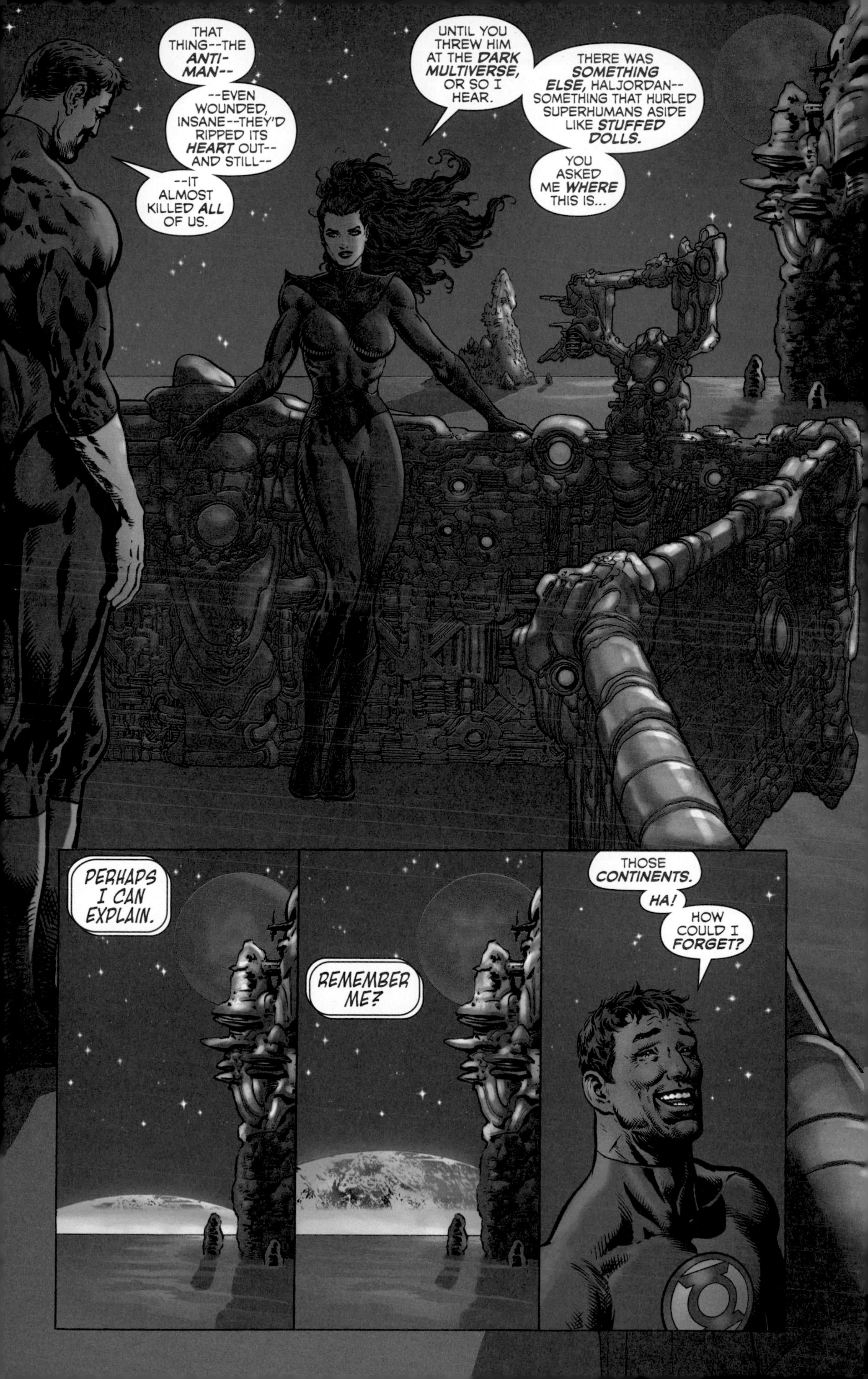
THAT THING--THE ANTI-MAN--
--EVEN WOUNDED, INSANE--THEY'D RIPPED ITS HEART OUT--AND STILL--
--IT ALMOST KILLED ALL OF US.
UNTIL YOU THREW HIM AT THE DARK MULTIVERSE, OR SO I HEAR.
THERE WAS SOMETHING ELSE, HALJORDAN--SOMETHING THAT HURLED SUPERHUMANS ASIDE LIKE STUFFED DOLLS.
YOU ASKED ME WHERE THIS IS...
PERHAPS I CAN EXPLAIN.
REMEMBER ME?
THOSE CONTINENTS.
HA!
HOW COULD I FORGET?

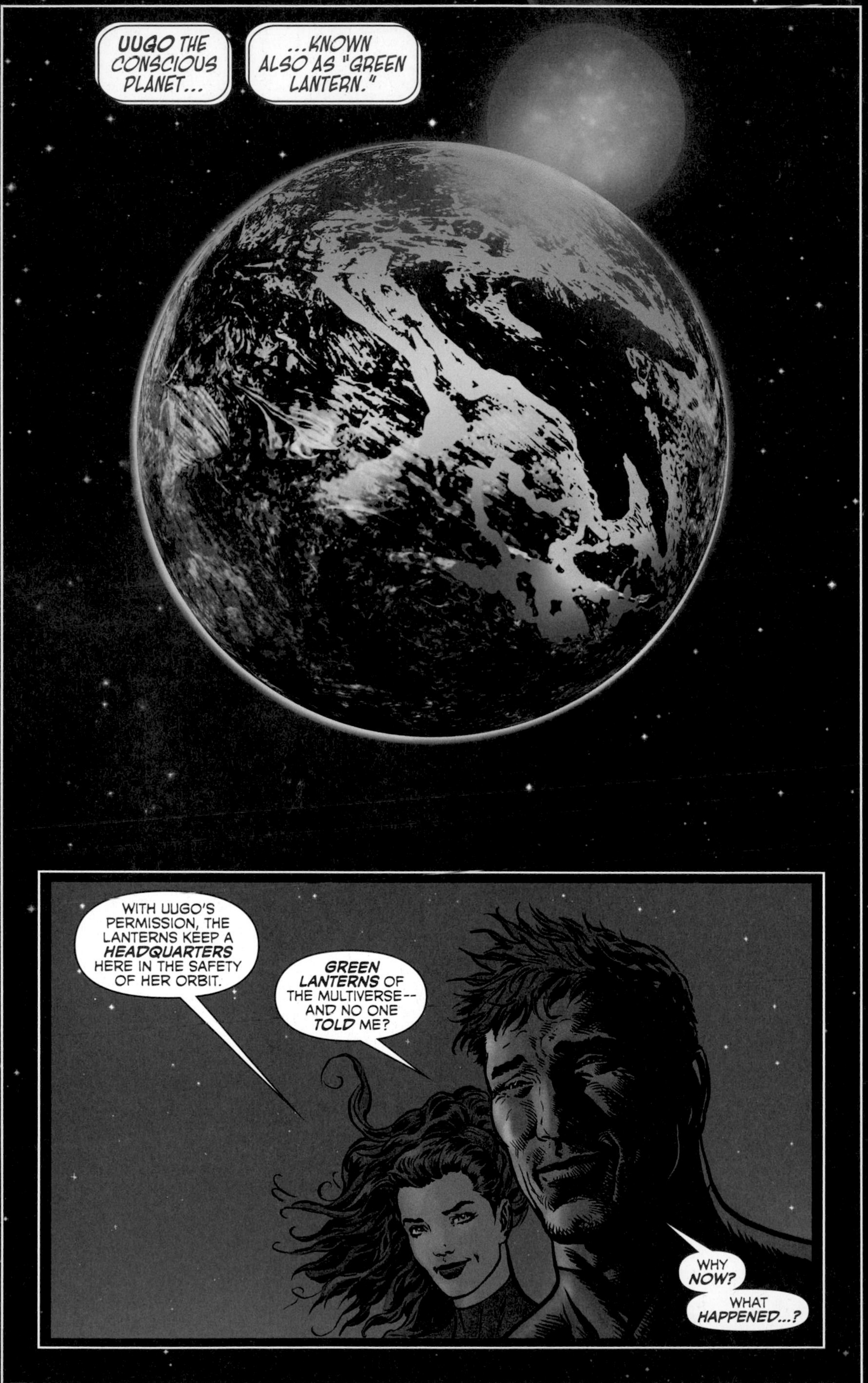
UUGO THE CONSCIOUS PLANET...
...KNOWN ALSO AS "GREEN LANTERN."
WITH UUGO'S PERMISSION, THE LANTERNS KEEP A HEADQUARTERS HERE IN THE SAFETY OF HER ORBIT.
GREEN LANTERNS OF THE MULTIVERSE-- AND NO ONE TOLD ME?
WHY NOW?
WHAT HAPPENED...?

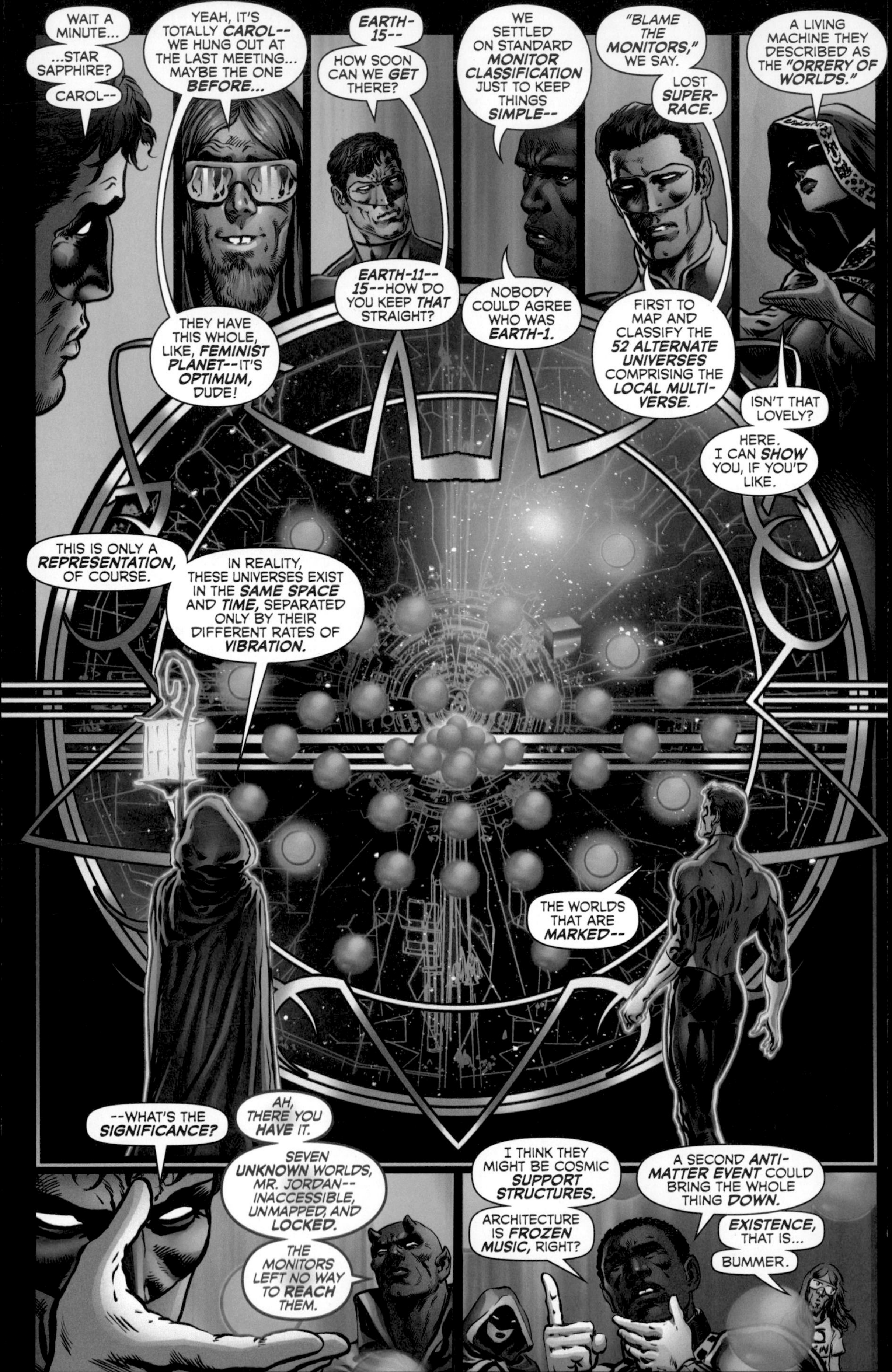

WAIT A MINUTE...
...STAR SAPPHIRE?
CAROL--
YEAH, IT'S TOTALLY CAROL-- WE HUNG OUT AT THE LAST MEETING... MAYBE THE ONE BEFORE...
THEY HAVE THIS WHOLE, LIKE, FEMINIST PLANET--IT'S OPTIMUM, DUDE!
EARTH-15--
HOW SOON CAN WE GET THERE?
EARTH-11--15--HOW DO YOU KEEP THAT STRAIGHT?
WE SETTLED ON STANDARD MONITOR CLASSIFICATION JUST TO KEEP THINGS SIMPLE--
NOBODY COULD AGREE WHO WAS EARTH-1.
"BLAME THE MONITORS," WE SAY.
LOST SUPER-RACE.
FIRST TO MAP AND CLASSIFY THE 52 ALTERNATE UNIVERSES COMPRISING THE LOCAL MULTI-VERSE.
A LIVING MACHINE THEY DESCRIBED AS THE "ORRERY OF WORLDS."
ISN'T THAT LOVELY?
HERE. I CAN SHOW YOU, IF YOU'D LIKE.
THIS IS ONLY A REPRESENTATION, OF COURSE.
IN REALITY, THESE UNIVERSES EXIST IN THE SAME SPACE AND TIME, SEPARATED ONLY BY THEIR DIFFERENT RATES OF VIBRATION.
THE WORLDS THAT ARE MARKED--
--WHAT'S THE SIGNIFICANCE?
AH, THERE YOU HAVE IT.
SEVEN UNKNOWN WORLDS, MR. JORDAN-- INACCESSIBLE, UNMAPPED, AND LOCKED.
THE MONITORS LEFT NO WAY TO REACH THEM.
I THINK THEY MIGHT BE COSMIC SUPPORT STRUCTURES.
ARCHITECTURE IS FROZEN MUSIC, RIGHT?
A SECOND ANTI-MATTER EVENT COULD BRING THE WHOLE THING DOWN.
EXISTENCE, THAT IS...
BUMMER.

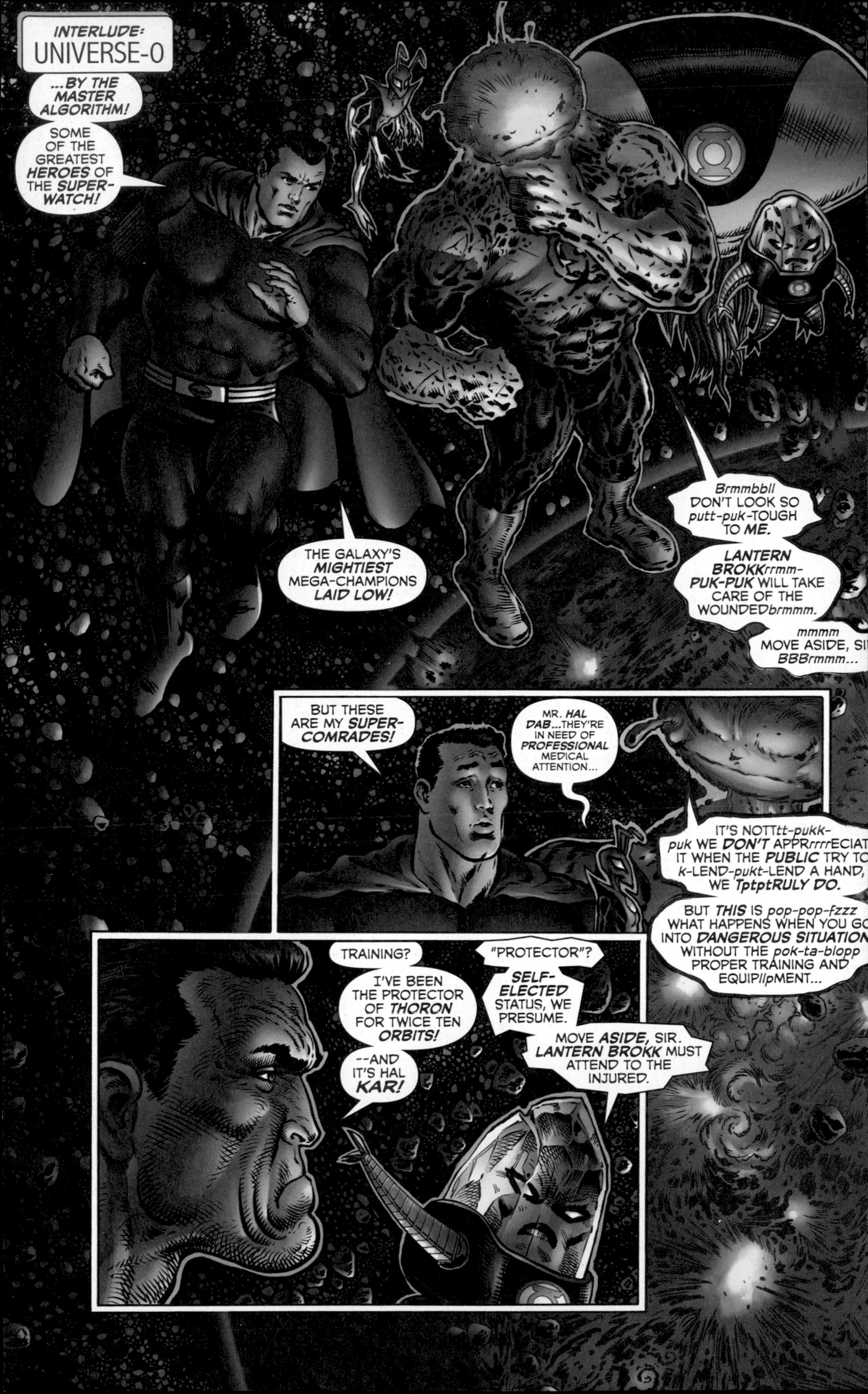
INTERLUDE: UNIVERSE-0
...BY THE MASTER ALGORITHM!
SOME OF THE GREATEST HEROES OF THE SUPER-WATCH!
THE GALAXY'S MIGHTIEST MEGA-CHAMPIONS LAID LOW!
Brmmbbll DON'T LOOK SO putt-puk-TOUGH TO ME.
LANTERN BROKKrrmm-PUK-PUK WILL TAKE CARE OF THE WOUNDEDbrmmm.
mmmm MOVE ASIDE, SI BBBrmmm...
BUT THESE ARE MY SUPER-COMRADES!
MR. HAL DAB...THEY'RE IN NEED OF PROFESSIONAL MEDICAL ATTENTION...
IT'S NOTTtt-pukk-puk WE DON'T APPRrrrrECIAT IT WHEN THE PUBLIC TRY TO k-LEND-pukt-LEND A HAND, WE TptptRULY DO.
BUT THIS IS pop-pop-fzzz WHAT HAPPENS WHEN YOU GO INTO DANGEROUS SITUATION WITHOUT THE pok-ta-blopp PROPER TRAINING AND EQUIPllpMENT...
TRAINING?
I'VE BEEN THE PROTECTOR OF THORON FOR TWICE TEN ORBITS!
--AND IT'S HAL KAR!
"PROTECTOR"?
SELF-ELECTED STATUS, WE PRESUME.
MOVE ASIDE, SIR. LANTERN BROKK MUST ATTEND TO THE INJURED.

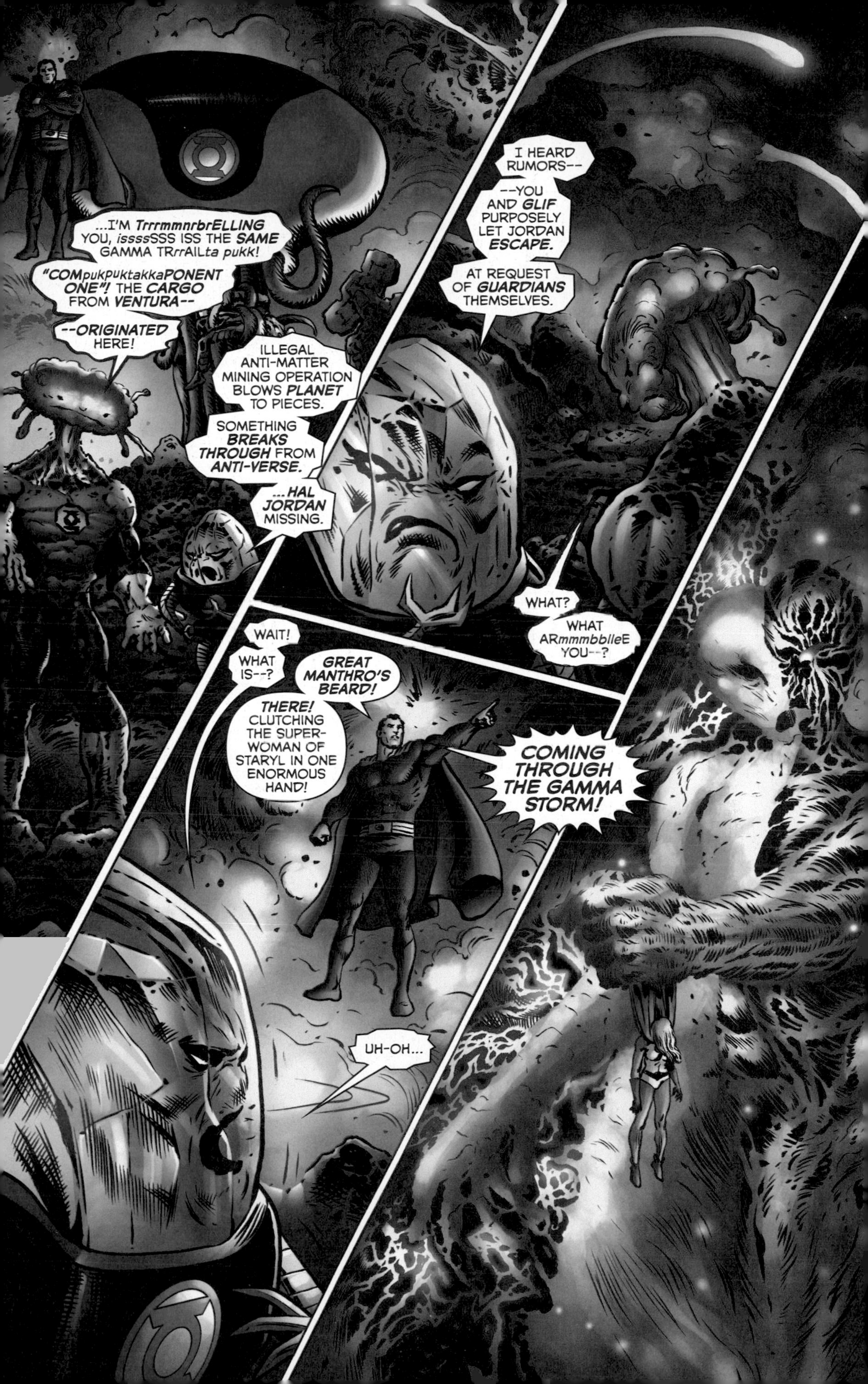

...I'M TrrrmmnrbrELLING YOU, issssSSS ISS THE SAME GAMMA TRrrAILta pukk!
"COMpukpuktakkaPONENT ONE"! THE CARGO FROM VENTURA--
--ORIGINATED HERE!
ILLEGAL ANTI-MATTER MINING OPERATION BLOWS PLANET TO PIECES.
SOMETHING BREAKS THROUGH FROM ANTI-VERSE.
...HAL JORDAN MISSING.
I HEARD RUMORS--
--YOU AND GLIF PURPOSELY LET JORDAN ESCAPE.
AT REQUEST OF GUARDIANS THEMSELVES.
WHAT?
WHAT ARmmmbbIleE YOU--?
WAIT!
WHAT IS--?
GREAT MANTHRO'S BEARD!
THERE! CLUTCHING THE SUPER-WOMAN OF STARYL IN ONE ENORMOUS HAND!
COMING THROUGH THE GAMMA STORM!
UH-OH...

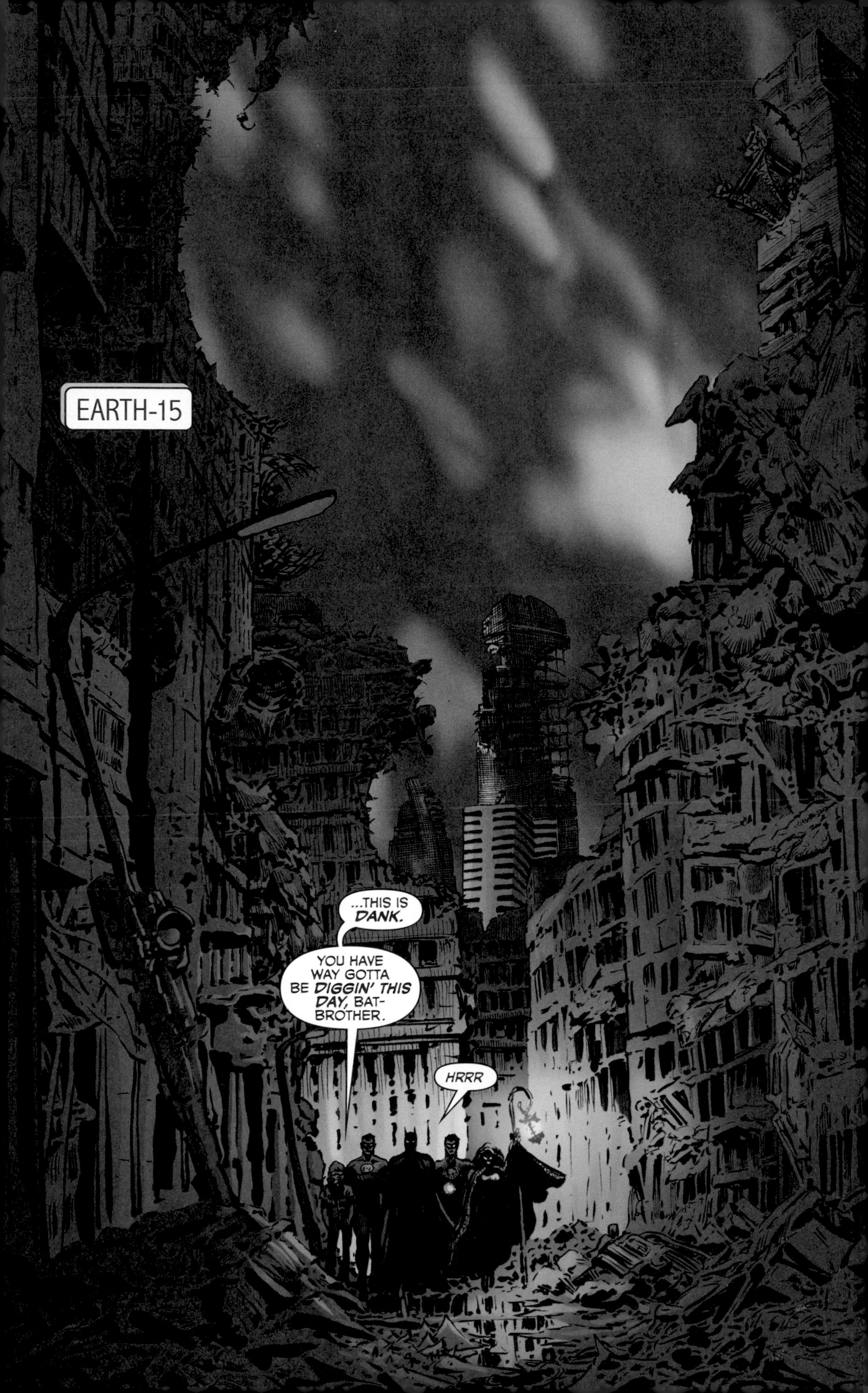
EARTH-15
...THIS IS DANK.
YOU HAVE WAY GOTTA BE DIGGIN' THIS DAY, BAT-BROTHER.
HRRR

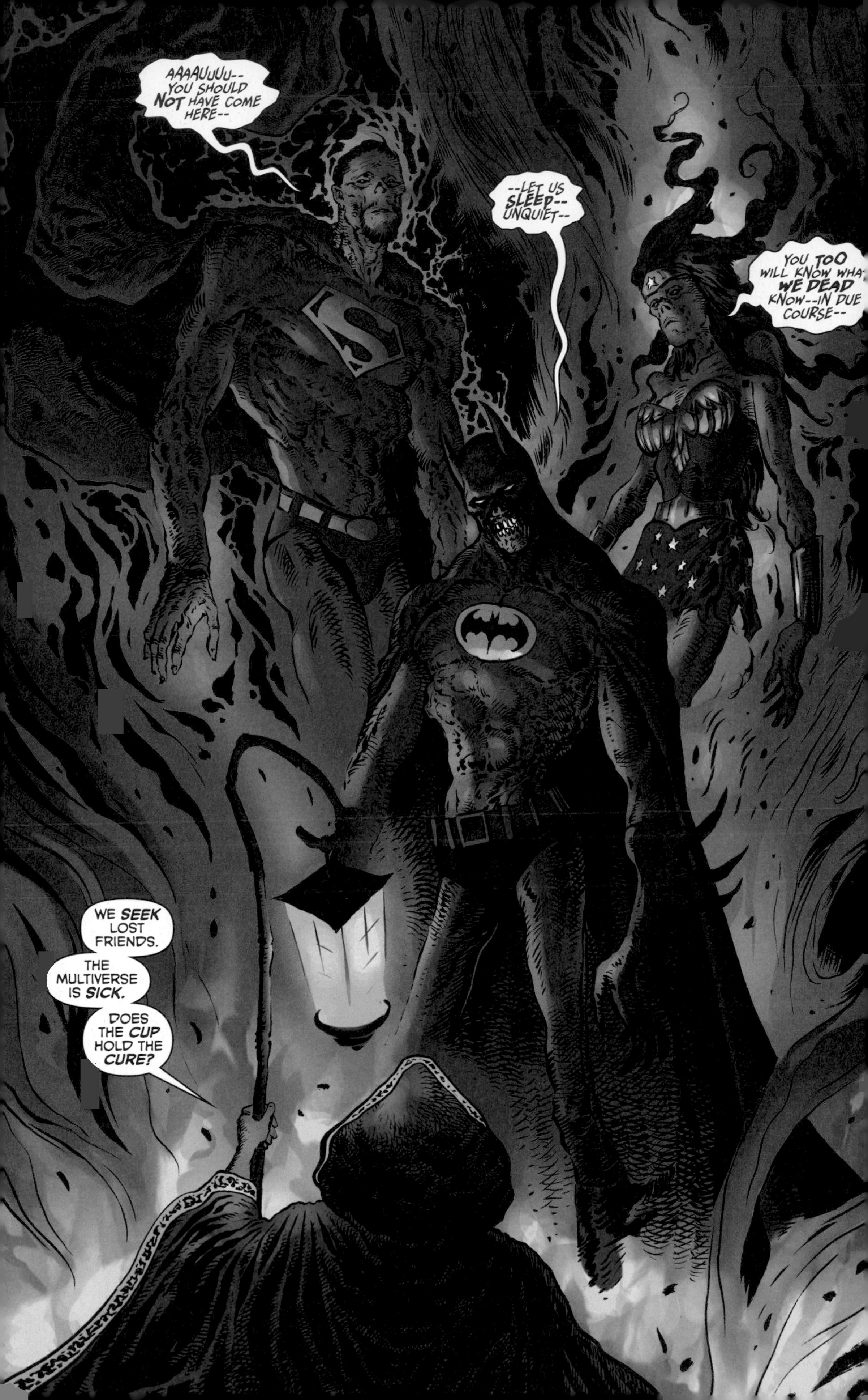
AAAAUUUU--
YOU SHOULD NOT HAVE COME HERE--
--LET US SLEEP--UNQUIET--
YOU TOO WILL KNOW WHA WE DEAD KNOW--IN DUE COURSE--
WE SEEK LOST FRIENDS.
THE MULTIVERSE IS SICK.
DOES THE CUP HOLD THE CURE?

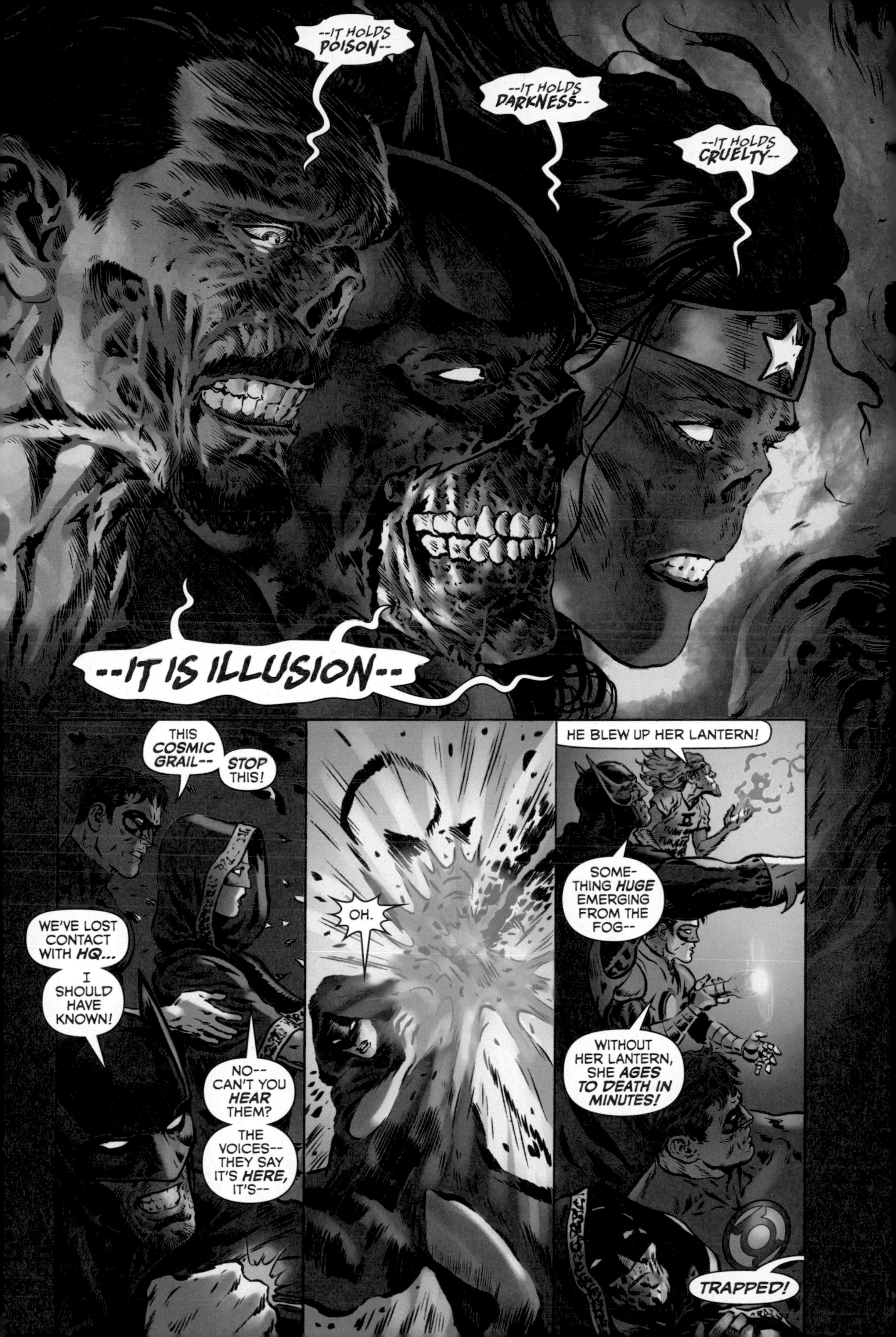
--IT HOLDS POISON--
--IT HOLDS DARKNESS--
--IT HOLDS CRUELTY--
--IT IS ILLUSION--
THIS COSMIC GRAIL--
STOP THIS!
WE'VE LOST CONTACT WITH HQ...
I SHOULD HAVE KNOWN!
NO-- CAN'T YOU HEAR THEM?
THE VOICES-- THEY SAY IT'S HERE, IT'S--
OH.
HE BLEW UP HER LANTERN!
SOME-THING HUGE EMERGING FROM THE FOG--
WITHOUT HER LANTERN, SHE AGES TO DEATH IN MINUTES!
TRAPPED!

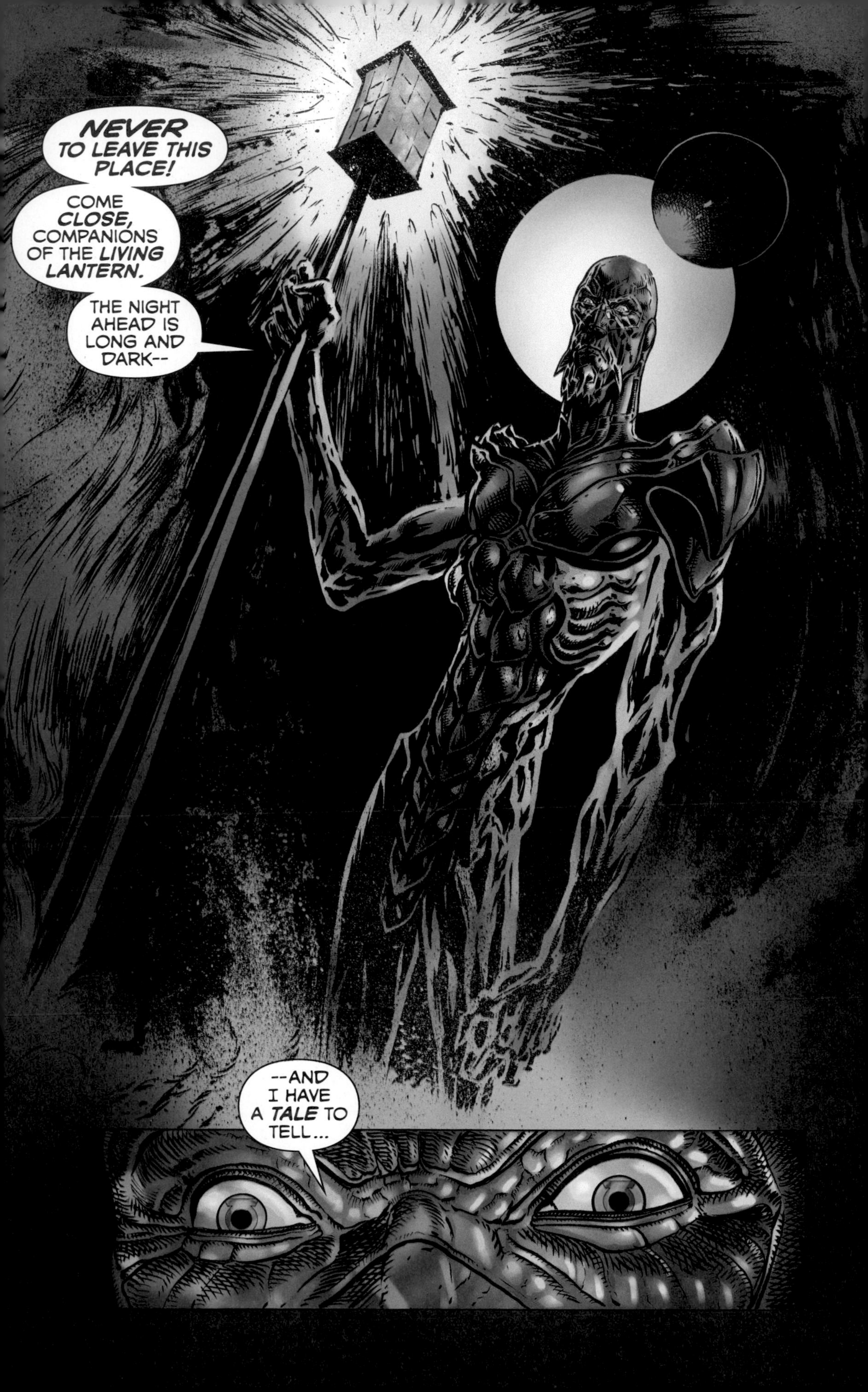
NEVER TO LEAVE THIS PLACE!
COME CLOSE, COMPANIONS OF THE LIVING LANTERN.
THE NIGHT AHEAD IS LONG AND DARK--
--AND I HAVE A TALE TO TELL...

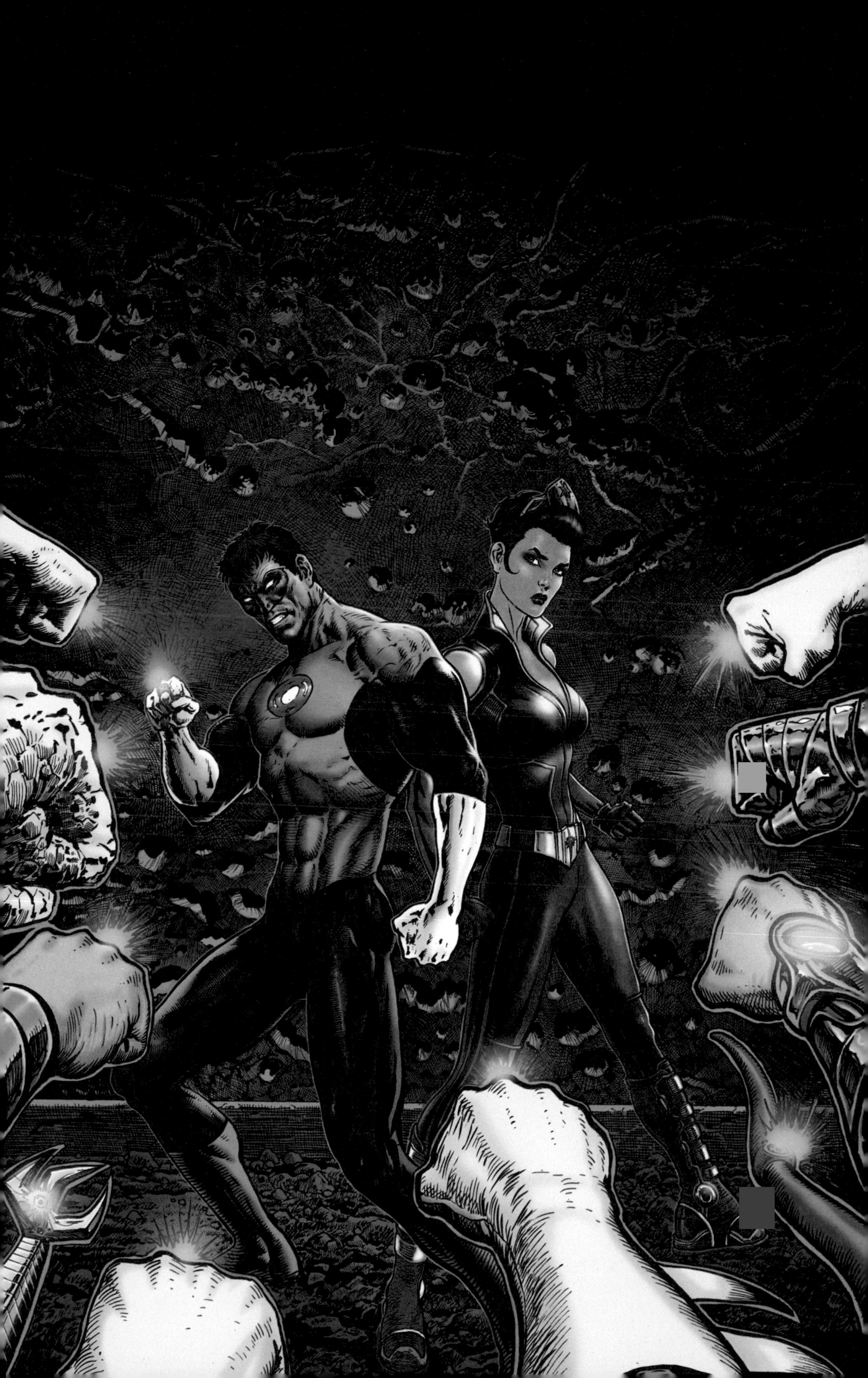

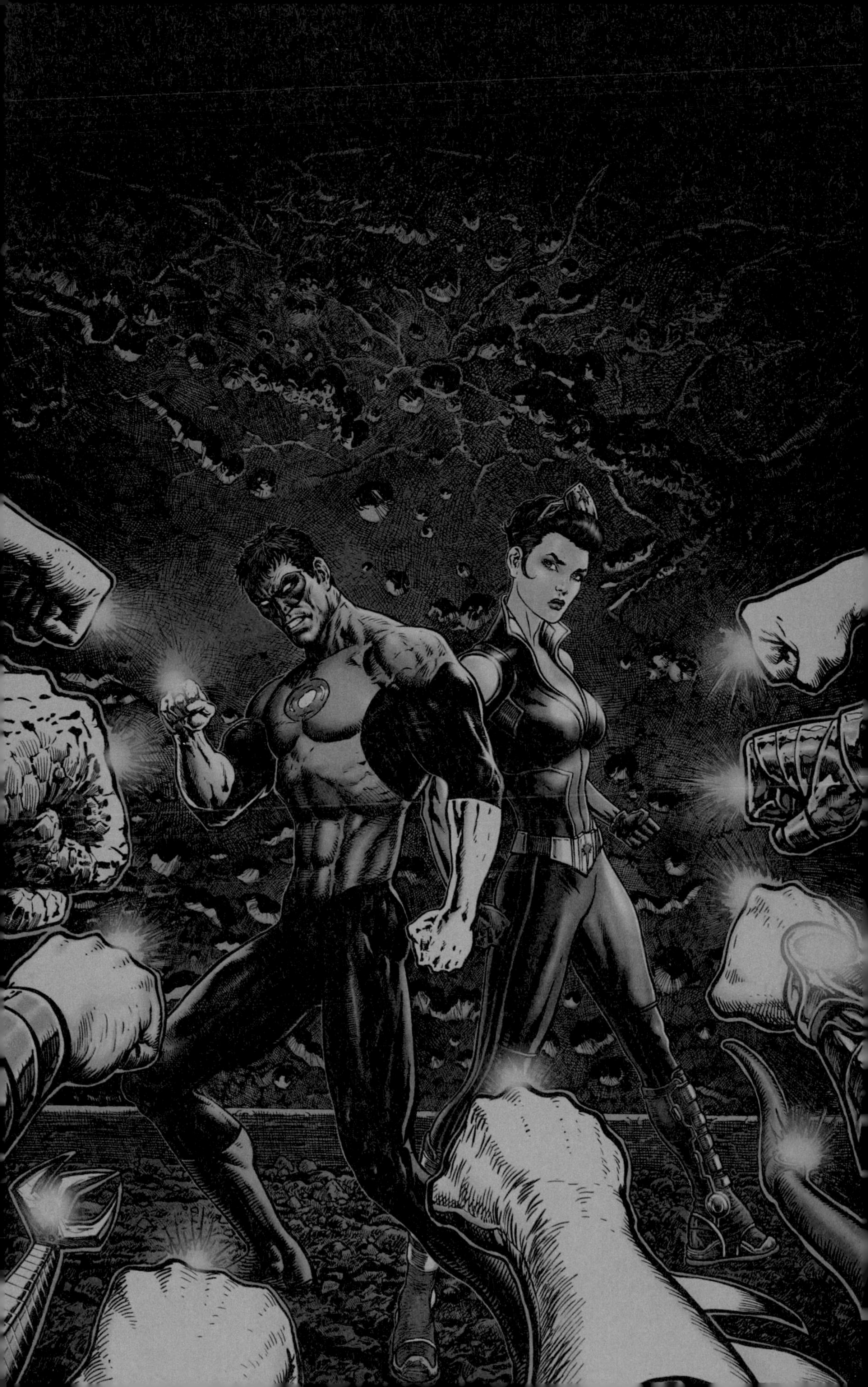

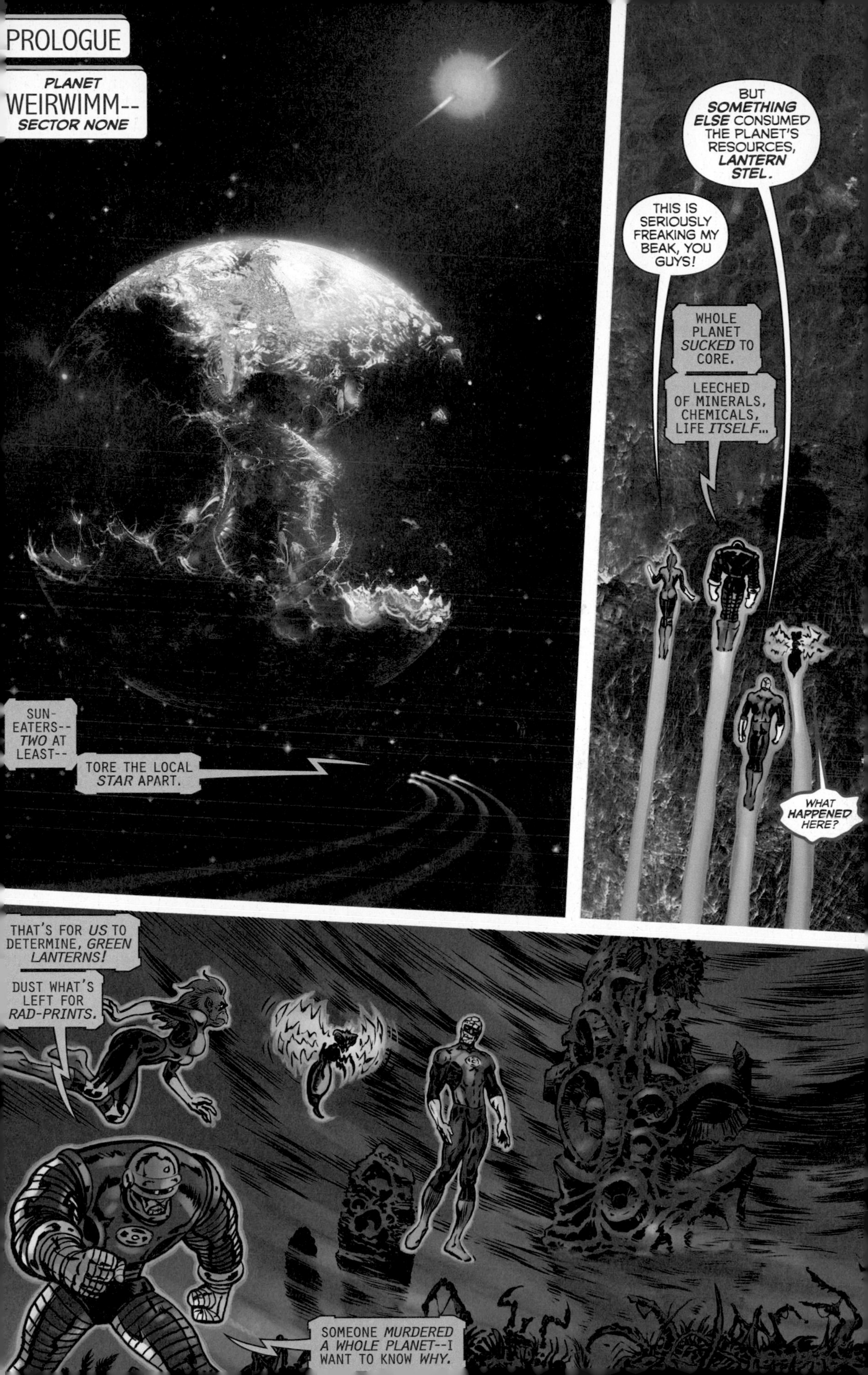
PROLOGUE
PLANET WEIRWIMM-- SECTOR NONE
SUN-EATERS--TWO AT LEAST--
TORE THE LOCAL STAR APART.
WHAT HAPPENED HERE?
WHOLE PLANET SUCKED TO CORE.
LEECHED OF MINERALS, CHEMICALS, LIFE ITSELF...
THIS IS SERIOUSLY FREAKING MY BEAK, YOU GUYS!
BUT SOMETHING ELSE CONSUMED THE PLANET'S RESOURCES, LANTERN STEL.
THAT'S FOR US TO DETERMINE, GREEN LANTERNS!
DUST WHAT'S LEFT FOR RAD-PRINTS.
SOMEONE MURDERED A WHOLE PLANET--I WANT TO KNOW WHY.

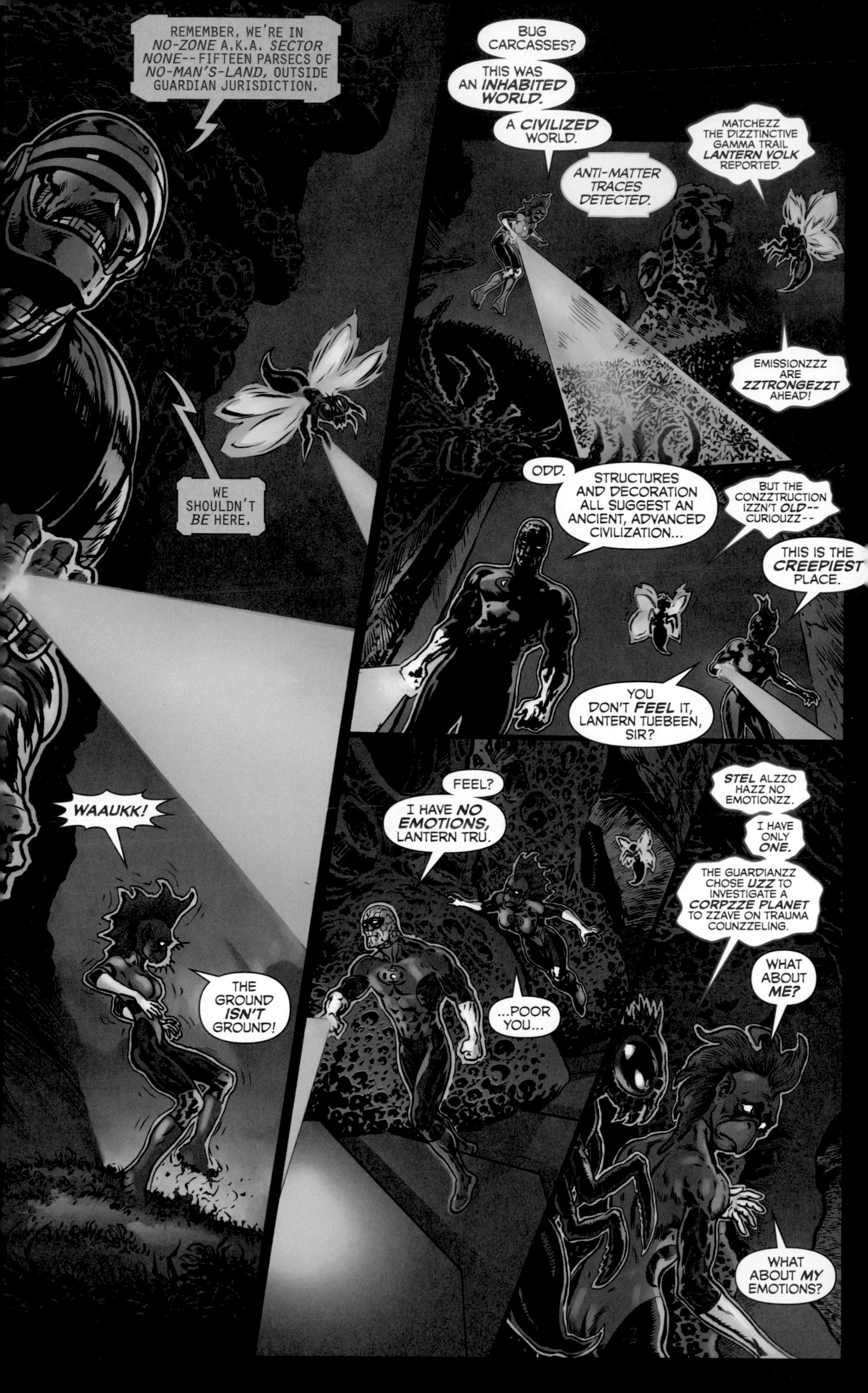

REMEMBER, WE'RE IN NO-ZONE A.K.A. SECTOR NONE--FIFTEEN PARSECS OF NO-MAN'S-LAND, OUTSIDE GUARDIAN JURISDICTION.
WE SHOULDN'T BE HERE.
BUG CARCASSES?
THIS WAS AN INHABITED WORLD.
A CIVILIZED WORLD.
ANTI-MATTER TRACES DETECTED.
MATCHEZZ THE DIZZTINCTIVE GAMMA TRAIL LANTERN VOLK REPORTED.
EMISSIONZZZ ARE ZZTRONGEZZT AHEAD!
ODD.
STRUCTURES AND DECORATION ALL SUGGEST AN ANCIENT, ADVANCED CIVILIZATION...
BUT THE CONZZTRUCTION IZZN'T OLD-- CURIOUZZ--
THIS IS THE CREEPIEST PLACE.
YOU DON'T FEEL IT, LANTERN TUEBEEN, SIR?
WAAUKK!
THE GROUND ISN'T GROUND!
FEEL?
I HAVE NO EMOTIONS, LANTERN TRU.
...POOR YOU...
STEL ALZZO HAZZ NO EMOTIONZZ.
I HAVE ONLY ONE.
THE GUARDIANZZ CHOSE UZZ TO INVESTIGATE A CORPZZE PLANET TO ZZAVE ON TRAUMA COUNZZELING.
WHAT ABOUT ME?
WHAT ABOUT MY EMOTIONS?

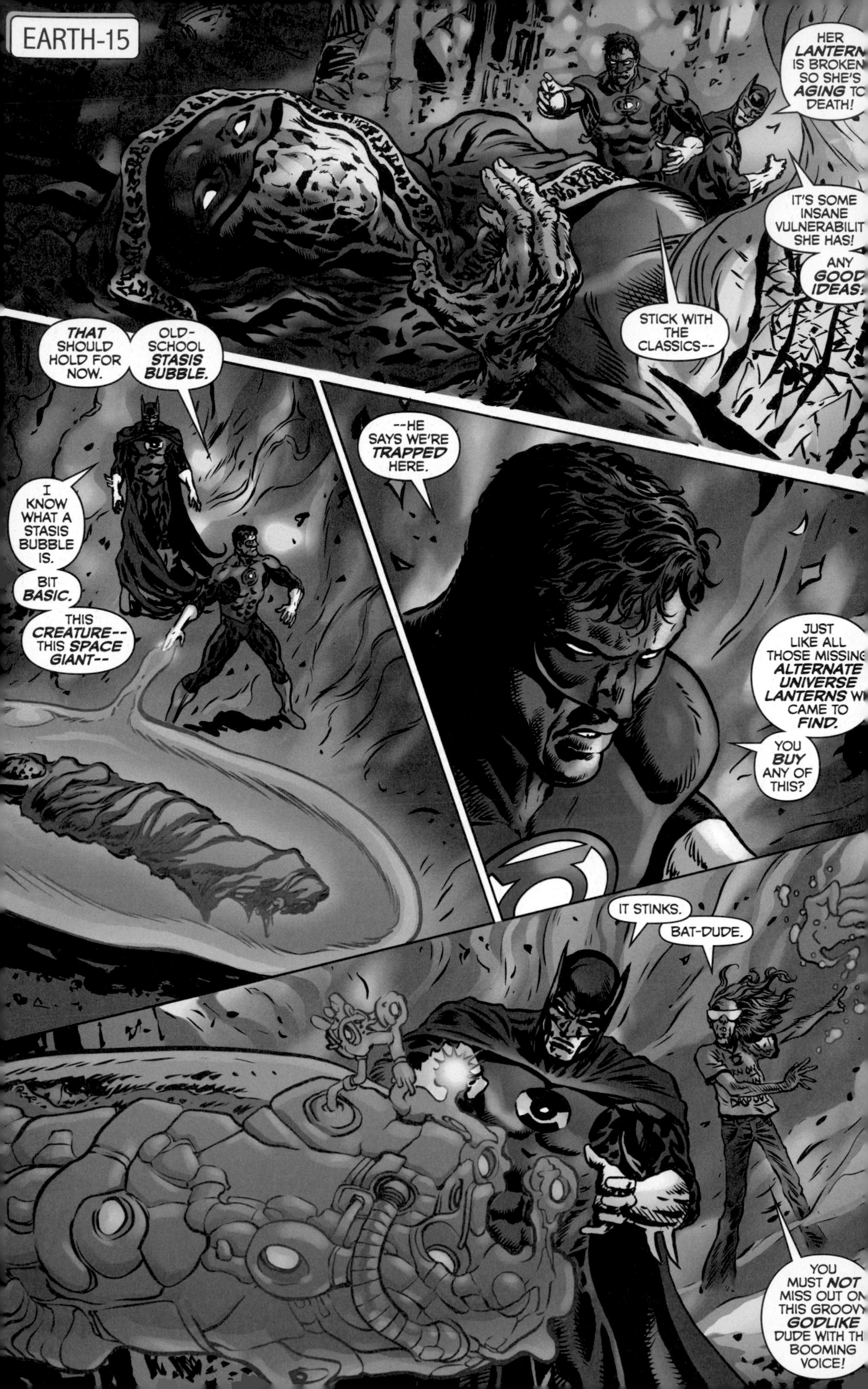
EARTH-15
HER LANTERN IS BROKEN SO SHE'S AGING TO DEATH!
IT'S SOME INSANE VULNERABILIT SHE HAS!
ANY GOOD IDEAS?
STICK WITH THE CLASSICS--
THAT SHOULD HOLD FOR NOW.
OLD-SCHOOL STASIS BUBBLE.
I KNOW WHAT A STASIS BUBBLE IS.
BIT BASIC.
THIS CREATURE-- THIS SPACE GIANT--
--HE SAYS WE'RE TRAPPED HERE.
JUST LIKE ALL THOSE MISSING ALTERNATE UNIVERSE LANTERNS W CAME TO FIND.
YOU BUY ANY OF THIS?
IT STINKS.
BAT-DUDE.
YOU MUST NOT MISS OUT ON THIS GROOVY GODLIKE DUDE WITH TH BOOMING VOICE!

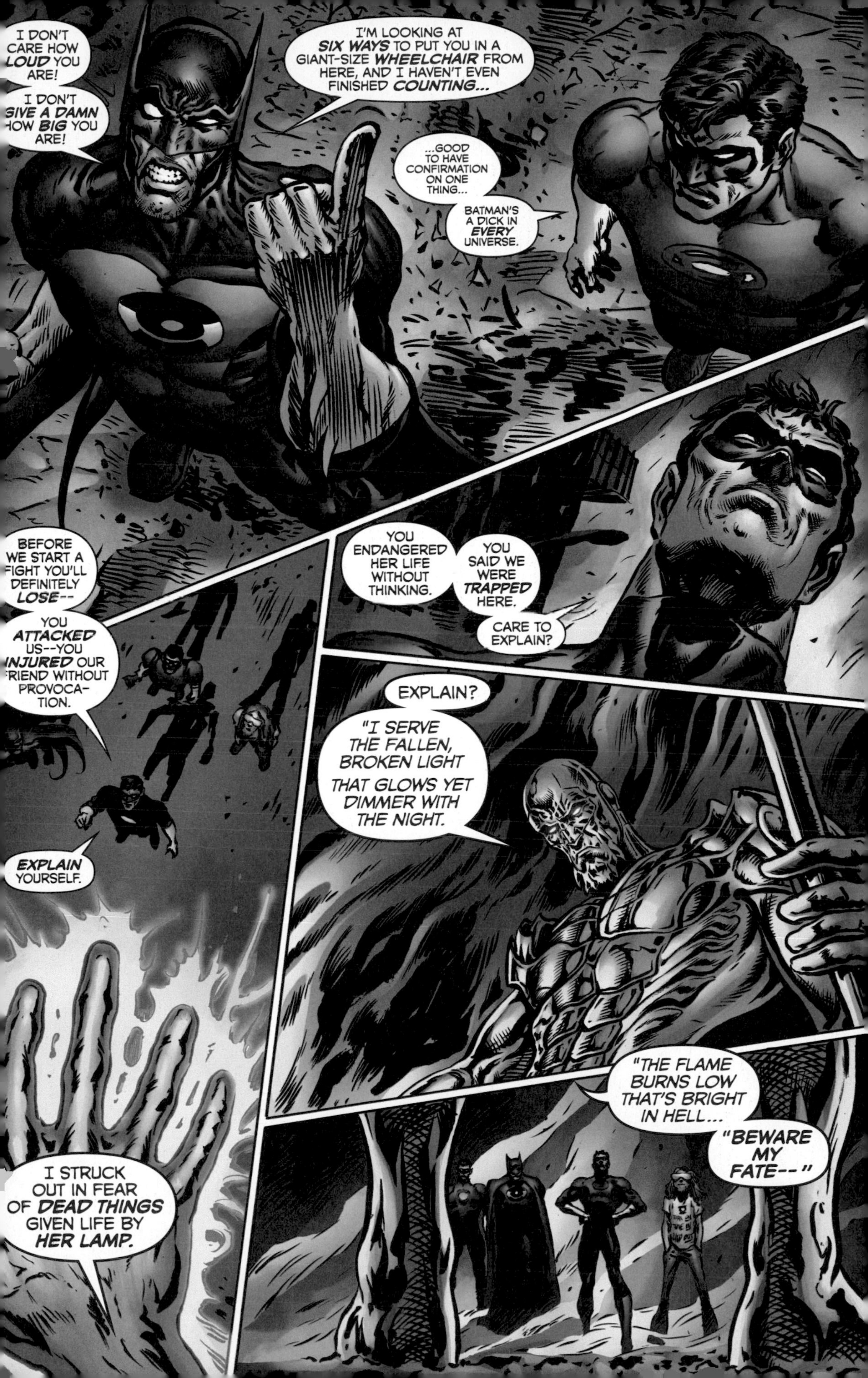
I DON'T CARE HOW LOUD YOU ARE!
I DON'T GIVE A DAMN HOW BIG YOU ARE!
I'M LOOKING AT SIX WAYS TO PUT YOU IN A GIANT-SIZE WHEELCHAIR FROM HERE, AND I HAVEN'T EVEN FINISHED COUNTING...
...GOOD TO HAVE CONFIRMATION ON ONE THING...
BATMAN'S A DICK IN EVERY UNIVERSE.
YOU ENDANGERED HER LIFE WITHOUT THINKING.
YOU SAID WE WERE TRAPPED HERE.
CARE TO EXPLAIN?
BEFORE WE START A FIGHT YOU'LL DEFINITELY LOSE--
YOU ATTACKED US--YOU INJURED OUR FRIEND WITHOUT PROVOCATION.
EXPLAIN YOURSELF.
EXPLAIN?
"I SERVE THE FALLEN, BROKEN LIGHT
THAT GLOWS YET DIMMER WITH THE NIGHT.
I STRUCK OUT IN FEAR OF DEAD THINGS GIVEN LIFE BY HER LAMP.
"THE FLAME BURNS LOW THAT'S BRIGHT IN HELL...
"BEWARE MY FATE--"

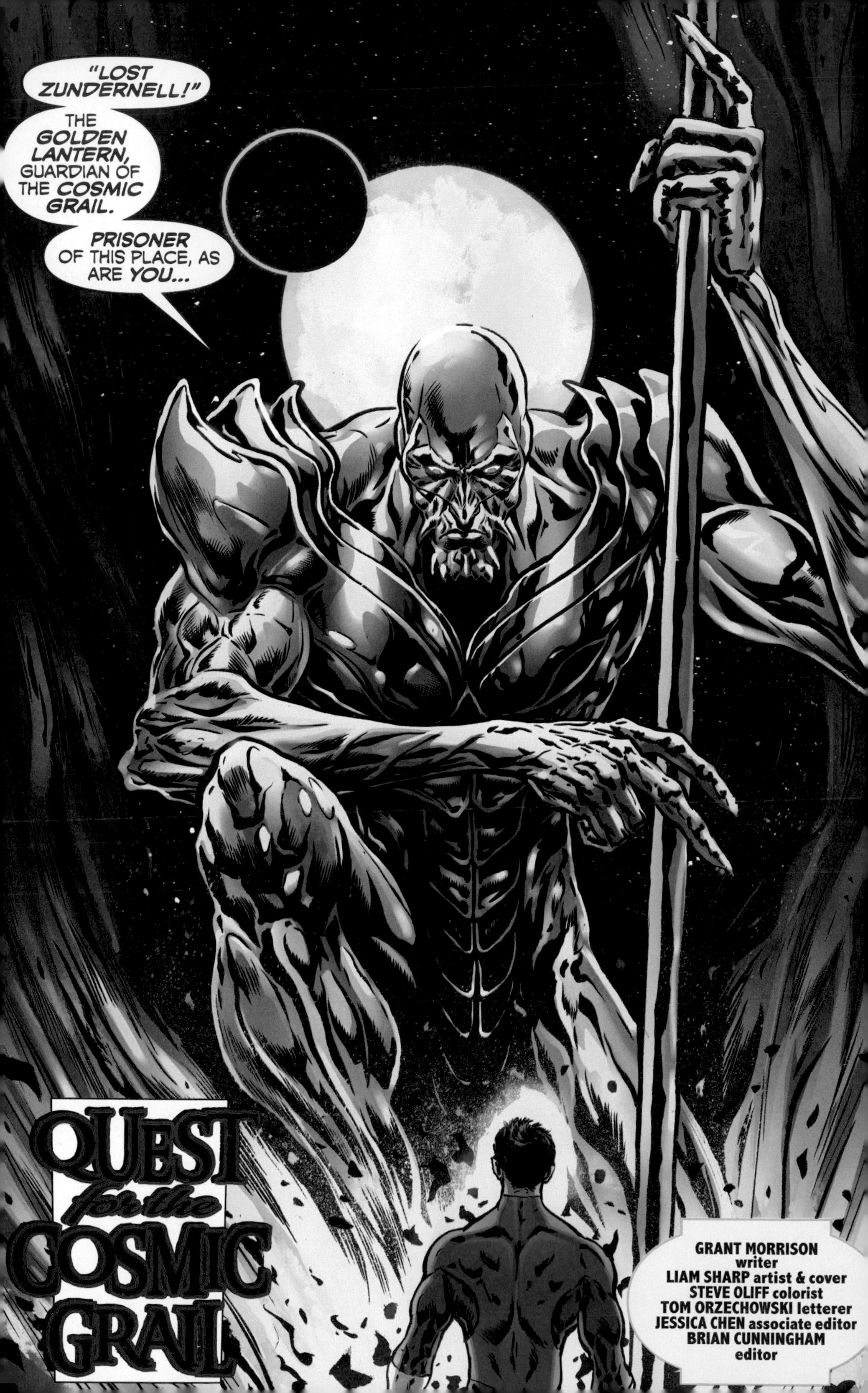
"LOST ZUNDERNELL!"
THE GOLDEN LANTERN, GUARDIAN OF THE COSMIC GRAIL.
PRISONER OF THIS PLACE, AS ARE YOU...
QUEST for the COSMIC GRAIL
GRANT MORRISON writer
LIAM SHARP artist & cover
STEVE OLIFF colorist
TOM ORZECHOWSKI letterer
JESSICA CHEN associate editor
BRIAN CUNNINGHAM editor

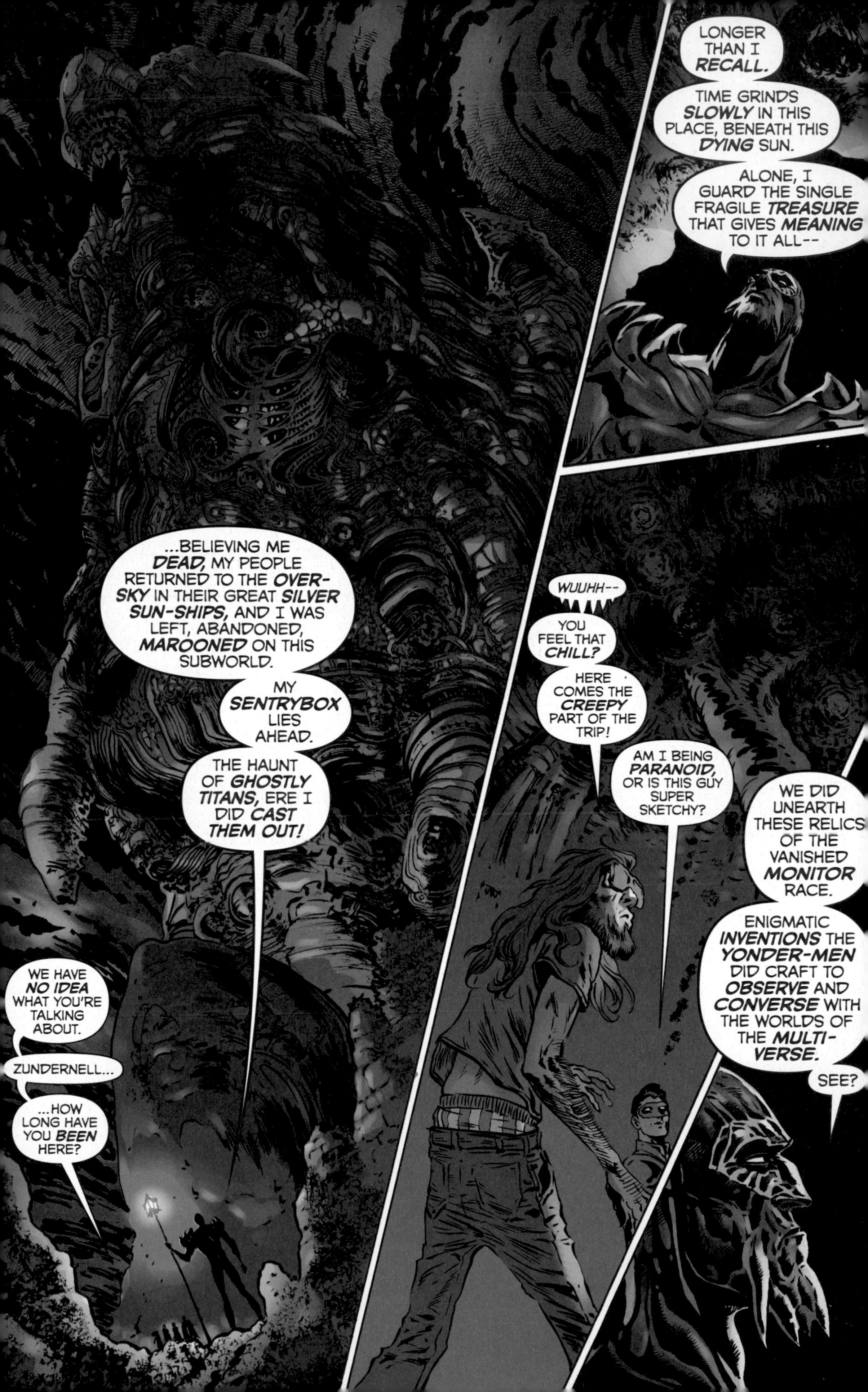
...BELIEVING ME DEAD, MY PEOPLE RETURNED TO THE OVER-SKY IN THEIR GREAT SILVER SUN-SHIPS, AND I WAS LEFT, ABANDONED, MAROONED ON THIS SUBWORLD.
MY SENTRYBOX LIES AHEAD.
THE HAUNT OF GHOSTLY TITANS, ERE I DID CAST THEM OUT!
WE HAVE NO IDEA WHAT YOU'RE TALKING ABOUT.
ZUNDERNELL...
...HOW LONG HAVE YOU BEEN HERE?
LONGER THAN I RECALL.
TIME GRINDS SLOWLY IN THIS PLACE, BENEATH THIS DYING SUN.
ALONE, I GUARD THE SINGLE FRAGILE TREASURE THAT GIVES MEANING TO IT ALL--
WUUHH--
YOU FEEL THAT CHILL?
HERE COMES THE CREEPY PART OF THE TRIP!
AM I BEING PARANOID, OR IS THIS GUY SUPER SKETCHY?
WE DID UNEARTH THESE RELICS OF THE VANISHED MONITOR RACE.
ENIGMATIC INVENTIONS THE YONDER-MEN DID CRAFT TO OBSERVE AND CONVERSE WITH THE WORLDS OF THE MULTI-VERSE.
SEE?

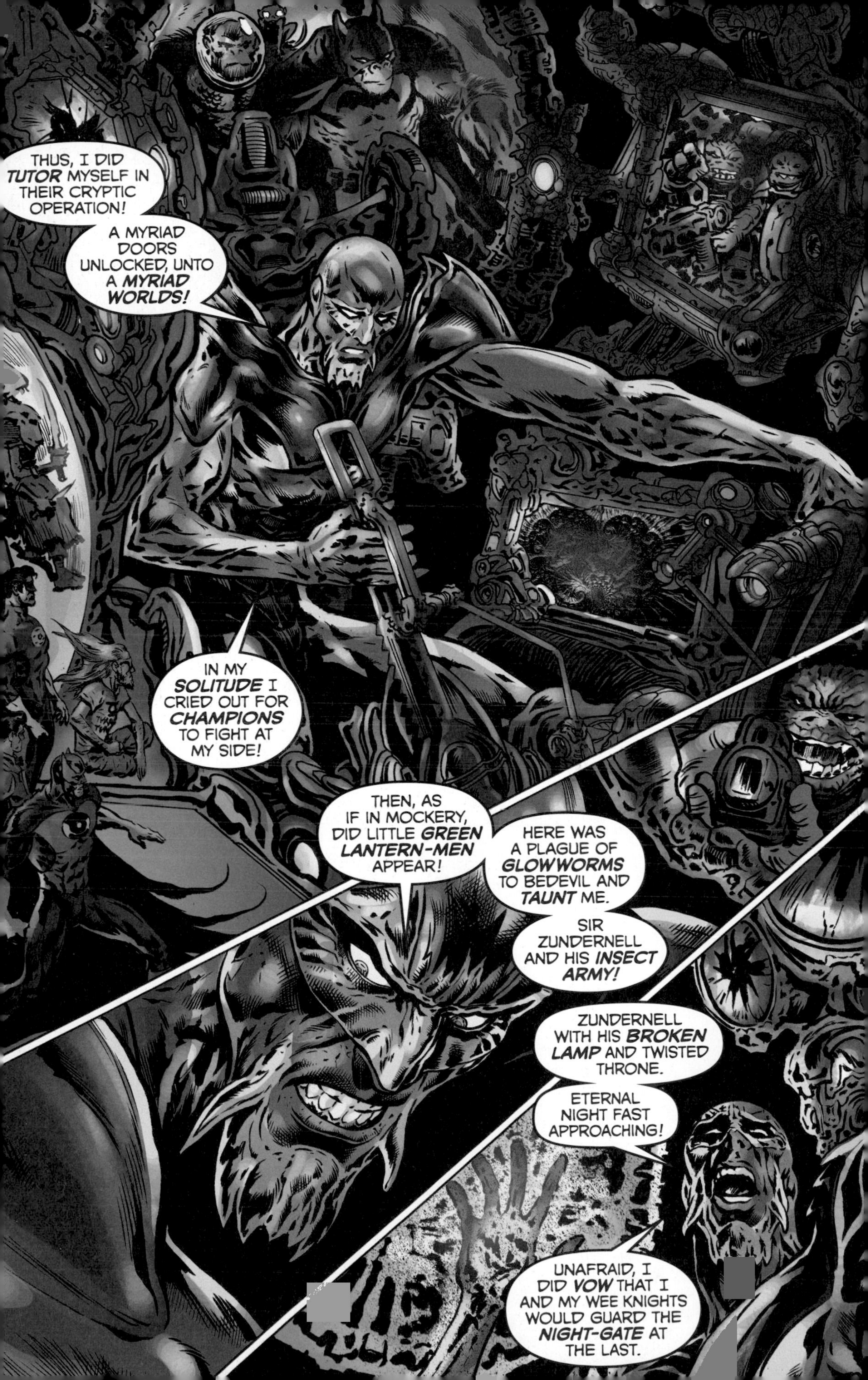
THUS, I DID TUTOR MYSELF IN THEIR CRYPTIC OPERATION!
A MYRIAD DOORS UNLOCKED, UNTO A MYRIAD WORLDS!
IN MY SOLITUDE I CRIED OUT FOR CHAMPIONS TO FIGHT AT MY SIDE!
THEN, AS IF IN MOCKERY, DID LITTLE GREEN LANTERN-MEN APPEAR!
HERE WAS A PLAGUE OF GLOWWORMS TO BEDEVIL AND TAUNT ME.
SIR ZUNDERNELL AND HIS INSECT ARMY!
ZUNDERNELL WITH HIS BROKEN LAMP AND TWISTED THRONE.
ETERNAL NIGHT FAST APPROACHING!
UNAFRAID, I DID VOW THAT I AND MY WEE KNIGHTS WOULD GUARD THE NIGHT-GATE AT THE LAST.

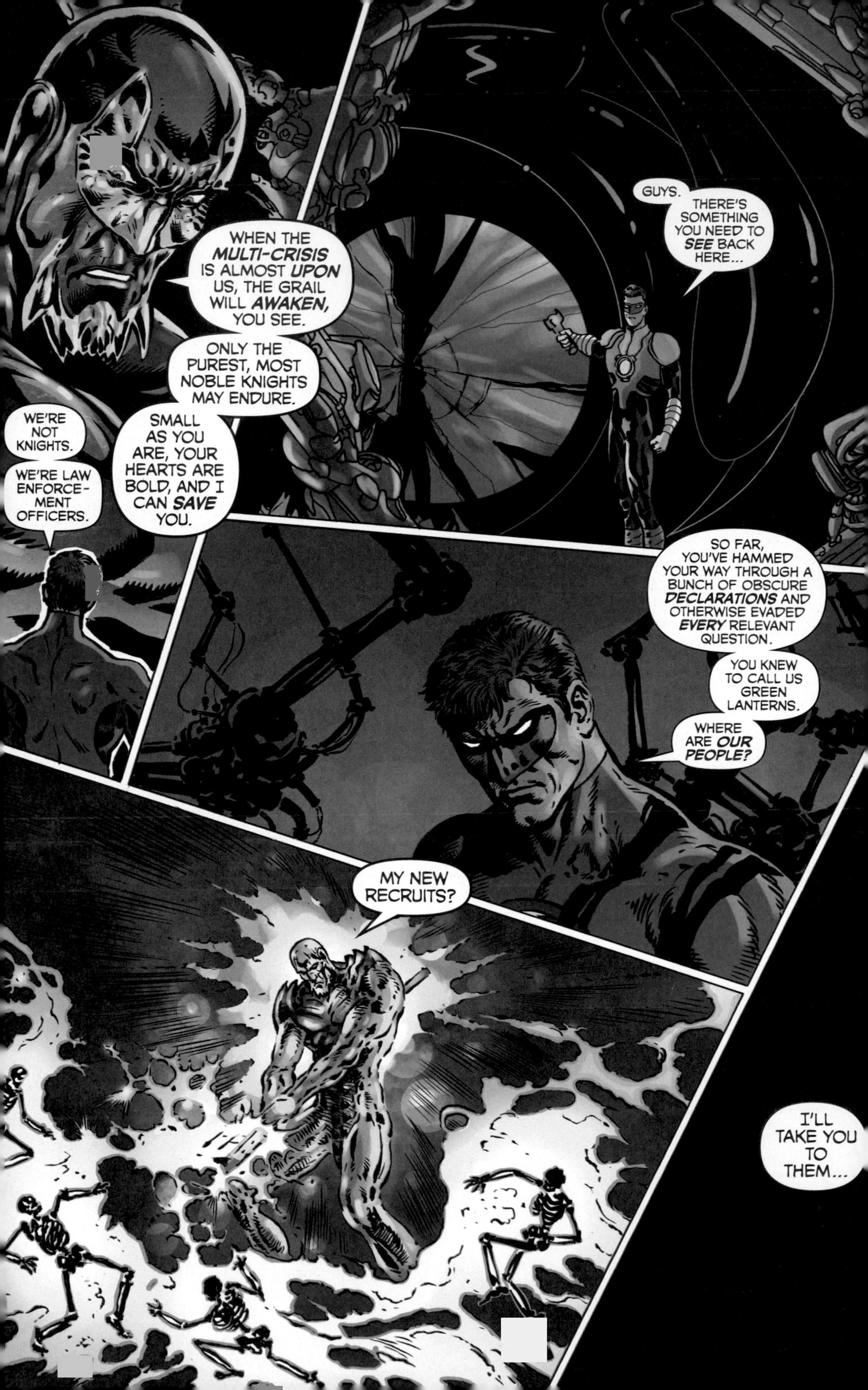
WHEN THE MULTI-CRISIS IS ALMOST UPON US, THE GRAIL WILL AWAKEN, YOU SEE.
ONLY THE PUREST, MOST NOBLE KNIGHTS MAY ENDURE.
WE'RE NOT KNIGHTS.
WE'RE LAW ENFORCE-MENT OFFICERS.
SMALL AS YOU ARE, YOUR HEARTS ARE BOLD, AND I CAN SAVE YOU.
GUYS.
THERE'S SOMETHING YOU NEED TO SEE BACK HERE...
SO FAR, YOU'VE HAMMED YOUR WAY THROUGH A BUNCH OF OBSCURE DECLARATIONS AND OTHERWISE EVADED EVERY RELEVANT QUESTION.
YOU KNEW TO CALL US GREEN LANTERNS.
WHERE ARE OUR PEOPLE?
MY NEW RECRUITS?
I'LL TAKE YOU TO THEM...

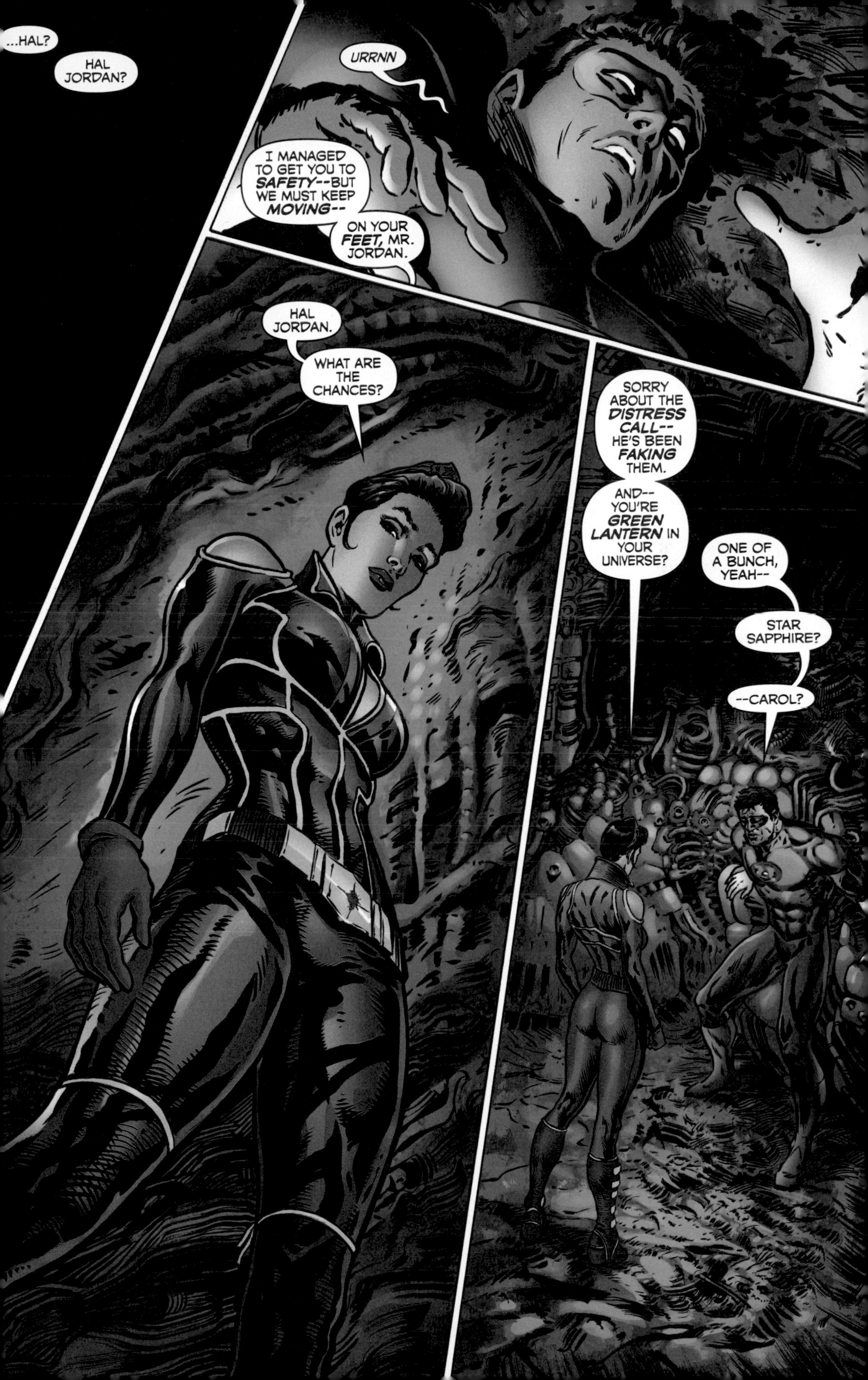
...HAL?
HAL JORDAN?
URRNN
I MANAGED TO GET YOU TO SAFETY--BUT WE MUST KEEP MOVING--
ON YOUR FEET, MR. JORDAN.
HAL JORDAN.
WHAT ARE THE CHANCES?
SORRY ABOUT THE DISTRESS CALL-- HE'S BEEN FAKING THEM.
AND-- YOU'RE GREEN LANTERN IN YOUR UNIVERSE?
ONE OF A BUNCH, YEAH--
STAR SAPPHIRE?
--CAROL?

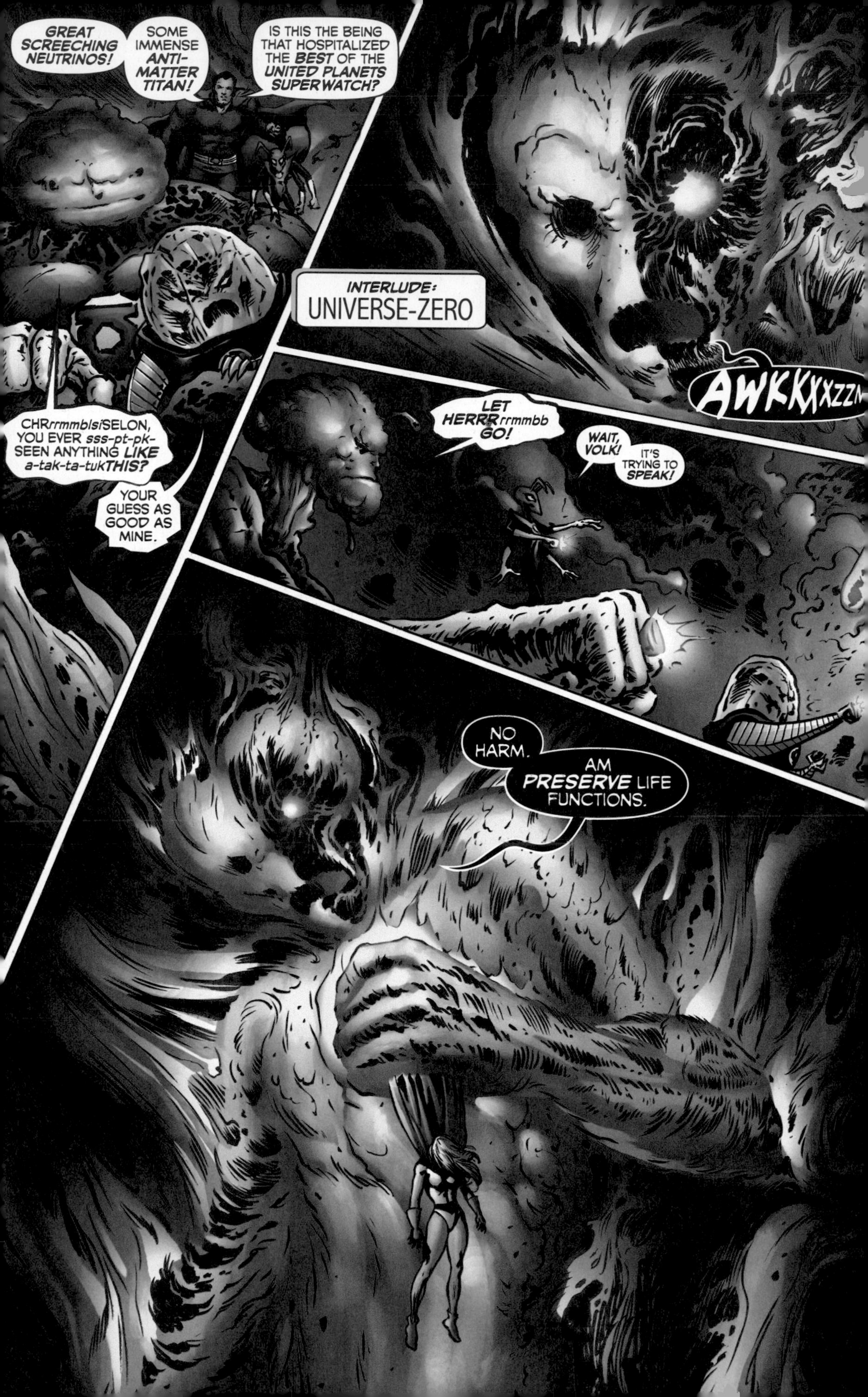
GREAT SCREECHING NEUTRINOS!
SOME IMMENSE ANTI-MATTER TITAN!
IS THIS THE BEING THAT HOSPITALIZED THE BEST OF THE UNITED PLANETS SUPERWATCH?
CHRrrmmblsiSELON, YOU EVER sss-pt-pk-SEEN ANYTHING LIKE a-tak-ta-tukTHIS?
YOUR GUESS AS GOOD AS MINE.
INTERLUDE:
UNIVERSE-ZERO
AWKKXXZZN
LET HERRRrrmmbb GO!
WAIT, VOLK!
IT'S TRYING TO SPEAK!
NO HARM.
AM PRESERVE LIFE FUNCTIONS.

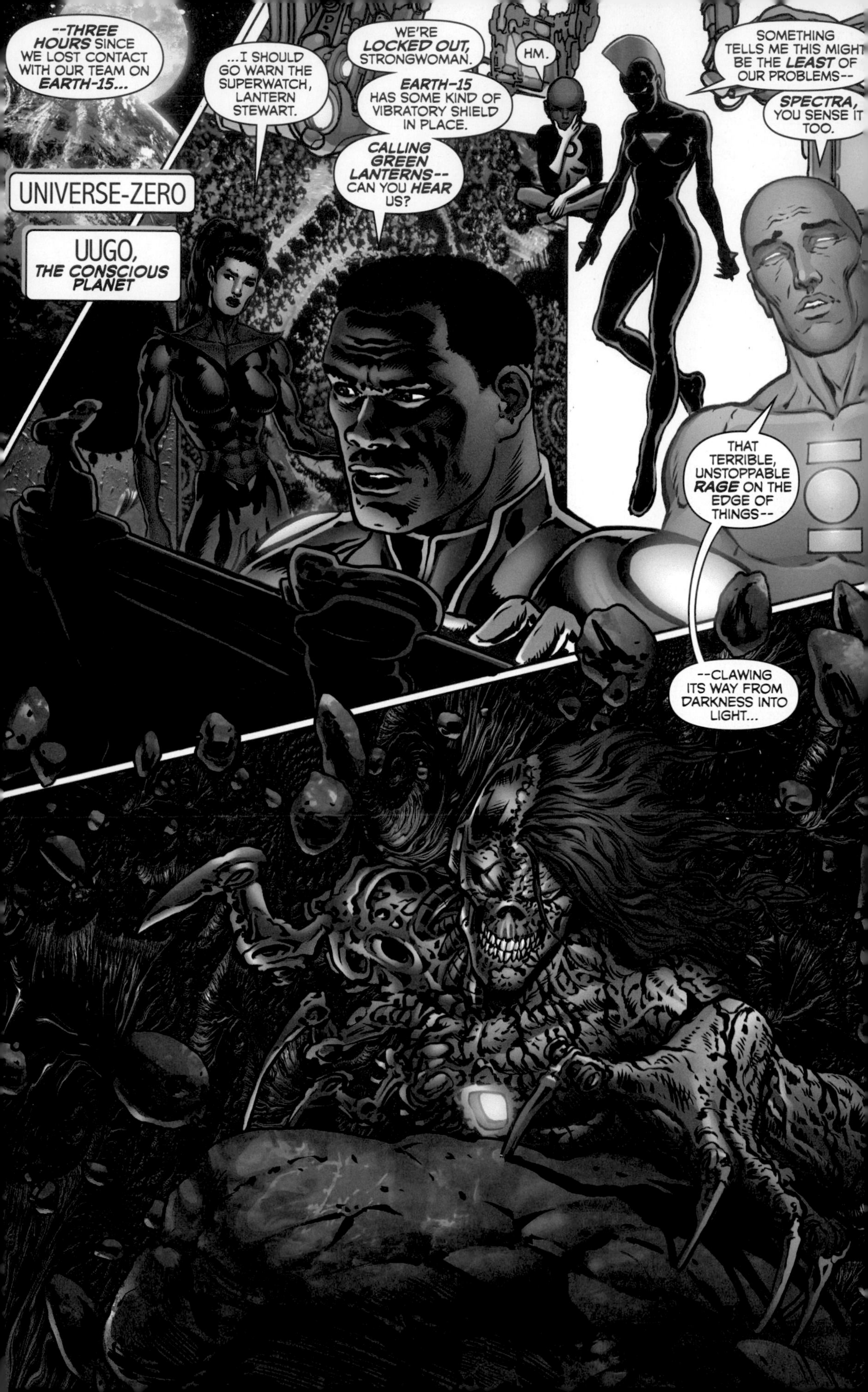
--THREE HOURS SINCE WE LOST CONTACT WITH OUR TEAM ON EARTH-15...
UNIVERSE-ZERO
UUGO, THE CONSCIOUS PLANET
...I SHOULD GO WARN THE SUPERWATCH, LANTERN STEWART.
WE'RE LOCKED OUT, STRONGWOMAN.
EARTH-15 HAS SOME KIND OF VIBRATORY SHIELD IN PLACE.
CALLING GREEN LANTERNS-- CAN YOU HEAR US?
HM.
SOMETHING TELLS ME THIS MIGHT BE THE LEAST OF OUR PROBLEMS--
SPECTRA, YOU SENSE IT TOO.
THAT TERRIBLE, UNSTOPPABLE RAGE ON THE EDGE OF THINGS--
--CLAWING ITS WAY FROM DARKNESS INTO LIGHT...

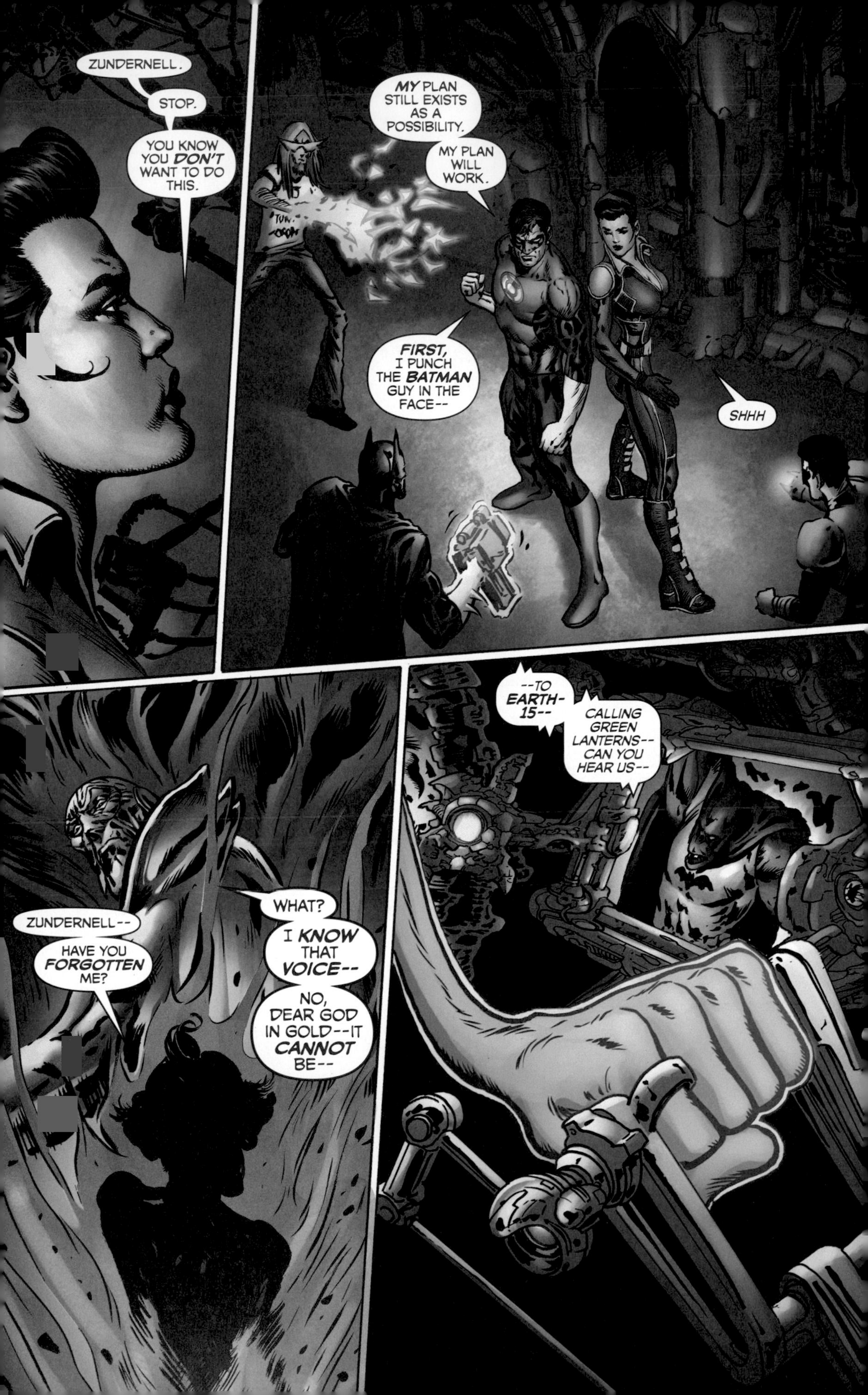
ZUNDERNELL.
STOP.
YOU KNOW YOU DON'T WANT TO DO THIS.
MY PLAN STILL EXISTS AS A POSSIBILITY.
MY PLAN WILL WORK.
FIRST, I PUNCH THE BATMAN GUY IN THE FACE--
SHHH
ZUNDERNELL--
HAVE YOU FORGOTTEN ME?
WHAT?
I KNOW THAT VOICE--
NO, DEAR GOD IN GOLD--IT CANNOT BE--
--TO EARTH-15--
CALLING GREEN LANTERNS--CAN YOU HEAR US--

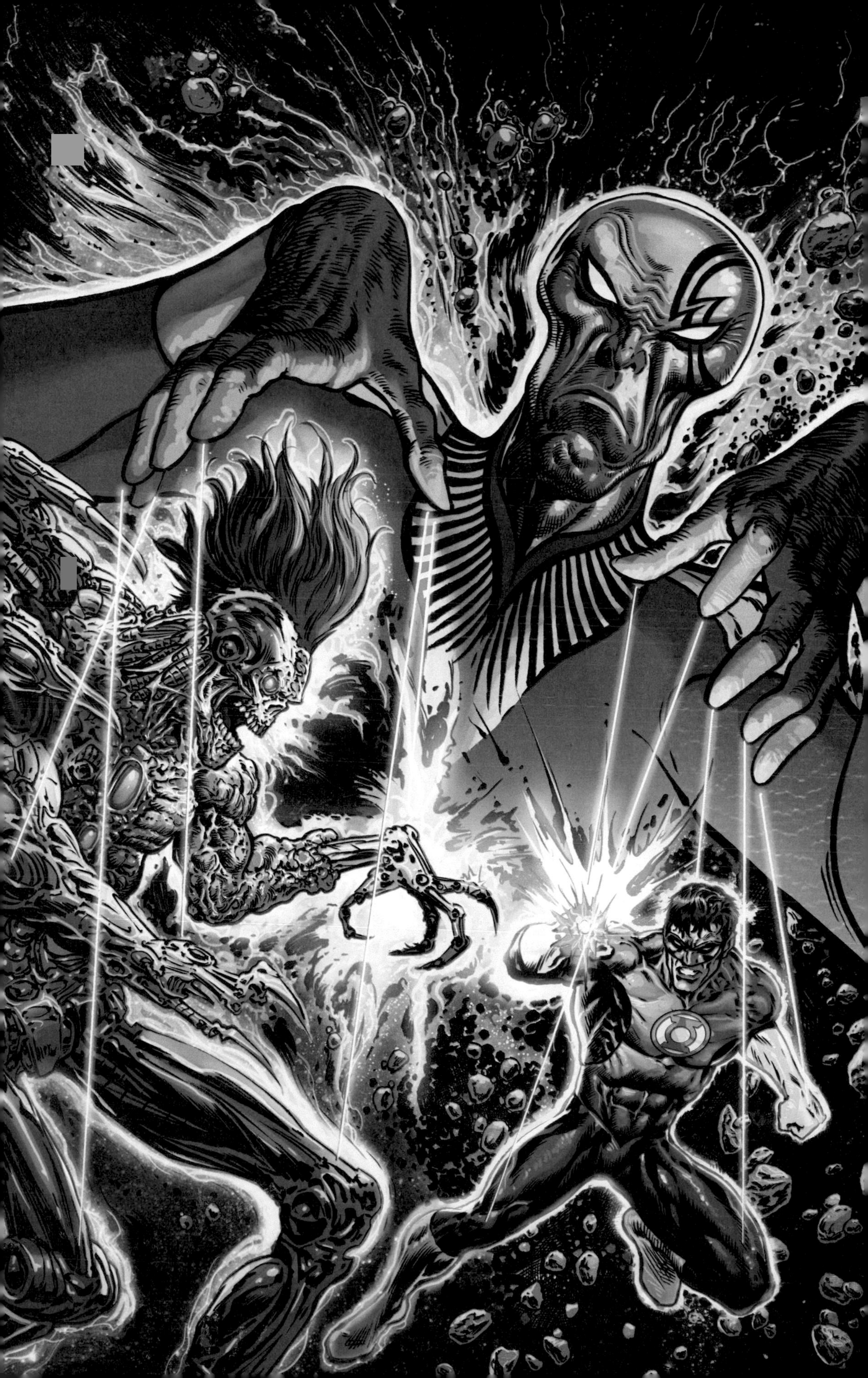

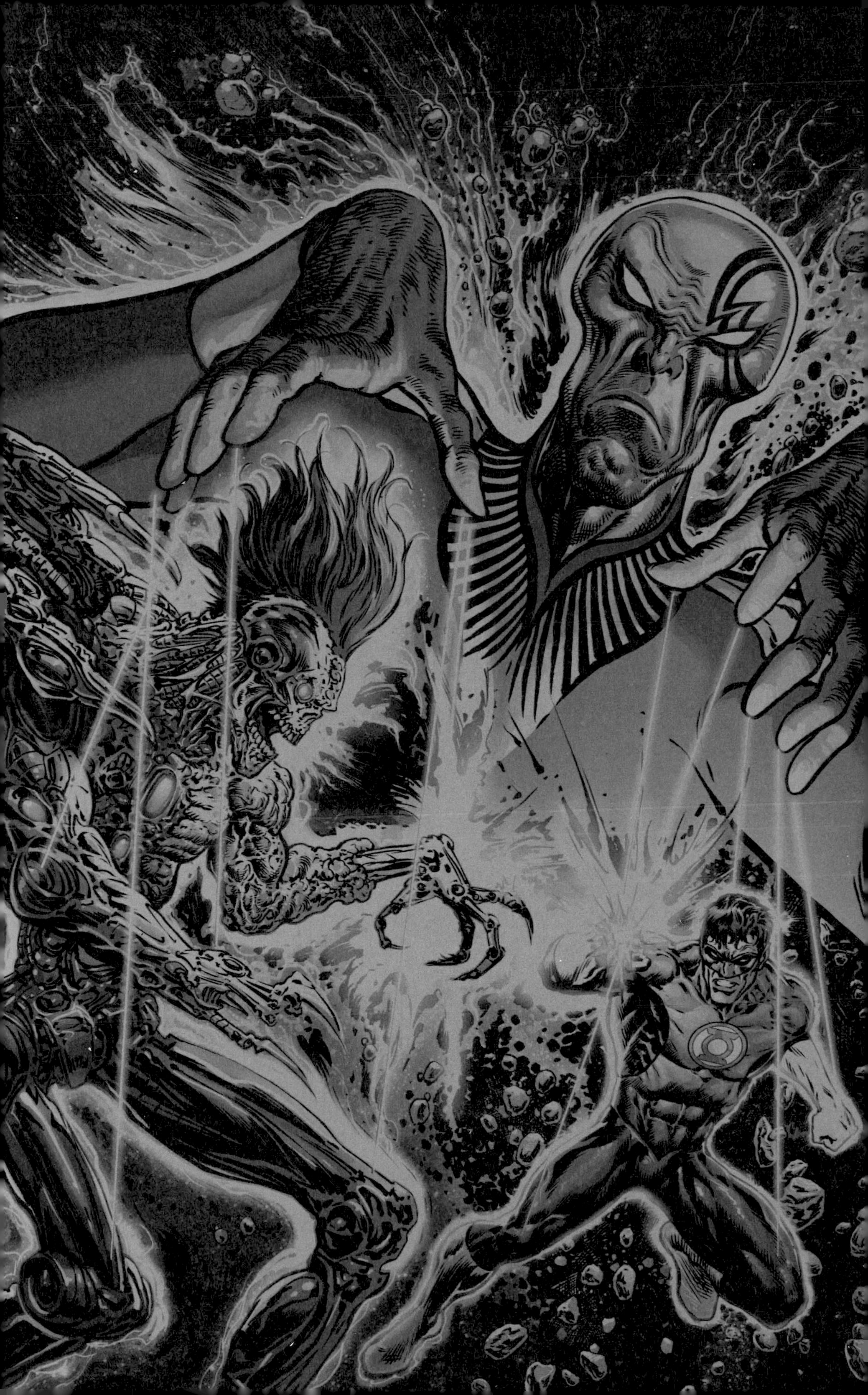

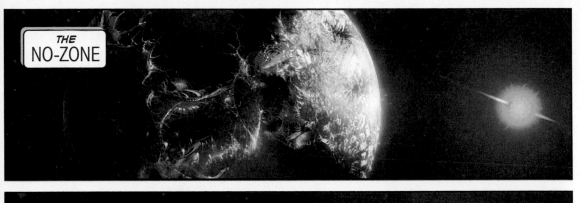

THE NO-ZONE

PLANET WEIRWIMM

HAL JORDAN HAS **FIFTEEN MINUTES** TO LIVE...

...FACE IT--

--YOUR EVIL **ANTI-MATTER DOPPELGÄNGER** WAS AN ACCIDENT **WAITING** TO HAPPEN.

IS THAT SO? HOW ABOUT YOU DO **YOUR** JOB.

AND I'LL DO **MINE.**

UNDER-STOOD!

NOBODY TELLS **YOU** WHAT TO DO, LANTERN JORDAN.

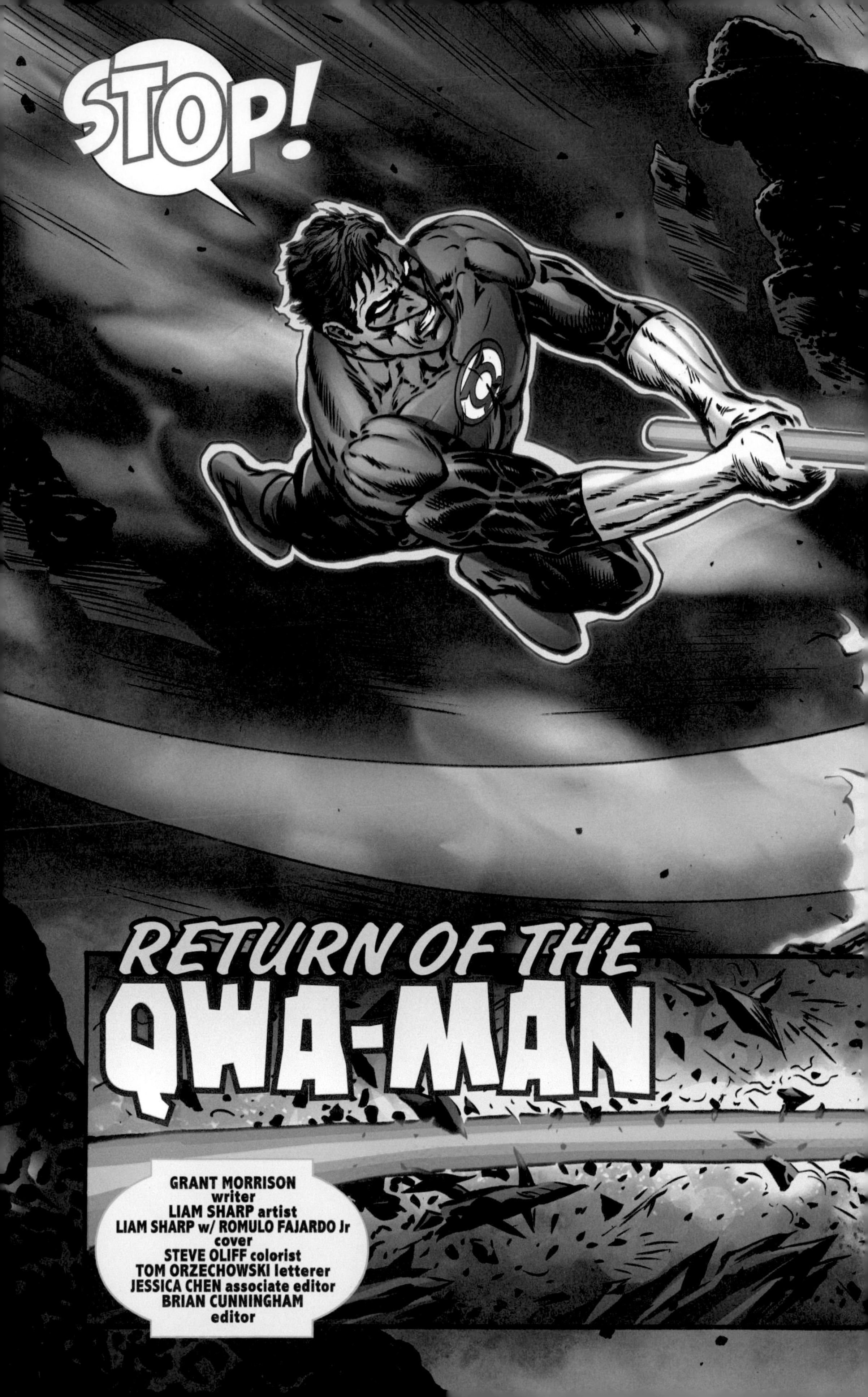

STOP!
RETURN OF THE
QWA-MAN
GRANT MORRISON
writer
LIAM SHARP artist
LIAM SHARP w/ ROMULO FAJARDO Jr
cover
STEVE OLIFF colorist
TOM ORZECHOWSKI letterer
JESSICA CHEN associate editor
BRIAN CUNNINGHAM
editor

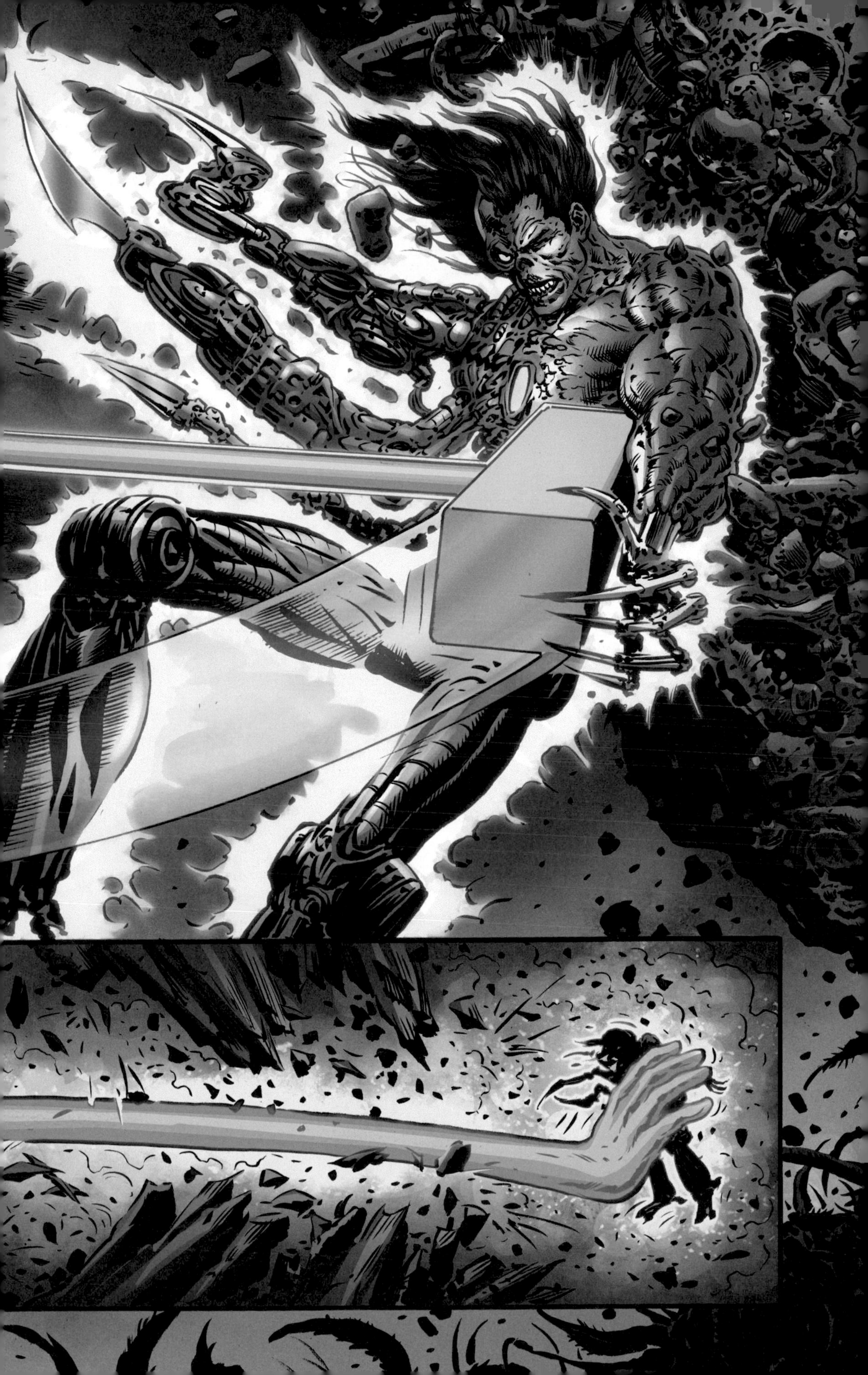

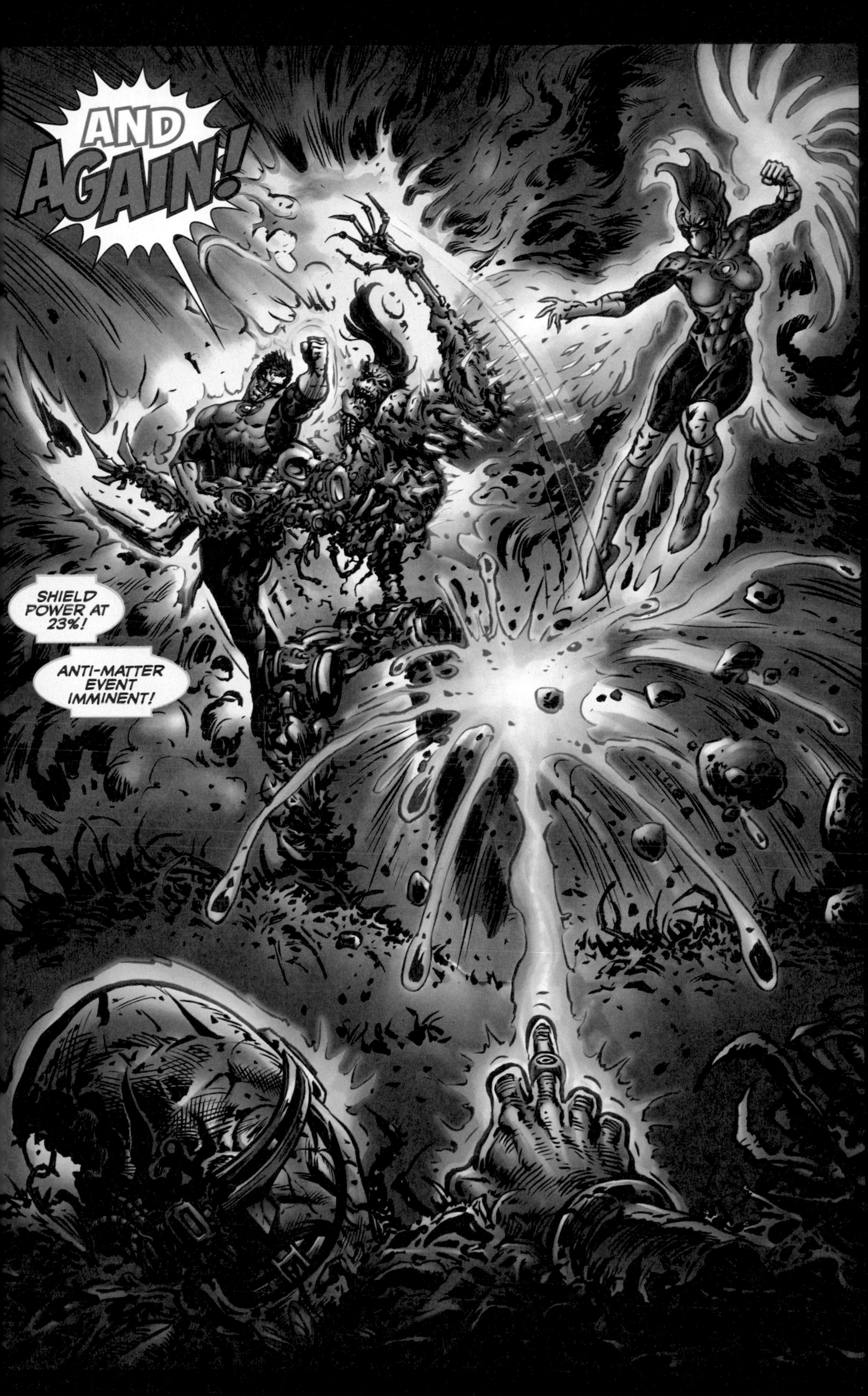
AND AGAIN!
SHIELD POWER AT 23%!
ANTI-MATTER EVENT IMMINENT!

WE COORDINATED THE DEATH OF *WORLDS* TO ORCHESTRATE *THIS MOMENT*--WE ORGANIZED THE FALL OF *CHAMPIONS* AND UNLEASHED AN ANTI-MATTER *DEMON.*

IT WILL CHANGE THE STARS *FOREVER.*

WE *CONTROL* YOU, AS YOU CONTROL YOUR *RING.*

YOU ARE THE *TRIGGER* WE PULL, YES?

MY RING-- IS OUT OF JUICE.

TOO BAD--

WE SHAPED *EVENTS* AROUND YOU ON A SCALE YOU ARE TOO *SMALL* AND SHORT-LIVED TO GRASP--ALL TO MAKE *THIS MOMENT.*

THE PLAN TOOK *SECONDS* TO CONCEIVE.

EXCEPT FOR THAT SPECIAL *FINAL IOTA* KEPT ALWAYS IN RESERVE.

THE *ANTI-MATTER WAR* WILL DESTROY *EVERYTHING.* YOU'LL *DIE* HERE AND NOW, UNLESS...

T MINUS THREE SECONDS.

WE ARE *MU'S WILL* IN ACTION, MU'S WILL BE *DONE*--PEACE AND UNIVERSAL HARMONY CAN BE *OURS* AT LAST.

ALL YOU NEED TO DO IS WISH THE WISH OF *CONTROLLER MU*--

ONCE A *BLACKSTAR, ALWAYS* A *BLACKSTAR...*

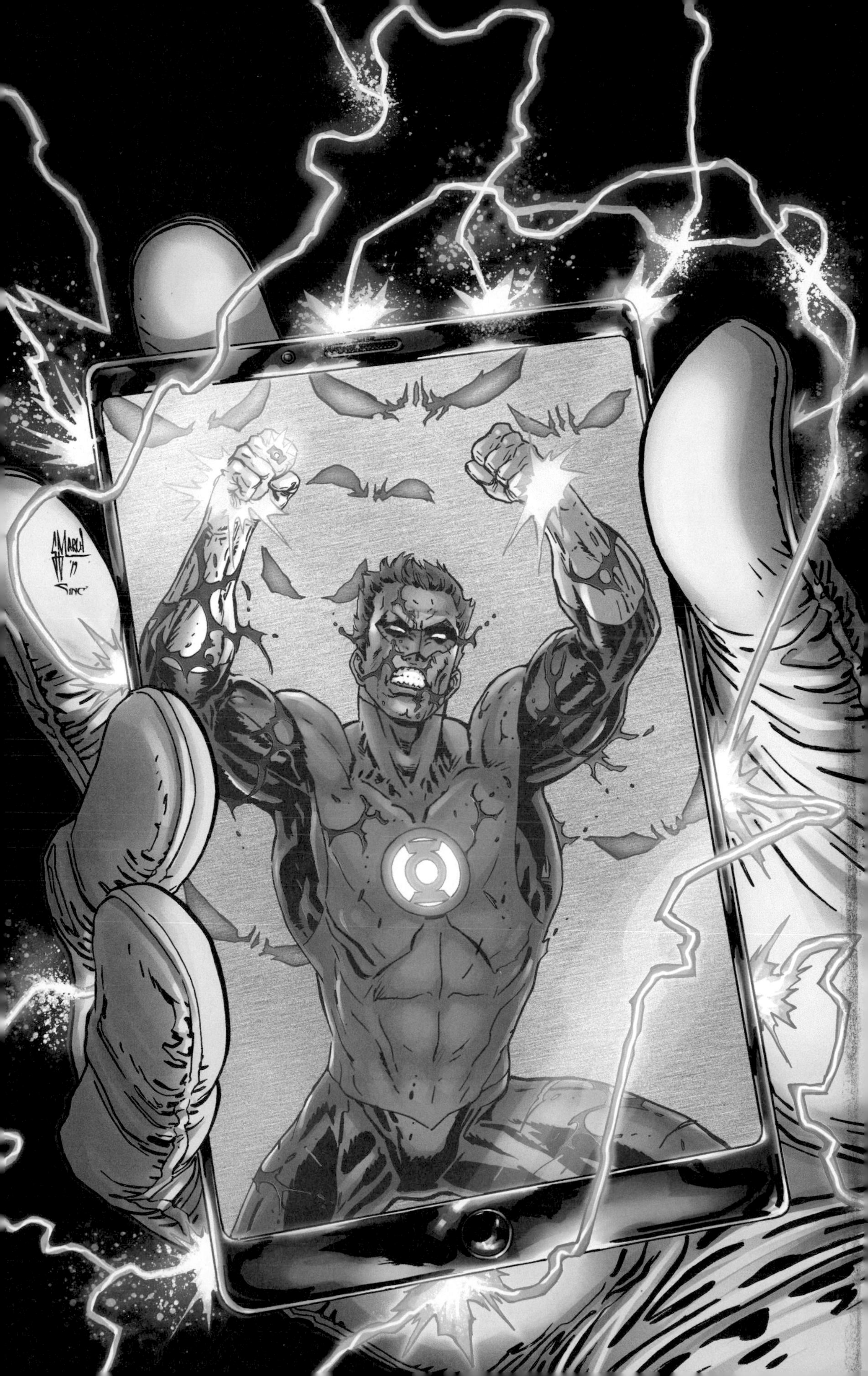

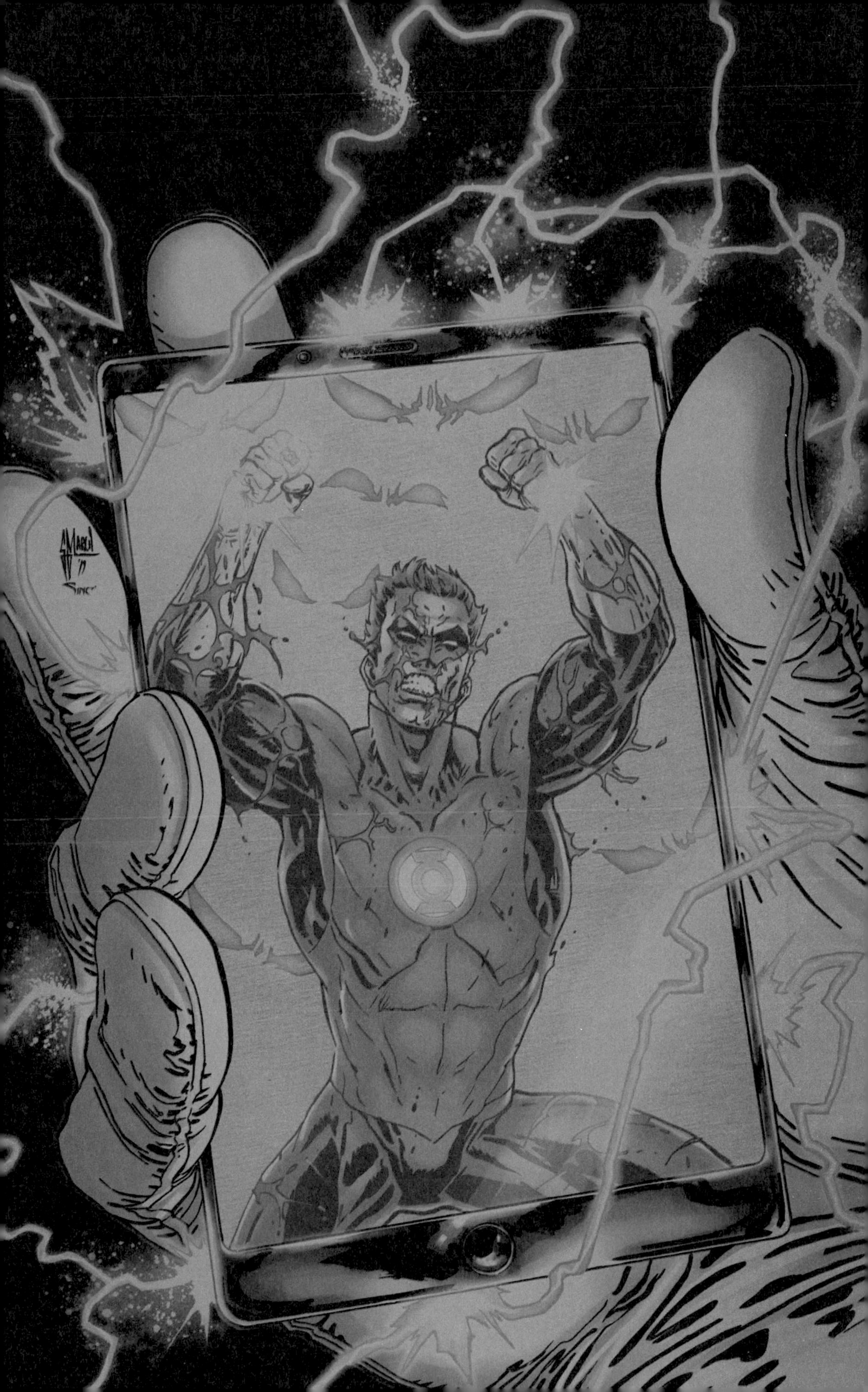

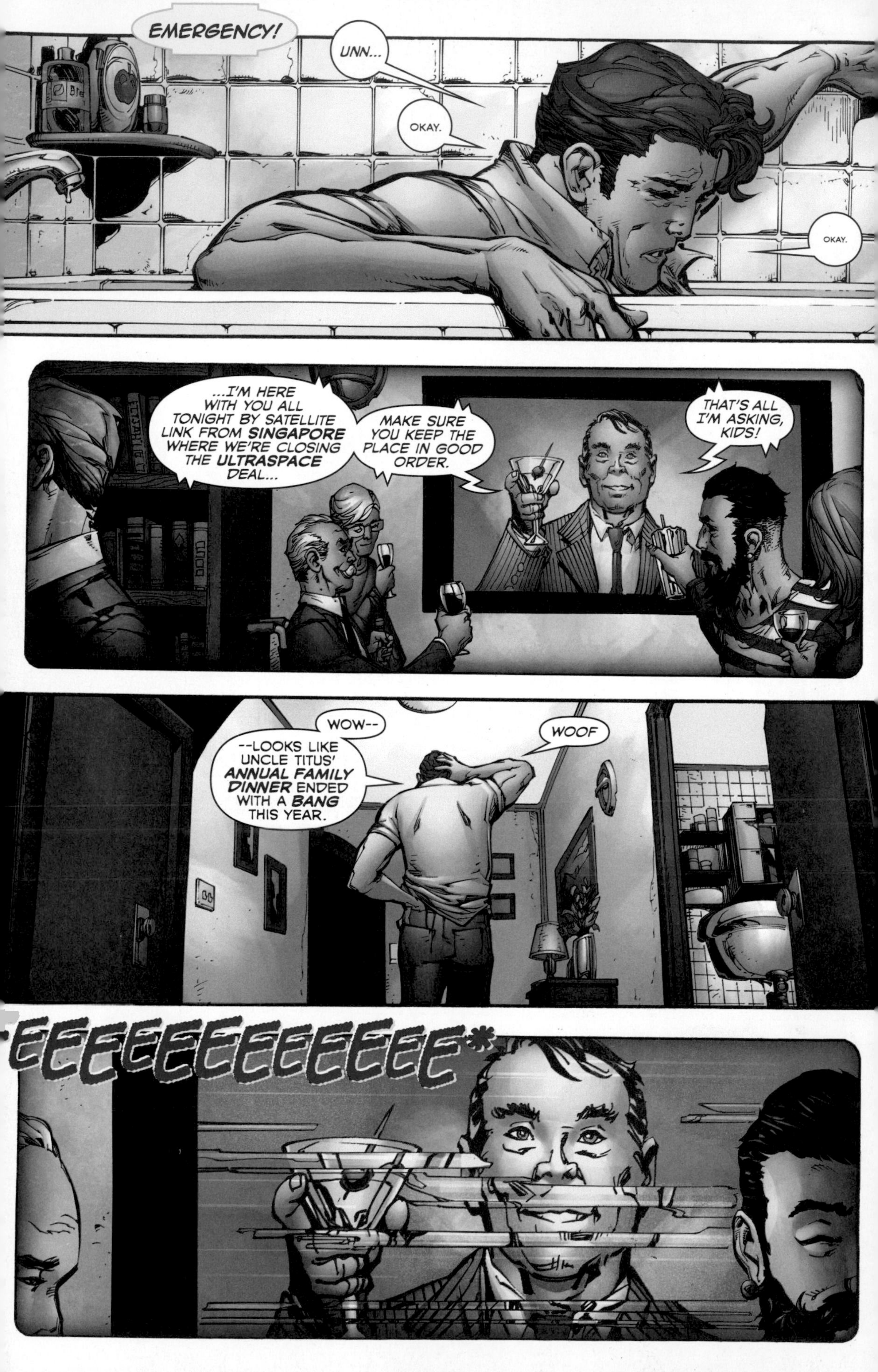
EMERGENCY!
UNN...
OKAY.
OKAY.
...I'M HERE WITH YOU ALL TONIGHT BY SATELLITE LINK FROM SINGAPORE WHERE WE'RE CLOSING THE ULTRASPACE DEAL...
MAKE SURE YOU KEEP THE PLACE IN GOOD ORDER.
THAT'S ALL I'M ASKING, KIDS!
WOW--
--LOOKS LIKE UNCLE TITUS' ANNUAL FAMILY DINNER ENDED WITH A BANG THIS YEAR.
WOOF
EEEEEEEEEEEEEE*

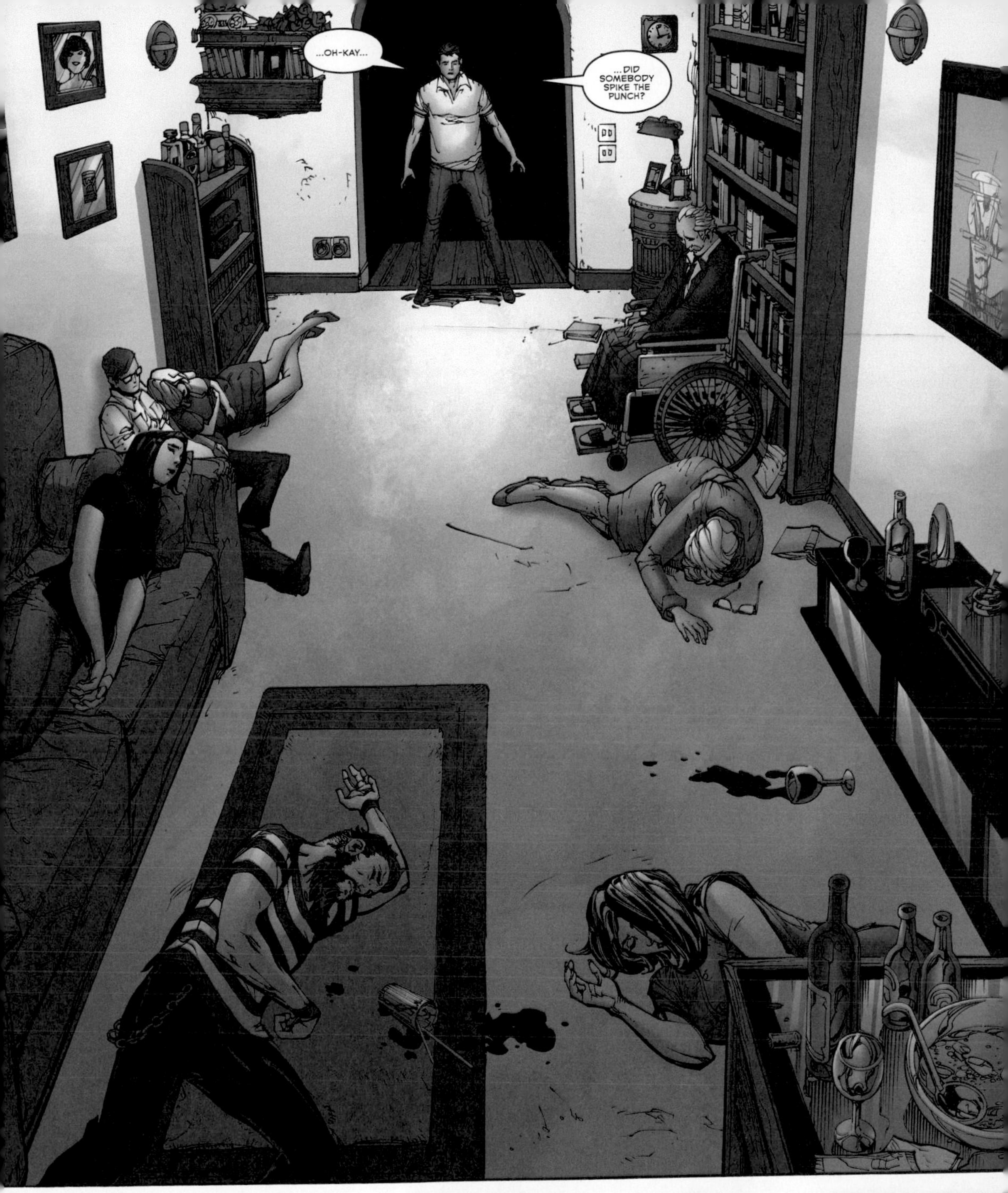
...OH-KAY...
...DID SOMEBODY SPIKE THE PUNCH?

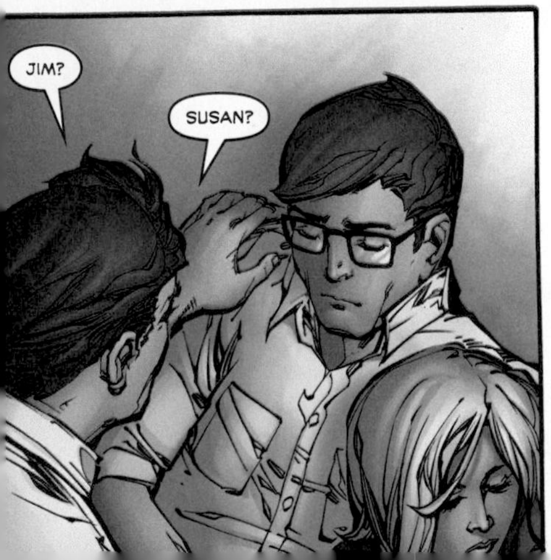
JIM?
SUSAN?

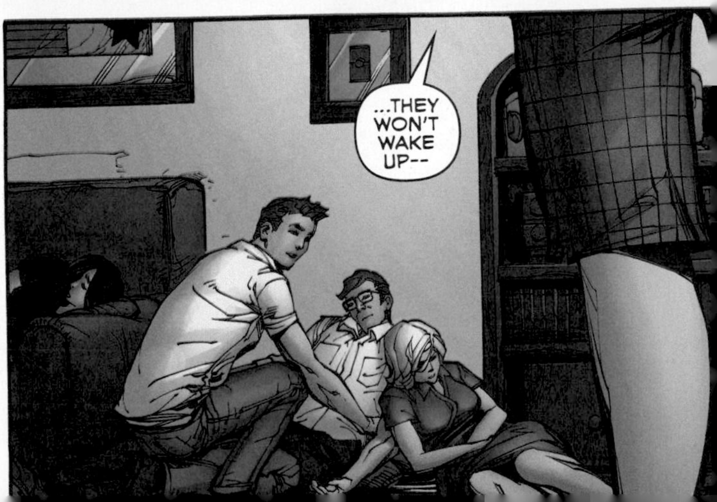
...THEY WON'T WAKE UP--

ALL THE ADULTS ARE *ASLEEP*, COUSIN HAL.

EXCEPT FOR *YOU*-- AND *ME*.

AND THAT'S NOT *ALL*--

HEY, UNCLE HAL.

WE ALREADY *TRIED*.

HOWIE...

HAL JR.?

HOWIE-- JASON--

WHAT'S THE *DEAL*?

YOU GOTTA *CHECK THIS OUT*, UNCLE HAL.

EVERYTHING LOOKS *NORMAL*, RIGHT?

EXCEPT--

--THIS *FUZZY* STUFF YOU CAN'T PUSH THROUGH--

SOME KIND OF *FORCE FIELD*.

SO...

...WHATEVER IT IS, THE WORLD *OUTSIDE* HASN'T BEEN AFFECTED.

WE CAN HANDLE A *FORCE* FIELD.

INVESTIGATING--

YEAH, RIGHT, COME *THIS* WAY...

HOW ABOUT YOU HOLD STILL AND *EXPLAIN* THIS TO ME.

SHOW, DON'T *TELL,* UNCLE HAL.

THIS IS SOME-THING YOU HAVE TO *SEE* FOR *YOURSELF.*

OH-KAY...

LOOKS LIKE I'M GONNA NEED YOUR *HELP,* KIDS--

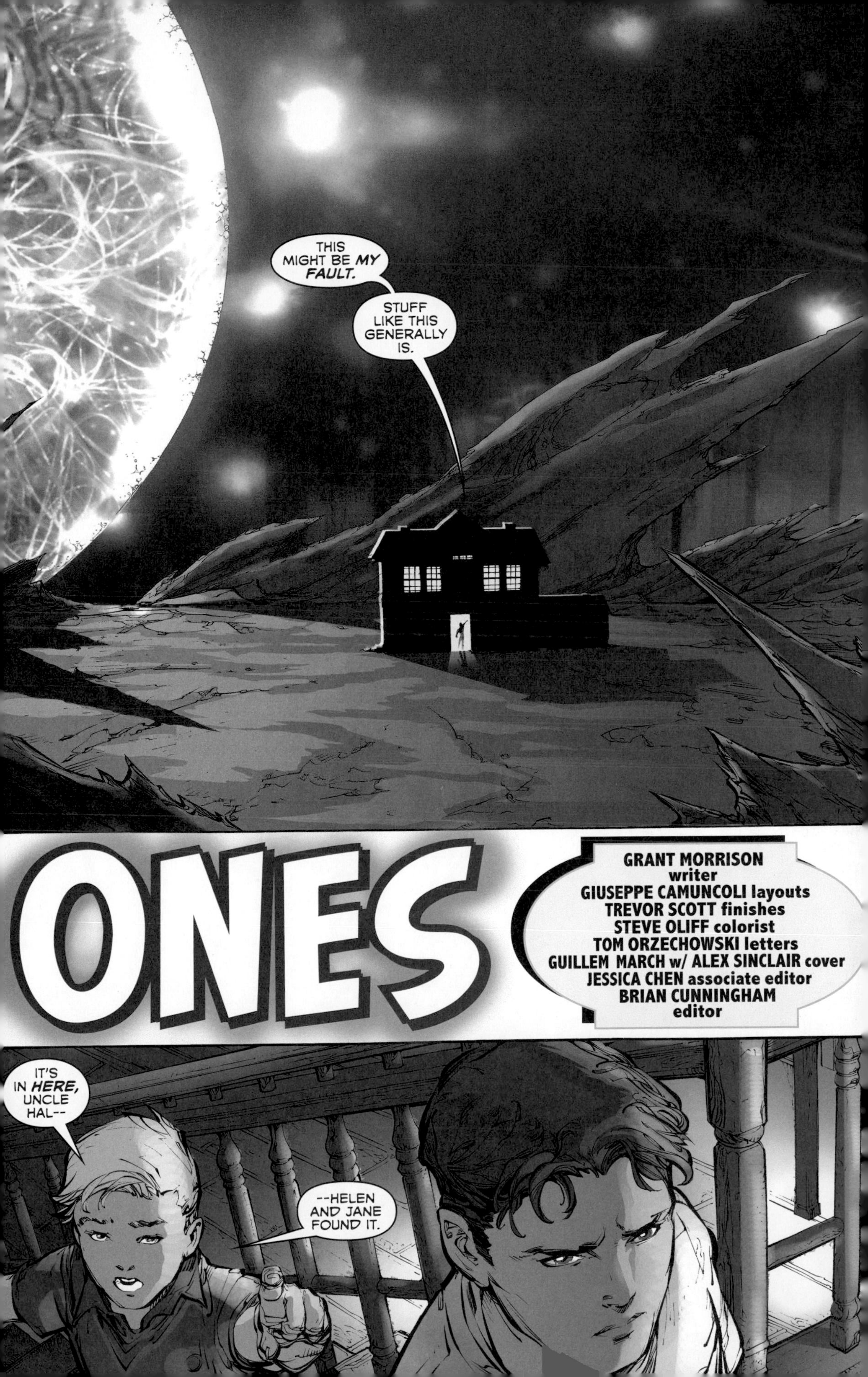
THIS MIGHT BE MY FAULT.
STUFF LIKE THIS GENERALLY IS.
ONES
GRANT MORRISON writer
GIUSEPPE CAMUNCOLI layouts
TREVOR SCOTT finishes
STEVE OLIFF colorist
TOM ORZECHOWSKI letters
GUILLEM MARCH w/ ALEX SINCLAIR cover
JESSICA CHEN associate editor
BRIAN CUNNINGHAM editor
IT'S IN HERE, UNCLE HAL--
--HELEN AND JANE FOUND IT.

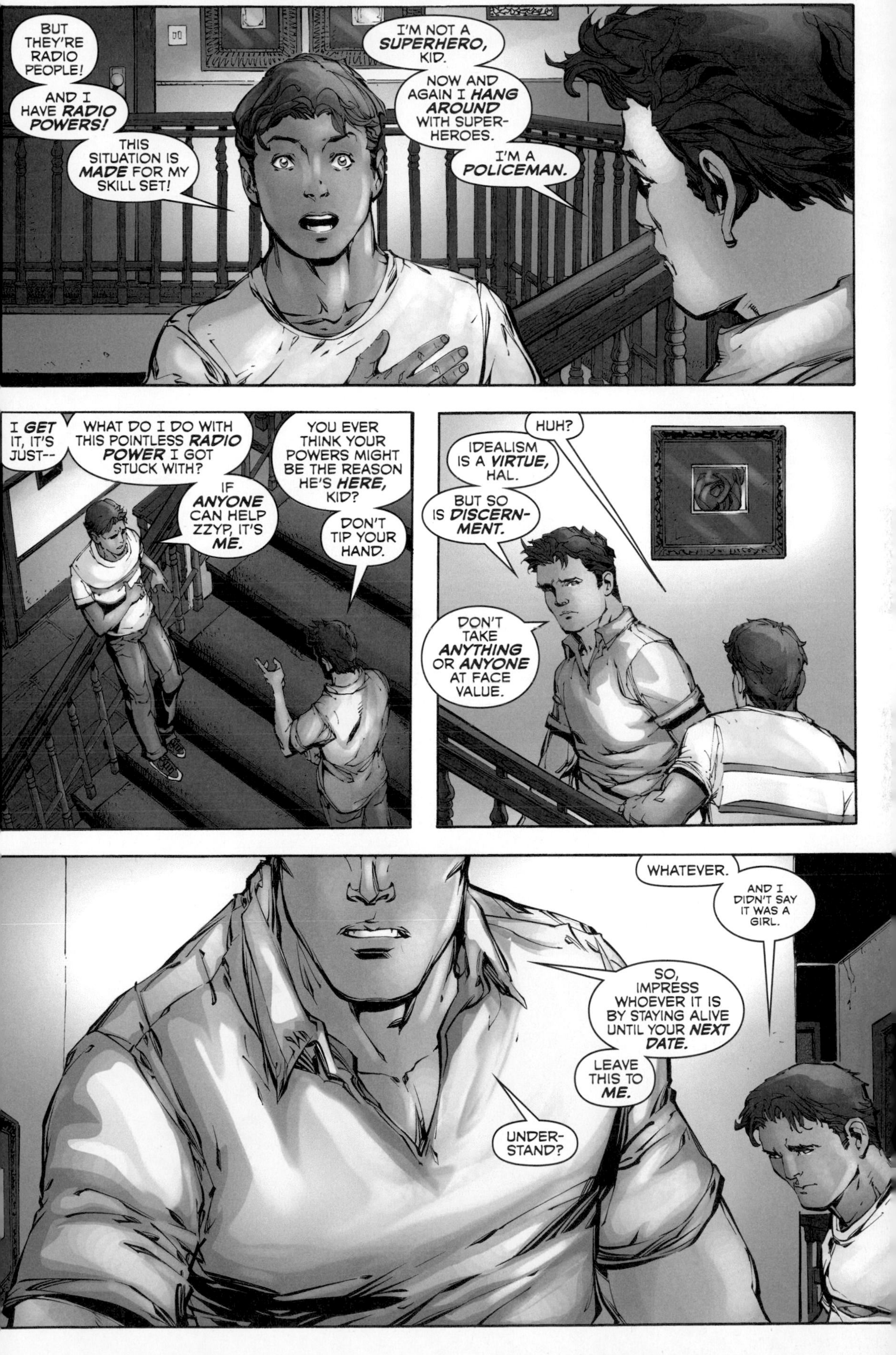
BUT THEY'RE RADIO PEOPLE!
AND I HAVE *RADIO POWERS!*
THIS SITUATION IS *MADE* FOR MY SKILL SET!
I'M NOT A *SUPERHERO,* KID.
NOW AND AGAIN I *HANG AROUND* WITH SUPER-HEROES.
I'M A *POLICEMAN.*
I *GET* IT, IT'S JUST--
WHAT DO I DO WITH THIS POINTLESS *RADIO POWER* I GOT STUCK WITH?
IF *ANYONE* CAN HELP ZZYP, IT'S *ME.*
YOU EVER THINK YOUR POWERS MIGHT BE THE REASON HE'S *HERE,* KID?
DON'T TIP YOUR HAND.
HUH?
IDEALISM IS A *VIRTUE,* HAL.
BUT SO IS *DISCERN-MENT.*
DON'T TAKE *ANYTHING* OR *ANYONE* AT FACE VALUE.
WHATEVER.
AND I DIDN'T SAY IT WAS A GIRL.
SO, IMPRESS WHOEVER IT IS BY STAYING ALIVE UNTIL YOUR *NEXT DATE.*
LEAVE THIS TO *ME.*
UNDER-STAND?

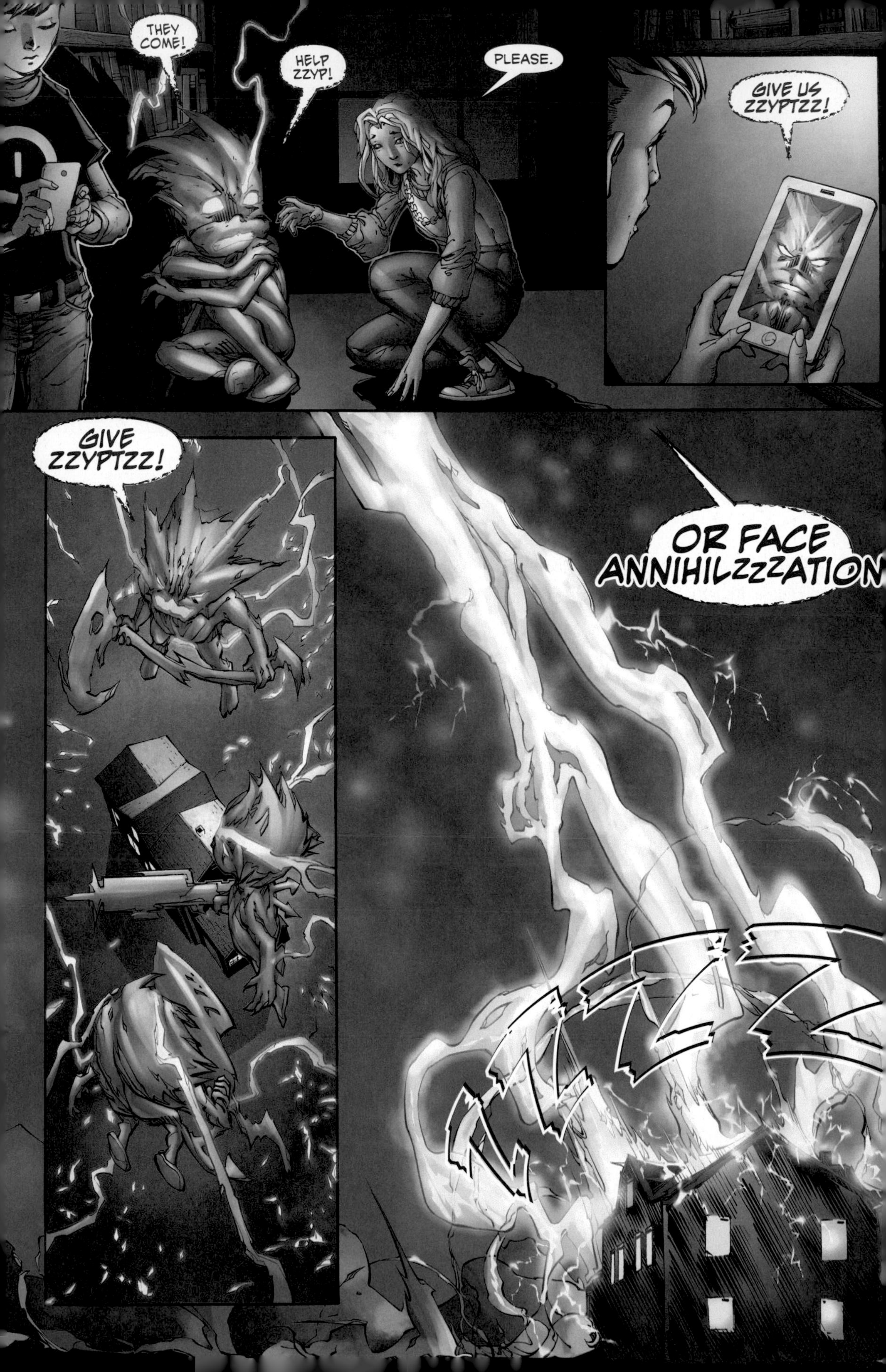
THEY COME!
HELP ZZYP!
PLEASE.
GIVE US ZZYPTZZ!
GIVE ZZYPTZZ!
OR FACE ANNIHILZZZATION

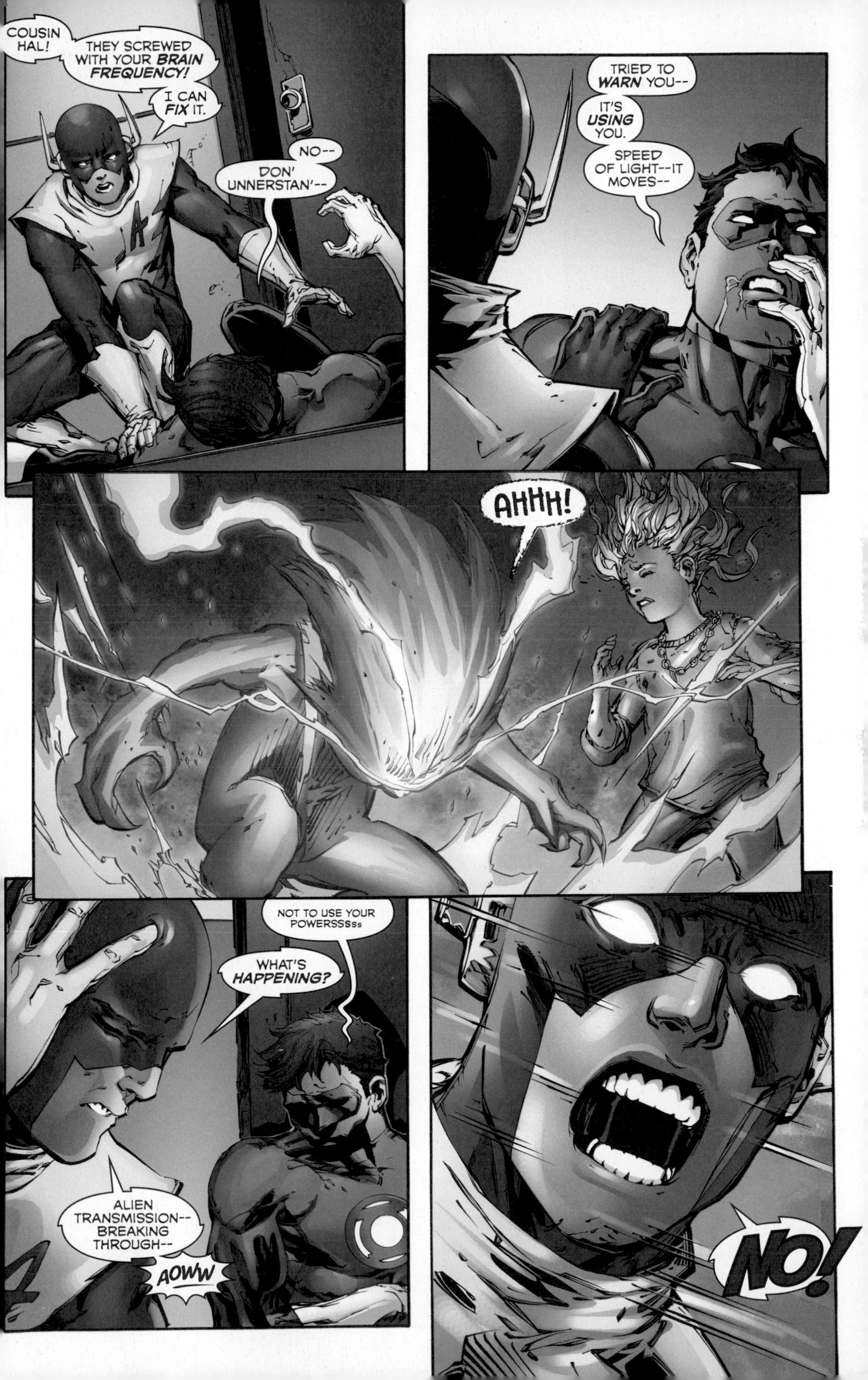
COUSIN HAL!
THEY SCREWED WITH YOUR BRAIN FREQUENCY!
I CAN FIX IT.
NO--
DON' UNNERSTAN'--
TRIED TO WARN YOU--
IT'S USING YOU.
SPEED OF LIGHT--IT MOVES--
AHHH!
NOT TO USE YOUR POWERSSSss
WHAT'S HAPPENING?
ALIEN TRANSMISSION-- BREAKING THROUGH--
AOWW
NO!

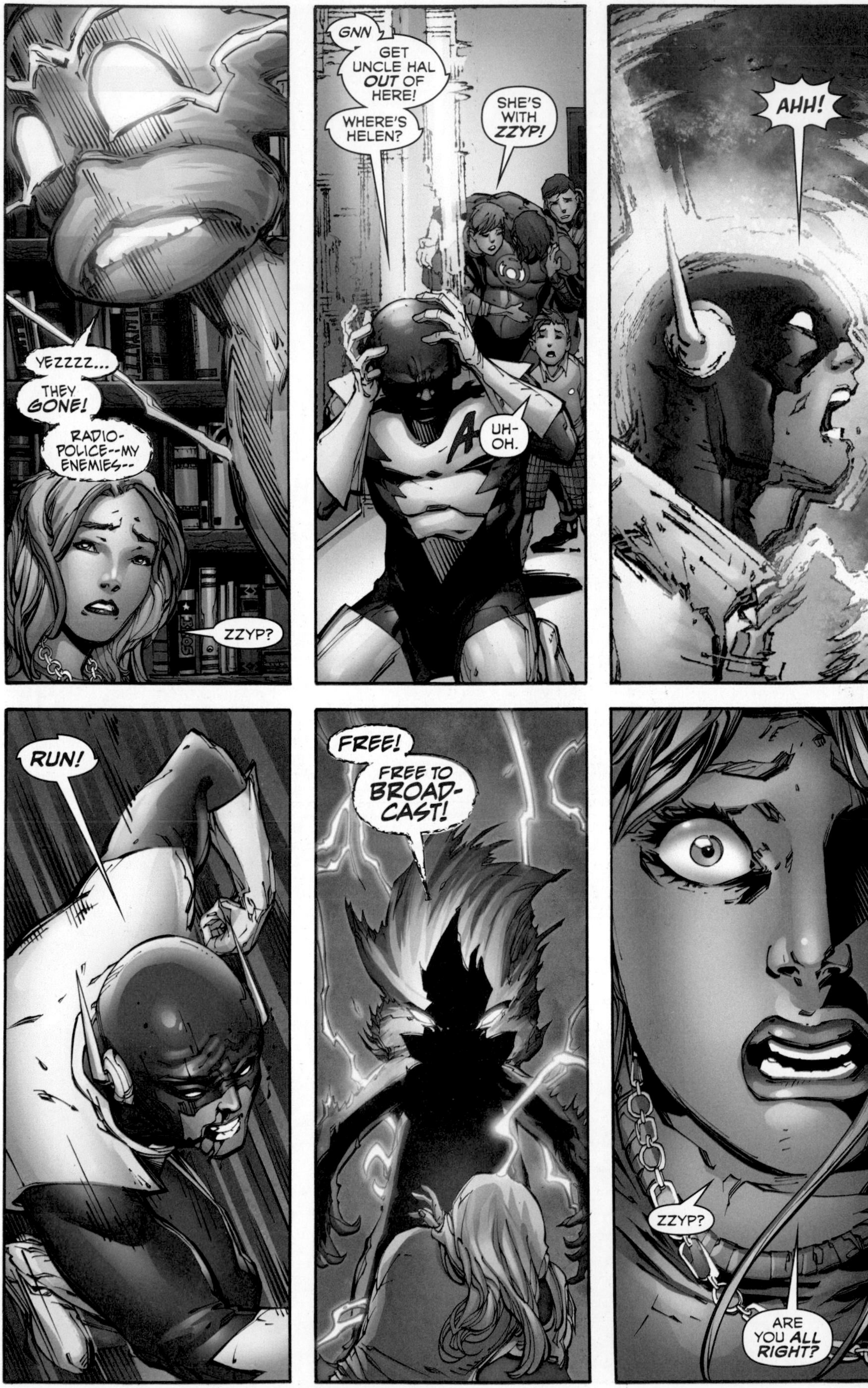
YEZZZZ...
THEY GONE!
RADIO-POLICE--MY ENEMIES--
ZZYP?
GNN
GET UNCLE HAL OUT OF HERE!
WHERE'S HELEN?
SHE'S WITH ZZYP!
UH-OH.
AHH!
RUN!
FREE!
FREE TO BROAD-CAST!
ZZYP?
ARE YOU ALL RIGHT?

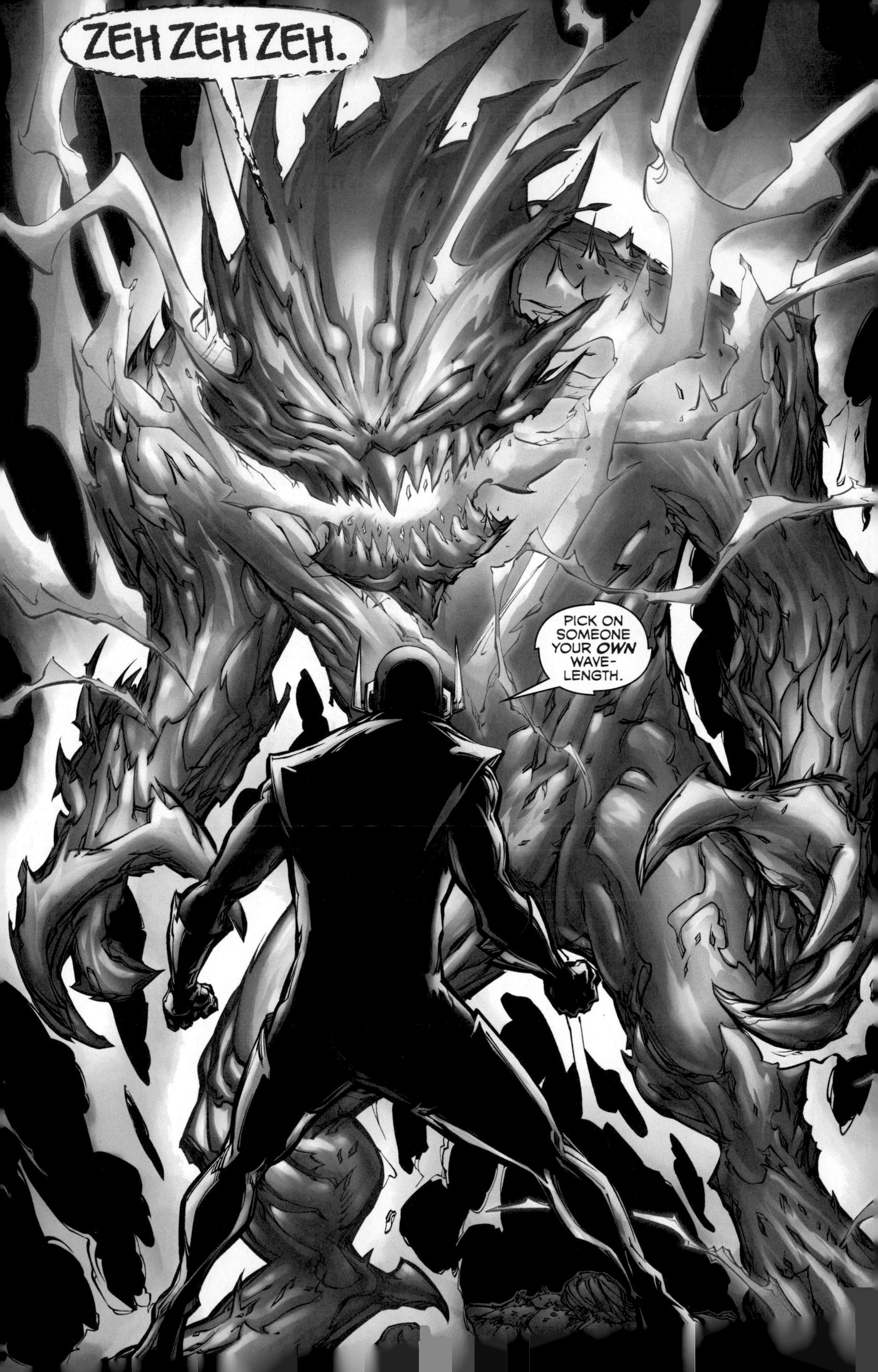
ZEH ZEH ZEH.
PICK ON SOMEONE YOUR OWN WAVE-LENGTH.

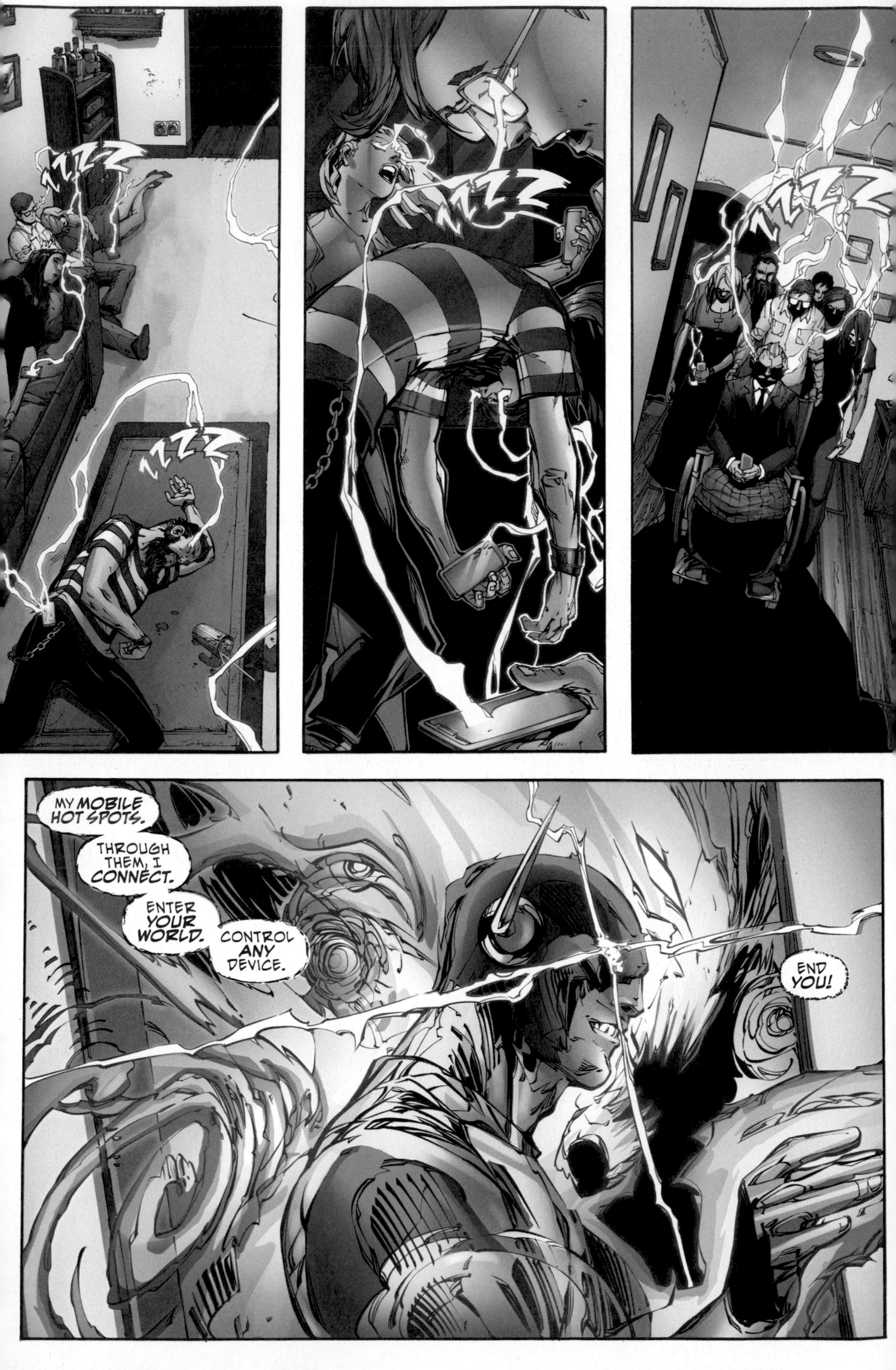
ZZZZ
ZZZZ
ZZZZ
ZZZZ
MY MOBILE HOT SPOTS.
THROUGH THEM, I CONNECT.
ENTER YOUR WORLD.
CONTROL ANY DEVICE.
END YOU!

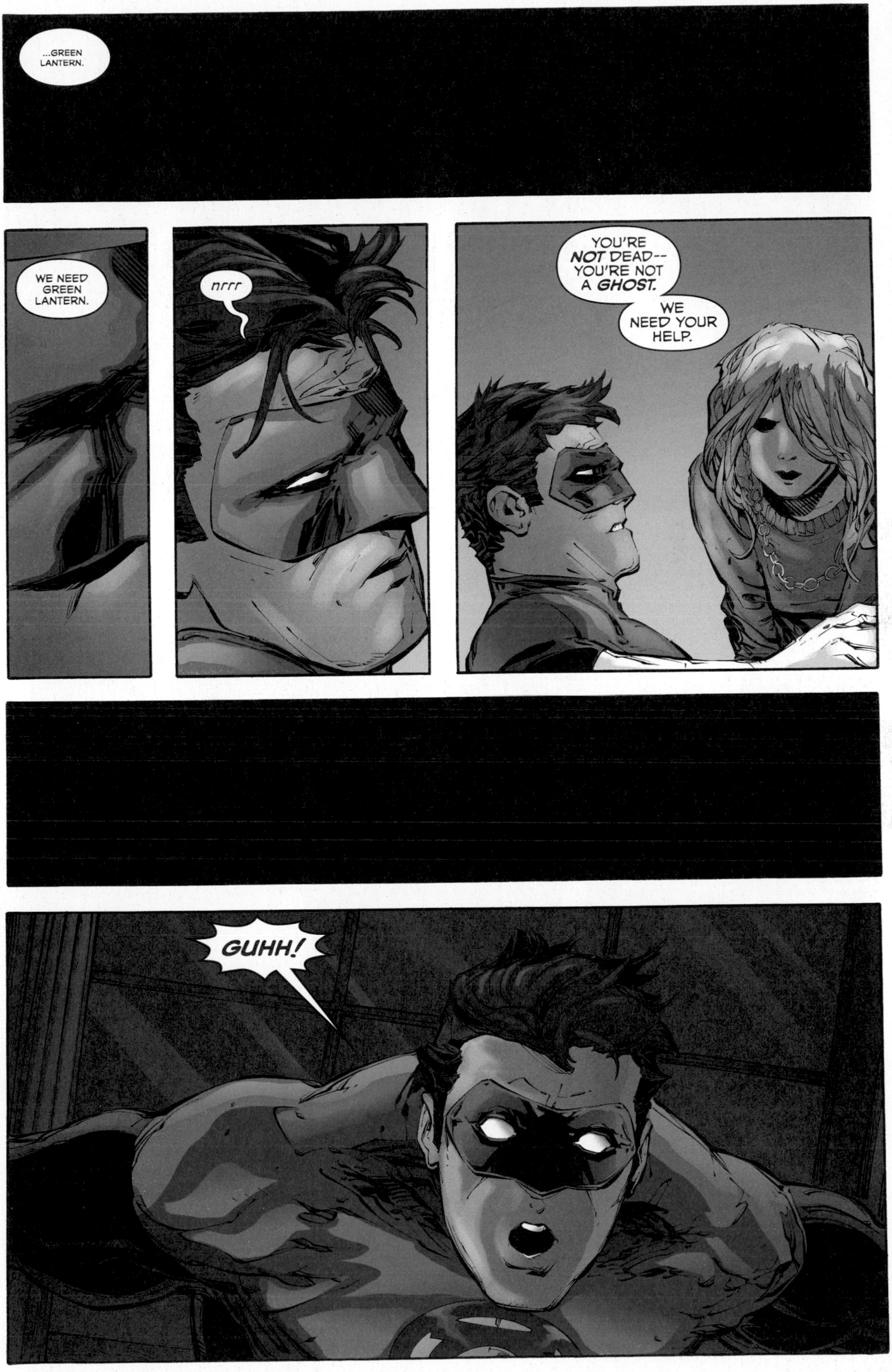
...GREEN LANTERN.
WE NEED GREEN LANTERN.
nrrr
YOU'RE *NOT* DEAD-- YOU'RE NOT A *GHOST.*
WE NEED YOUR HELP.
GUHH!

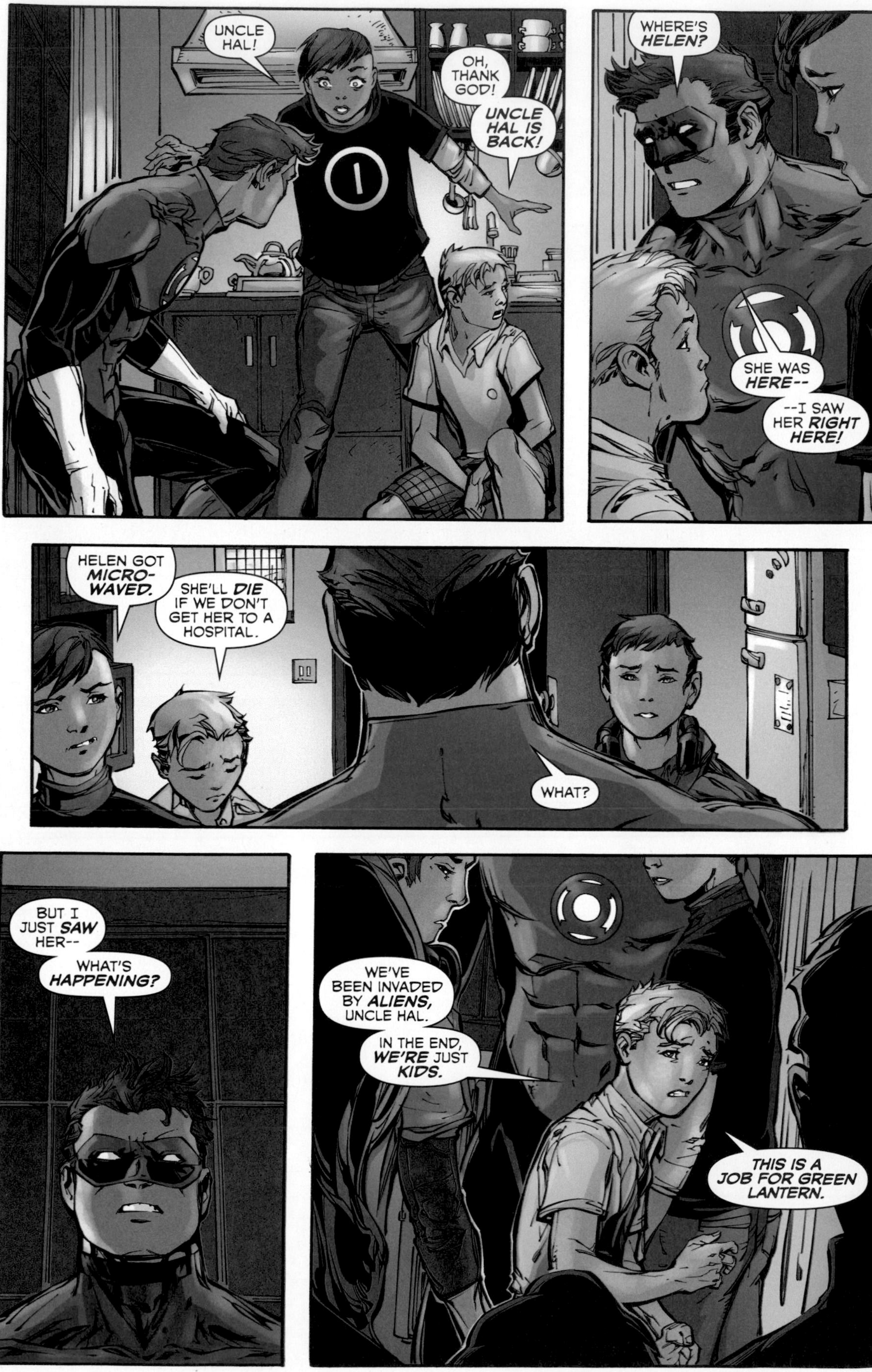
UNCLE HAL!
OH, THANK GOD!
UNCLE HAL IS BACK!
WHERE'S HELEN?
SHE WAS HERE--
--I SAW HER RIGHT HERE!
HELEN GOT MICRO-WAVED.
SHE'LL DIE IF WE DON'T GET HER TO A HOSPITAL.
WHAT?
BUT I JUST SAW HER--
WHAT'S HAPPENING?
WE'VE BEEN INVADED BY ALIENS, UNCLE HAL.
IN THE END, WE'RE JUST KIDS.
THIS IS A JOB FOR GREEN LANTERN.

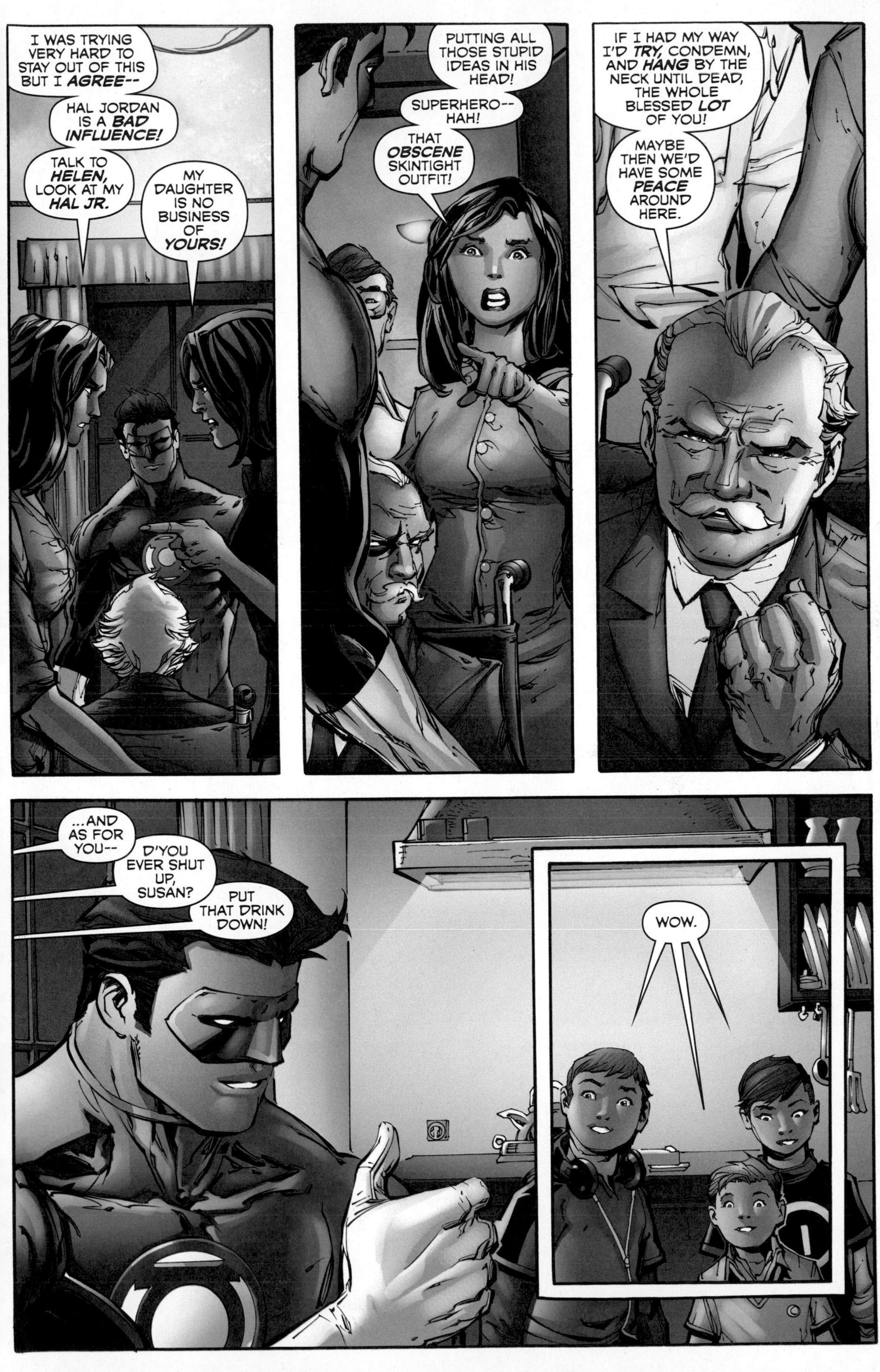
I WAS TRYING VERY HARD TO STAY OUT OF THIS BUT I AGREE--
HAL JORDAN IS A BAD INFLUENCE!
TALK TO HELEN, LOOK AT MY HAL JR.
MY DAUGHTER IS NO BUSINESS OF YOURS!
PUTTING ALL THOSE STUPID IDEAS IN HIS HEAD!
SUPERHERO-- HAH!
THAT OBSCENE SKINTIGHT OUTFIT!
IF I HAD MY WAY I'D TRY, CONDEMN, AND HANG BY THE NECK UNTIL DEAD, THE WHOLE BLESSED LOT OF YOU!
MAYBE THEN WE'D HAVE SOME PEACE AROUND HERE.
...AND AS FOR YOU--
D'YOU EVER SHUT UP, SUSAN?
PUT THAT DRINK DOWN!
WOW.

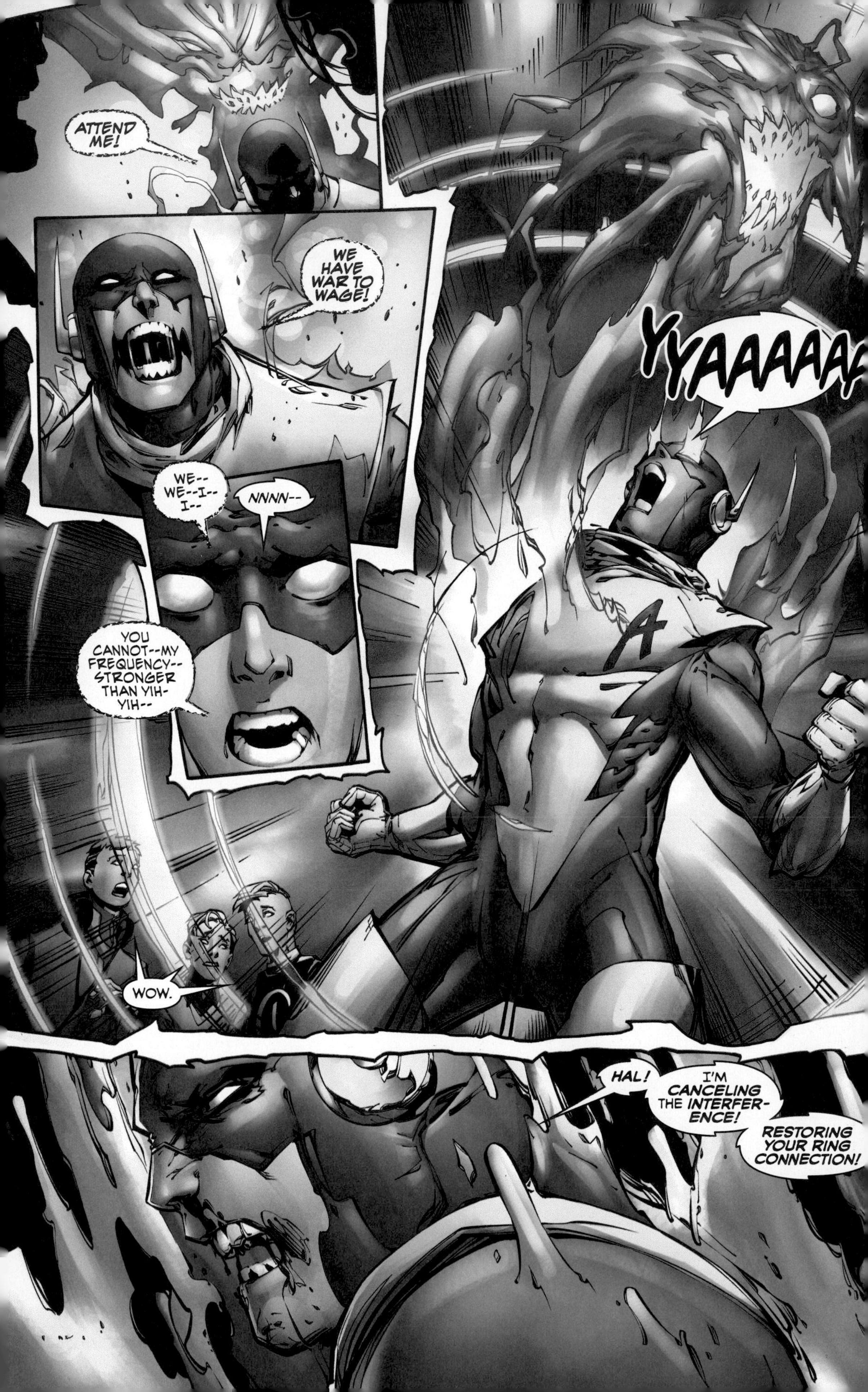
ATTEND ME!
WE HAVE WAR TO WAGE!
WE-- WE--I-- I--
NNNN--
YOU CANNOT--MY FREQUENCY--STRONGER THAN YIH-YIH--
YYAAAAA
WOW.
HAL!
I'M CANCELING THE INTERFERENCE!
RESTORING YOUR RING CONNECTION!

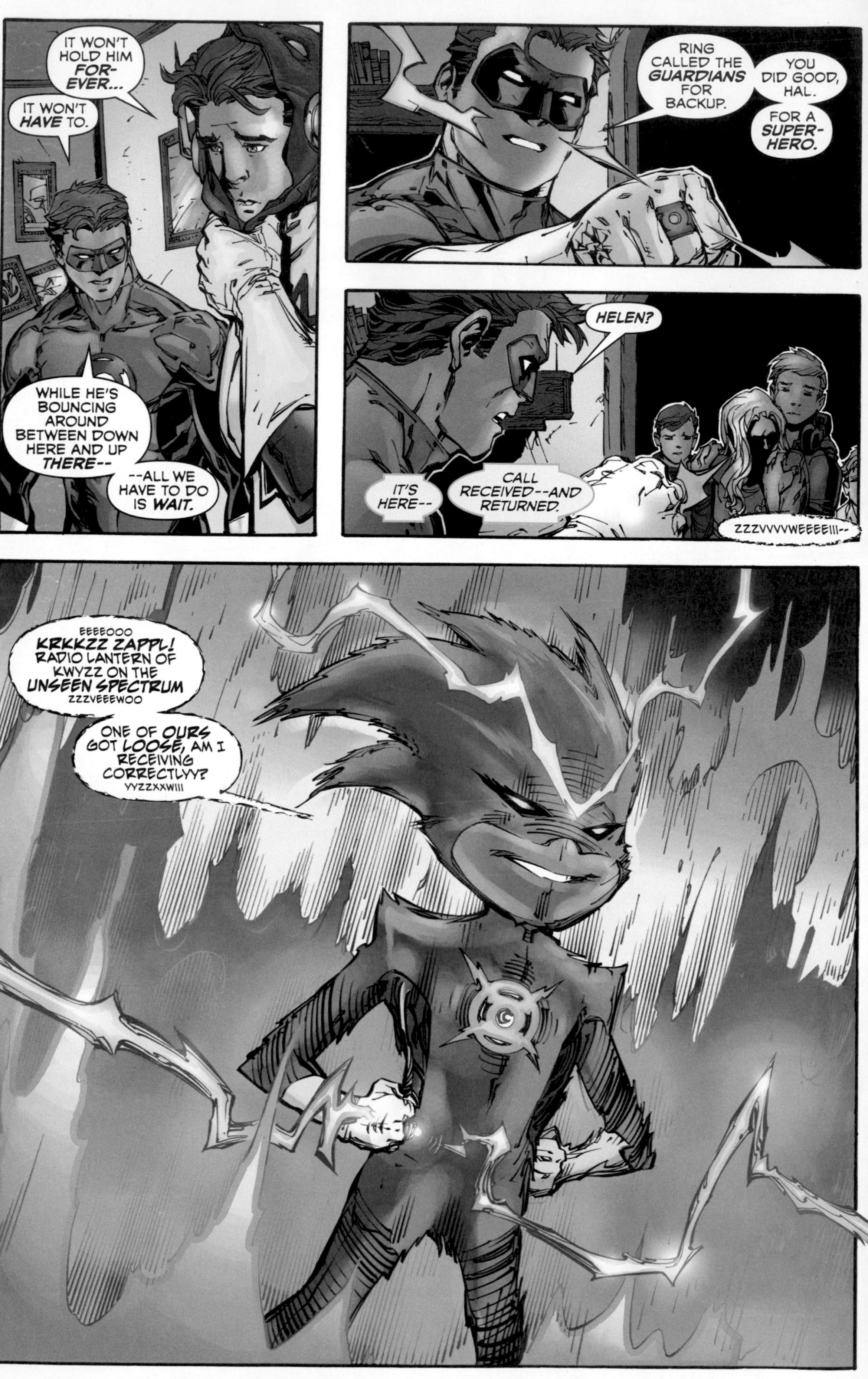

IT WON'T HOLD HIM FOR-EVER...
IT WON'T HAVE TO.
WHILE HE'S BOUNCING AROUND BETWEEN DOWN HERE AND UP THERE--
--ALL WE HAVE TO DO IS WAIT.
RING CALLED THE GUARDIANS FOR BACKUP.
YOU DID GOOD, HAL.
FOR A SUPER-HERO.
HELEN?
IT'S HERE--
CALL RECEIVED--AND RETURNED.
ZZZVVVVWEEEEIII--
EEEEOOO KRKKZZ ZAPPL! RADIO LANTERN OF KWYZZ ON THE UNSEEN SPECTRUM ZZZVEEEWOO
ONE OF OURS GOT LOOSE, AM I RECEIVING CORRECTLYY? YYZZXXWIII

ZZZVVVVWBEEEIII-- THANKS FOR APPREHENDING WAVE-BANDIT ZZYPTZZ IIIIEEEOOOUU

BUT ZZYP HAD A *POINT!*

WE STOLE HIS TERRITORY AND FILLED IT WITH CRAPPY *POP SONGS* AND *PROPAGANDA.*

THIS IS AN *ENVIRONMENTAL* ISSUE.

EARTH CHILDREN.

THEY TEND TO SUPPORT THE UNDERDOG.

WE'LL LOOK INTO ZZYPTZZ'S CASE ZVEEPPZZZZ

VKRRKVVTZZ AS FAR AS I KNOW *HUMAN-CELL* FREQUENCIES ARE SO FAR OUT ON THE *BOUNDARIES* WE RARELY NOTICE *WHAT GOES ON THERE*VVZZZIIIEVVV

WELL... MAYBE OUT ON THE *BOUNDARIES* IS WHERE TROUBLE GETS *STARTED.*

JUST SAYING.

LET'S PUT THE DUBIOUS MORALITY OF OUR ACTIONS ASIDE.

THE *JORDAN FAMILY* DOES IT AGAIN.

ONE FOR ALL AND ALL--

TOGETHER!

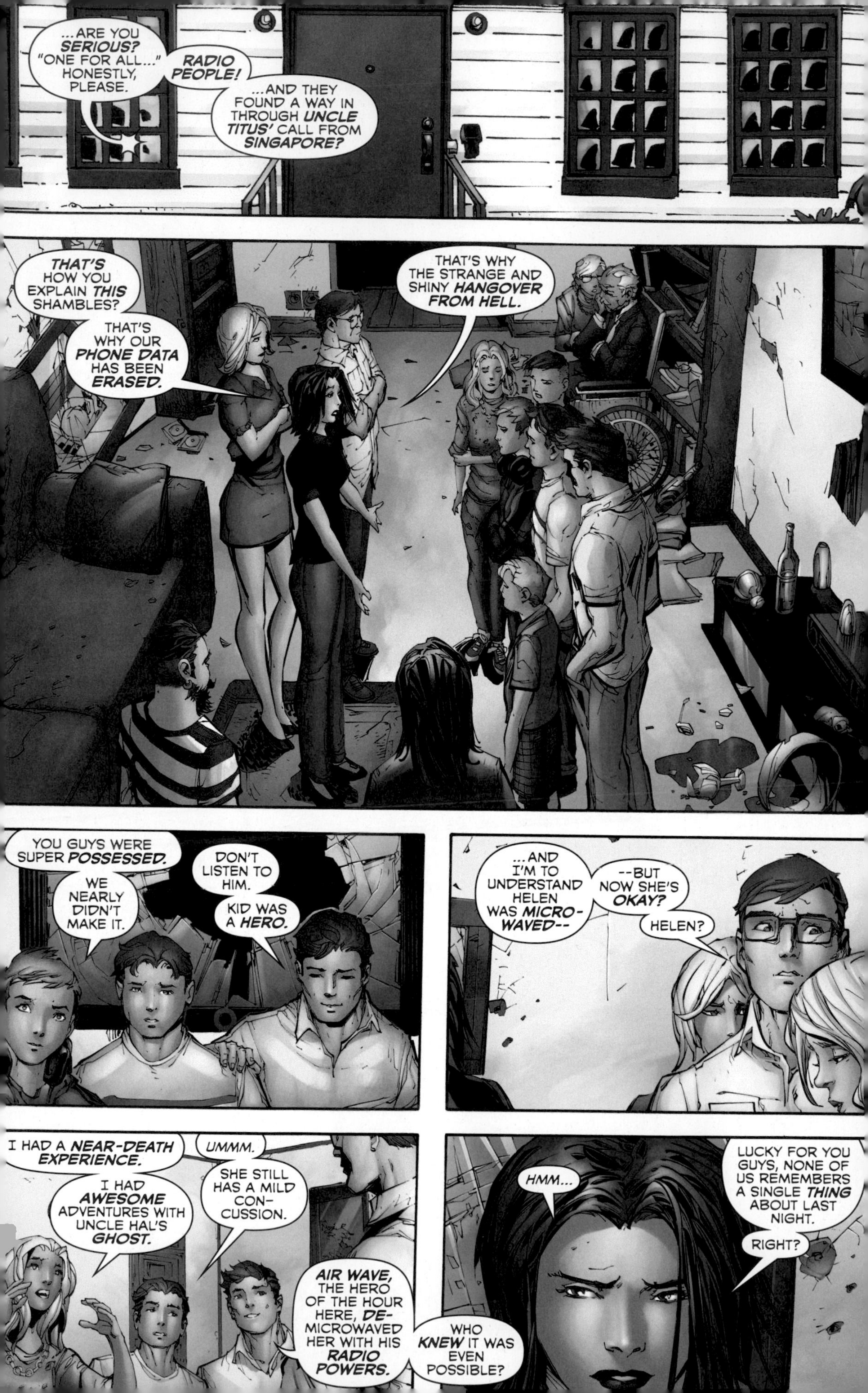

...ARE YOU SERIOUS? "ONE FOR ALL..." HONESTLY, PLEASE.
RADIO PEOPLE!
...AND THEY FOUND A WAY IN THROUGH UNCLE TITUS' CALL FROM SINGAPORE?
THAT'S HOW YOU EXPLAIN THIS SHAMBLES?
THAT'S WHY OUR PHONE DATA HAS BEEN ERASED.
THAT'S WHY THE STRANGE AND SHINY HANGOVER FROM HELL.
YOU GUYS WERE SUPER POSSESSED.
WE NEARLY DIDN'T MAKE IT.
DON'T LISTEN TO HIM.
KID WAS A HERO.
...AND I'M TO UNDERSTAND HELEN WAS MICRO-WAVED--
--BUT NOW SHE'S OKAY?
HELEN?
I HAD A NEAR-DEATH EXPERIENCE.
I HAD AWESOME ADVENTURES WITH UNCLE HAL'S GHOST.
UMMM.
SHE STILL HAS A MILD CON-CUSSION.
AIR WAVE, THE HERO OF THE HOUR HERE, DE-MICROWAVED HER WITH HIS RADIO POWERS.
WHO KNEW IT WAS EVEN POSSIBLE?
HMM...
LUCKY FOR YOU GUYS, NONE OF US REMEMBERS A SINGLE THING ABOUT LAST NIGHT.
RIGHT?

...I CAN'T BELIEVE THEY **BOUGHT** IT!

NEVER AGAIN!

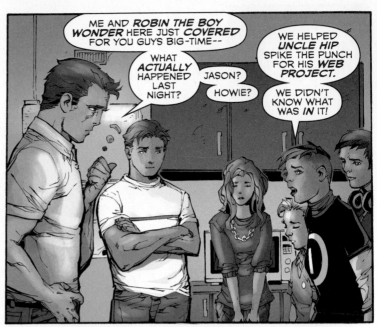

ME AND **ROBIN THE BOY WONDER** HERE JUST **COVERED** FOR YOU GUYS BIG-TIME--

WHAT **ACTUALLY** HAPPENED LAST NIGHT?

JASON?

HOWIE?

WE HELPED **UNCLE HIP** SPIKE THE PUNCH FOR HIS **WEB PROJECT.**

WE DIDN'T KNOW WHAT WAS **IN** IT!

UNCLE "HIP"?

DOUG JORDAN PUT YOU UP TO THIS?

...JACK JORDAN WAS A **SAINT!**

=CHUCKLE=

A **MARTYR** TO SEX ADDICTION, YOU MEAN!

...I DIDN'T ASK TO BE THE **BLACK SHEEP** OF THE FAMILY BUT IF I GOTTA BE--

WEB PROJECT?

VARIANT COVER GALLERY

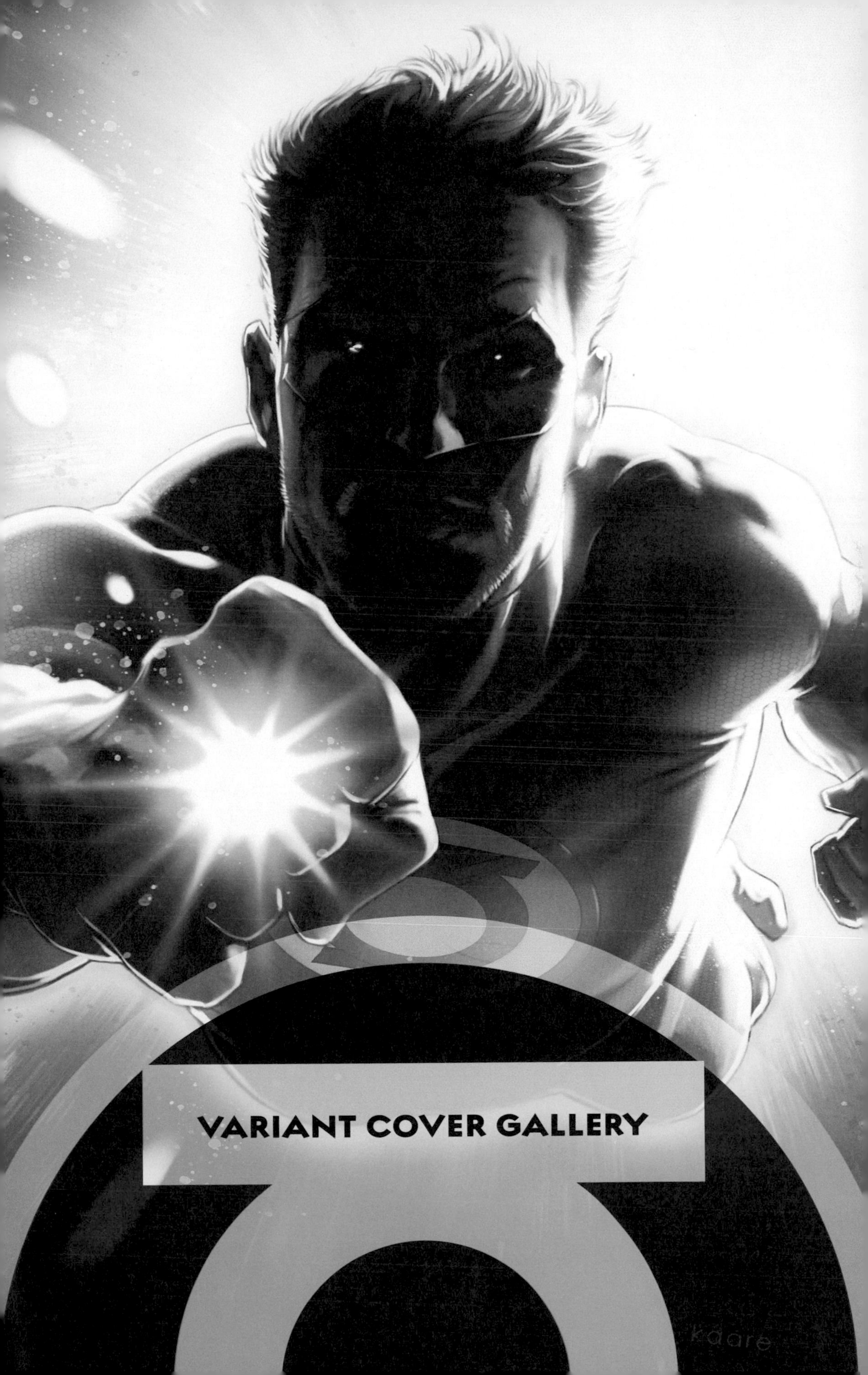
kaare

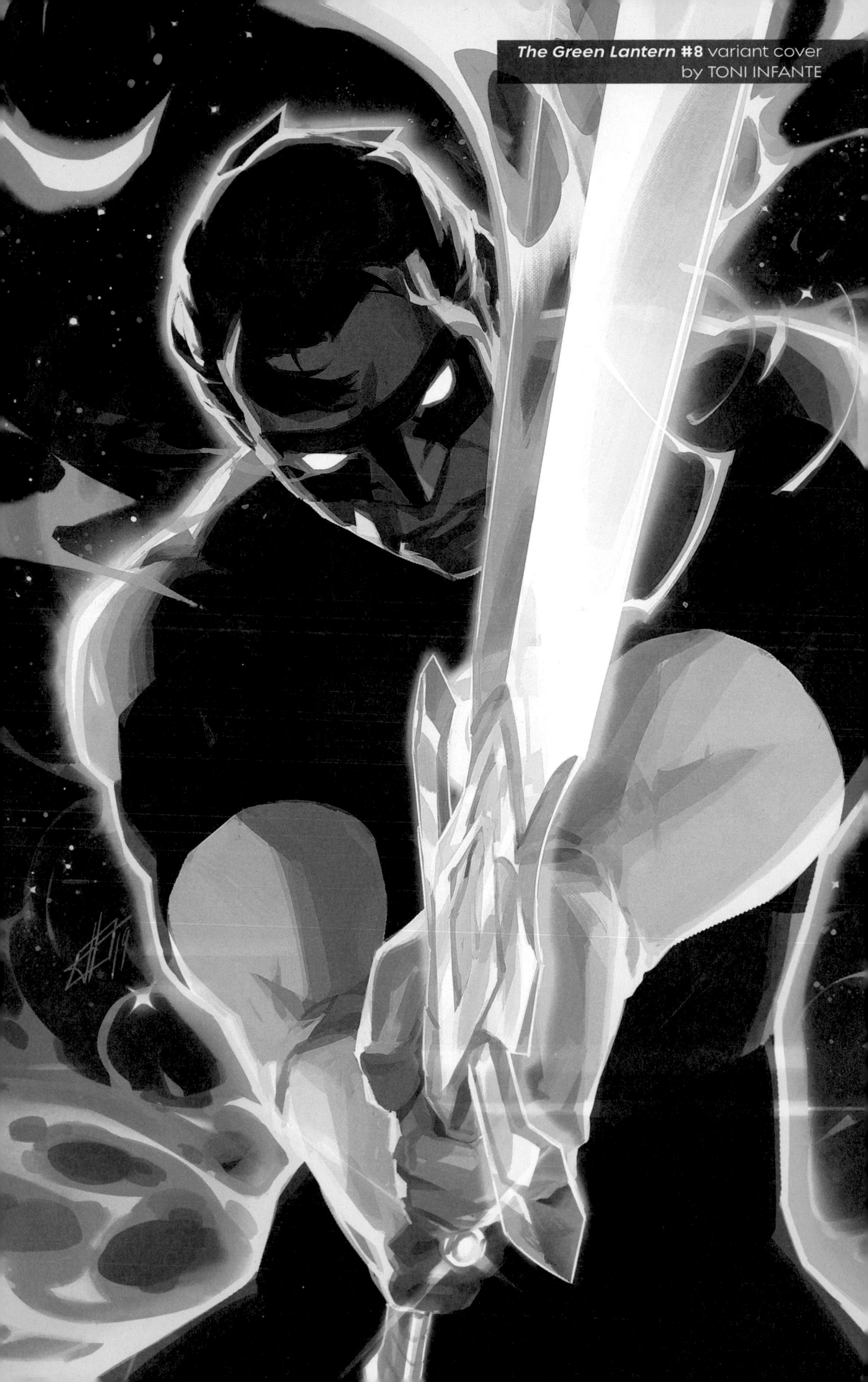

***The Green Lantern* #8** variant cover
by TONI INFANTE

The Green Lantern **#9** variant cover
by JEFF DEKAL

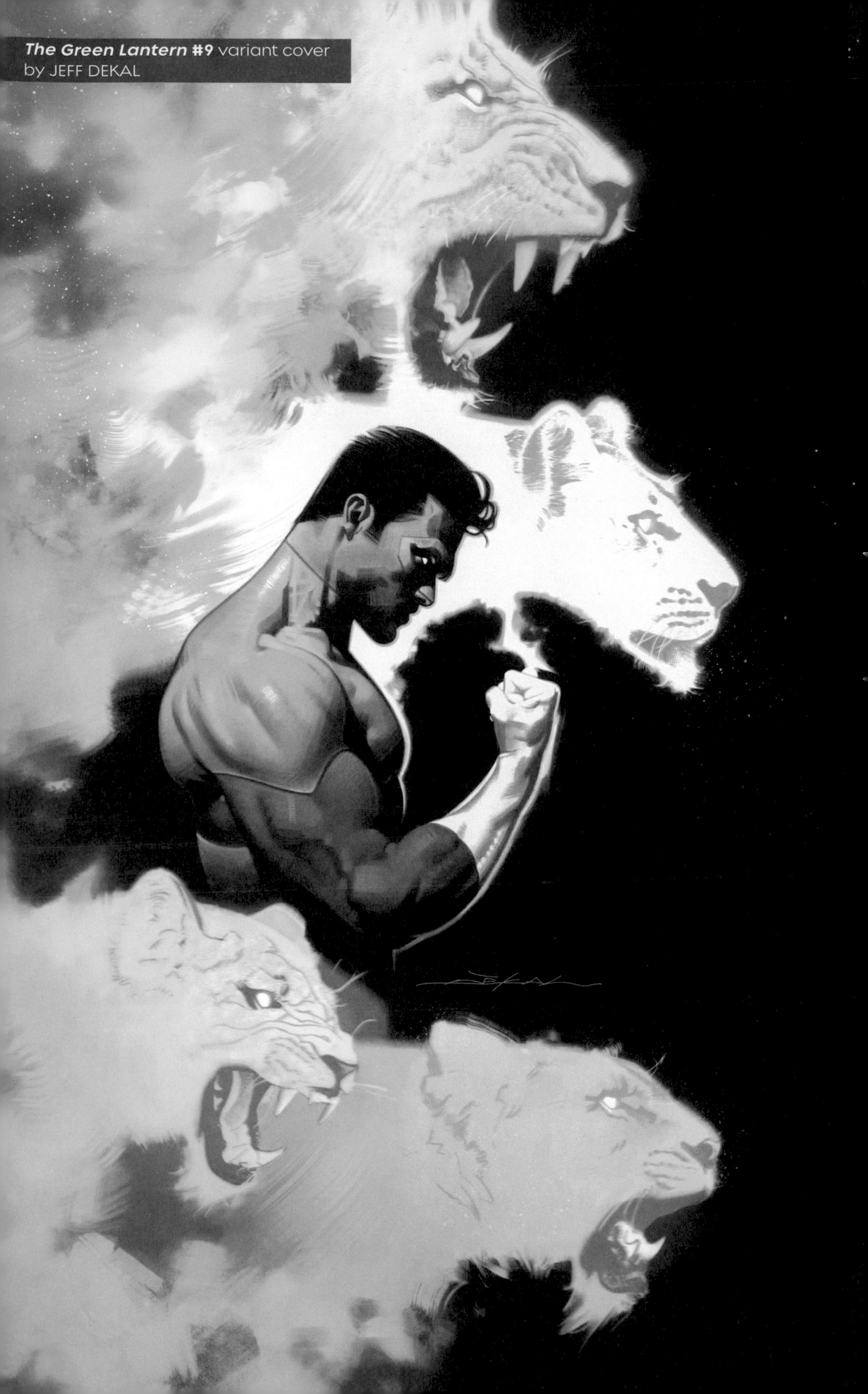

The Green Lantern **#10** variant cover
by KAARE ANDREWS

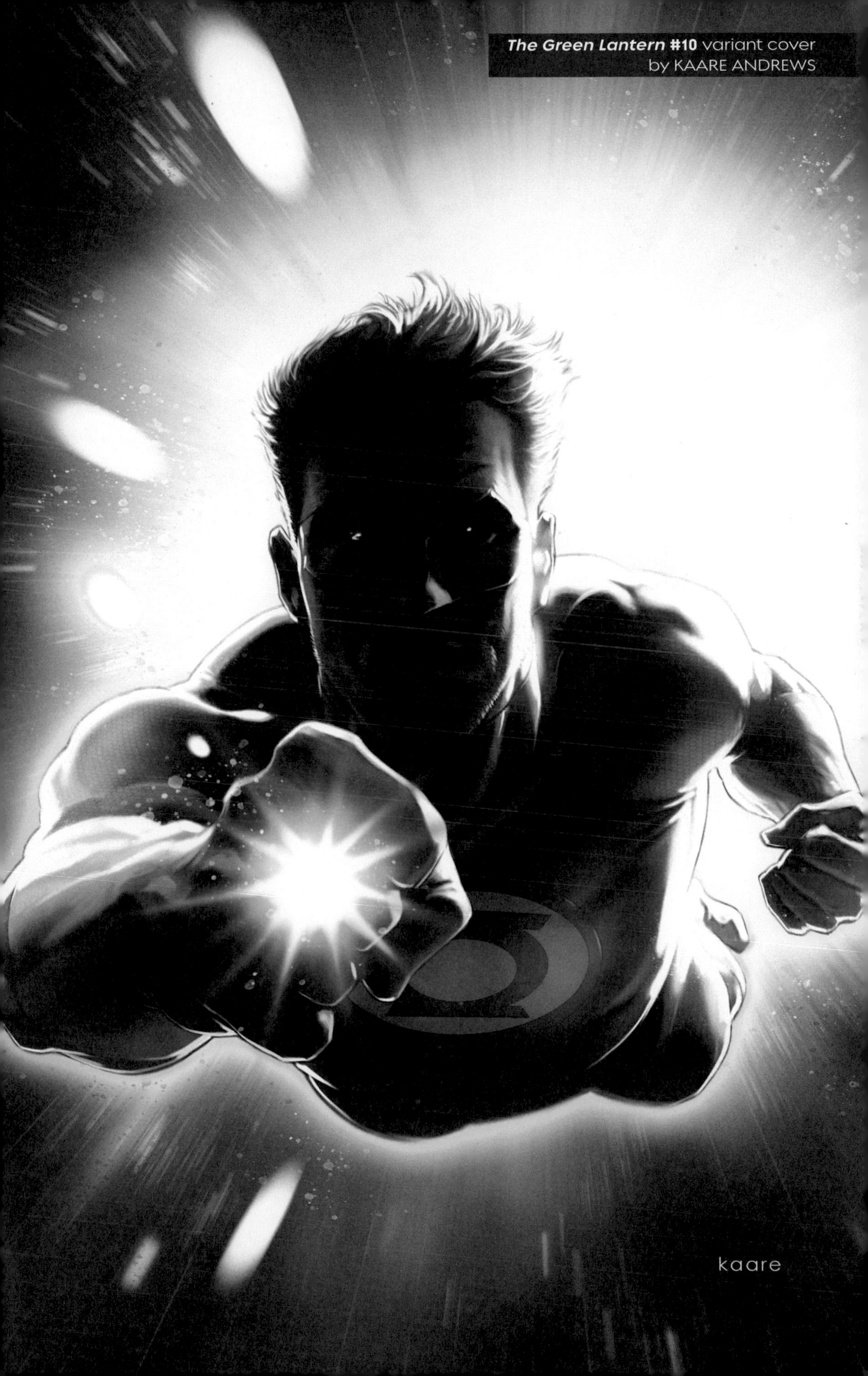
kaare

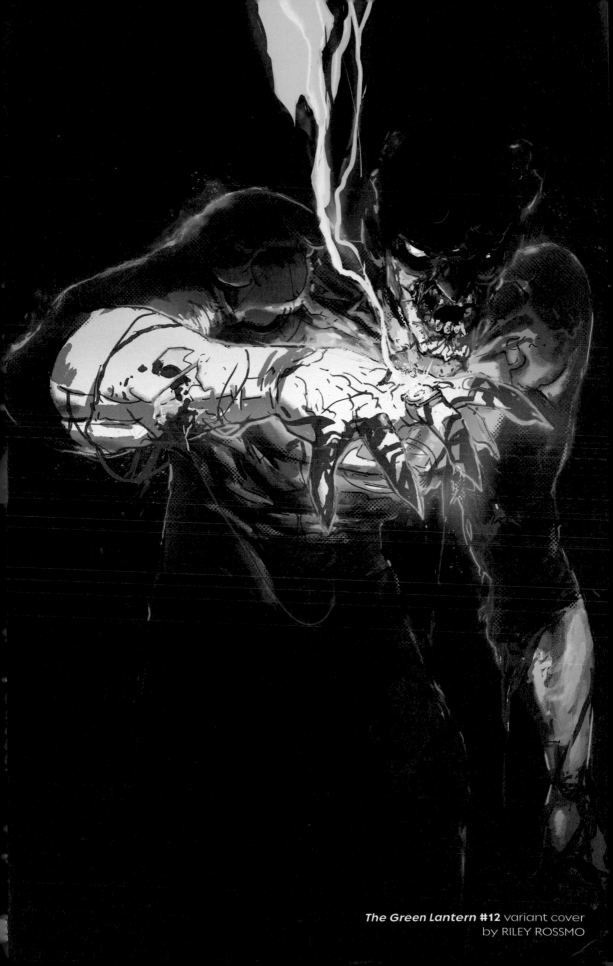

The Green Lantern **#12** variant cover
by RILEY ROSSMO

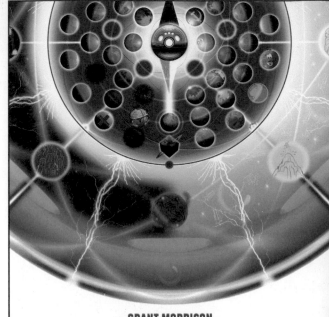

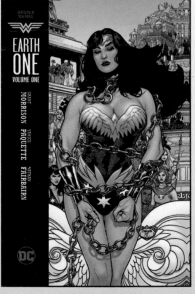
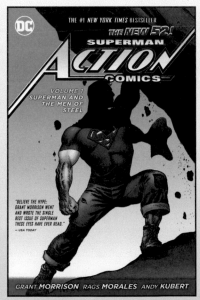
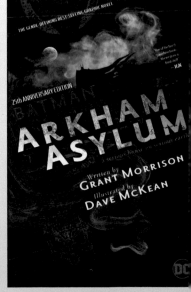